Environment for Man

The Next Fifty Years

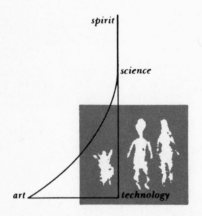

Based on papers commissioned for the American Institute of Planners' two-year consultation, Part I: Optimum Environment with Man as the Measure, Portland, Oregon, August 14-18, 1966

ENVIRONMENT FOR MAN

THE NEXT FIFTY YEARS

Edited by WILLIAM R. EWALD, JR.

INDIANA UNIVERSITY PRESS

Bloomington & London

Contents

Preface

In 1866 there were three cities in the United States that had reached a population of 300,000 persons—New York, Philadelphia, and St. Louis. There is little or no record of any particularly troublesome problems of the kind that we face today.

In 1916, fifty years later, we had become aware of the slum, had experienced the first massive traffic congestion problem— on the approaches to the Brooklyn Bridge—and had adopted the first comprehensive zoning ordinance to attempt control of chaotic growth and development. Other problems were recognized and discussed, as disclosed by the proceedings of the National Conference on City Planning in the five years immediately preceding. So significant was the nature of the emerging problems that some fifty landscape architects, engineers, architects, and socially minded citizens organized a professional planning institute, The American Institute of Planners.

To commemorate that beginning almost fifty years ago, AIP, being an institute of planners, has mounted a two-year national consultation to look into THE NEXT FIFTY YEARS / 1967-2017, and the future environment of this democracy, as well as attempting an appraisal of past professional planning successes and failures.

This book results from Part I of that consultation: the papers presented August 14-18, 1966 in Portland, Oregon at a conference on the theme of Optimum Environment with Man as the Measure. Our concern there was to explore, with the several professional disciplines most concerned with its creation, the kind of environment we should build. We face the awesome fact of a future population double its present size with 80-90 per cent living in urban areas, an entirely new condition that warrants new means to meet it and new multidisciplinary efforts. The fact that so many people, half of whom were not members of the Institute, overcame the air strike to attend the Portland conference is an indication of the awareness of the importance of the undertaking.

These Part I papers are concerned with the physiological, psychological, and sociological impact of the physical environment. Part II (papers from the Washington, D.C. conference, October 1-6, 1967) will move on to a philosophy for the future, current rates of change, and specific policy and program statements for planning over THE NEXT FIFTY YEARS. These will be the work of special commissions and will be published by the Indiana University Press in two more volumes.

The membership of the Institute has been joined in this large undertaking, well beyond its own resources, with generous support (to date) from:

> Episcopal Church
> Ford Foundation
> General Electric Company
> National Council of Churches
> U.S. Public Health Service
> Urban America, Inc.
> United Presbyterian Church
> University of California (Berkeley)

Many professional groups have cooperated with the American
Institute of Planners to insure widespread notice and utilization
of this unprecedented effort, including:

American Academy of Arts and Sciences
American Academy of Political and Social Sciences
American Institute of Architects
American Society of Civil Engineers
American Society of Landscape Architects
American Society of Planning Officials
Building Research Institute
Committee for Economic Development
Department of Housing and Urban Development
General Electric Company
National Association of Housing and Redevelopment
   Officials
U.S. Public Health Service
The Rand Corporation
Science Information Exchange, Smithsonian Institution
Society for Applied Anthropology
Society for the Psychological Study of Social Issues
Stanford Research Institute
Trans-action
Urban America, Inc.

There is no way to thank here the many who are helping to
create the AIP's two-year consultation, but those who have
contributed to producing this volume must certainly be identified: Gail O'Gorman, Leah B. Biller, and Linda A. Feick.

HARLAND BARTHOLOMEW, Chairman
Fiftieth Anniversary Committee
American Institute of Planners

Washington, D.C.
November 1, 1966

Environment for Man

The Next Fifty Years

William R. Ewald, Jr.

Consultant to the AIP project on The Next Fifty Years

Introduction

If we had the technology and the economy—both said to be imminent—to build an ideal environment, what kind would we build? What could environment contribute to a "good" day? Do we know how to define and work toward "Optimum Environment with Man as the Measure"? To date neither optimum nor environment has been defined, nor have we made an adequate beginning at measuring man.

Part I of the American Institute of Planners' two-year consultation was constructed to *begin* the answers to such questions. But the fact is, the professionals of our society are trained and oriented toward avoiding disasters and achieving universal minimums. "Optimum" is a word taboo to the pragmatist. He is concerned with the best he can do in the here and now. We submit, however, that in discussions of man's environment pragmatism itself must be redefined, from something that works now to something that will work in the future.

The very discipline of an optimum perspective consciously introduces society's values into the process of deciding what priorities should be assigned. The "trade-offs"—choices among priorities—that are necessary in the real world, where optimum environment is not yet achievable, can be much better evaluated if we have a clearer grasp of what optimum environment really might be for man.

The papers in this book are intended to begin the definition of optimum environment, its controllable variables, and its functions. By looking into "the next fifty years" in this way, an attempt is being made to develop an understanding both of the present state of the art of city planning and of the scope of the intellectual enterprise that is yet to be evolved if we are to develop a truly human environment.

Part II of the Institute's consultation, the Washington Conference (October 1-6, 1967) will begin the articulation of a philosophy for the next fifty years. How should the future environment be created in an open pluralistic society in which the responsible individual counts? Albert Camus tells us that: "The aim of life can only be to increase the sense of freedom and responsibility to be found in every man in the world." How does this affect our utilization of the expert? Implicit in this conference will be an identification of the rate of change we will be moving through in the next fifty years.

Having tried to understand the values of our society and the great changes that lie ahead, Part II will also propose specific policies and programs of the sort that *must* be considered if we really *do* understand. The Washington conference will be followed by Part III, six to ten regional conferences to refine and test the conclusions of Part II—continuing the nationwide dialogue begun in Portland and Washington.

The scope of the two-year consultation on the future environment of a democracy thus runs from defining environment and the application of science in creating it, to the philosophic and moral values involved, to what we actually propose to do, step by step over the next fifty years—in pragmatic terms. For this consultation what the American Institute of Planners' charter has defined as the "art and science of city planning" has been expanded to include the role of art, spirit, science, and technology in creating the future environment of a democracy. It is clear that we will be including nonempirical data that won't go through the computer, as well as making the fullest appropriate use of that powerful machine.

As it is, we seem to know more about the environmental requirements of bees, Santa Gertrudis cattle, and chickens than we do about human environment. The reason may be that we like to treat human environmental needs as a matter of folklore or of serendipity. Perhaps there is so little research because there is "no money in it." Or is it because we have had other priorities in our society? Perhaps we have just lacked the capacity to really tackle the subject.

The true reason we are so backward in our understanding of human environment is probably some kind of blend of all four of these suppositions, and others. There are four reasons for thinking that the time is ripe for a new effort to define what men need from their environment. (1) With increasing numbers and concentrations of people, the costs of dealing with environment on a hit-or-miss basis are becoming increasingly obvious. (2) The market is growing so large and the state of the housing industry is so decrepit that there is now an opportunity for profit for many different industries in new concepts of environment. (3) The attainments of our affluent society have moved human environment into a priority political position. (4) With computers and skilled computer personnel now available to planners, politicians, and the public, we now have the capacity to study seriously the real-life multivariable complex interrelationships of the environment which the human mind could not possibly manage unaided.

Thus, a comprehensive effort to understand human environment might begin with identification of the functions of environment; its controllable variables; the relationship of the variables to one another; the relationship between functions and variables; the trade-off between functions (priorities).

In the beginning we should not be too careful. This is a new endeavor, and as Bertrand Russell has said: "It is a peculiar fact about the genesis and growth of new disciplines that too much rigor too early imposed stifles the imagination and stultifies invention. A certain freedom from the strictures of sustained formality tends to promote the development of a subject in its early stages even if this means the risk of a certain amount of error."

We *expect* to make errors in our effort at multivariable, multifunctional thinking about the future environment, but we believe it is a bigger error not to attempt this approach. There are undoubtedly errors as well as fresh insights in the papers in this book. And we must somehow learn to allow for subjective human values. The priority given to cancer and polio research, for instance, was a value judgment made by society. Statistically, these diseases are not the greatest causes of human deaths, yet they are given the highest priority because they represent to our society the greatest of all human suffering. Within the limits of practicality, the values of a society will select the alternatives to be pursued. Although we propose logic (including mathematics and the computer) as one tool in this development of the future environment, we do not consider it an exclusive tool.

The papers in this book are concerned mainly with the contribution of science and the professions toward creating optimum human environments defined in physiological, psychological, and sociological terms. We expect no single optimum environment; men are not animals in a zoo. The concept of a single optimum environment is for the human *animal*, not the human being; it is a "zoo view" of humanity that precludes human dignity.

The great contribution of science to this endeavor is best understood if we agree with Jacob Bronowski that "science is not a set of facts but a way of giving order, and therefore of giving unity and intelligibility, to the facts of nature."

The Matrix Approach

As a background for the chapters that follow, it may be useful to describe the ordering of the functions and variables of the environment known as the "matrix" approach.* In this attempt to bring order to our thinking on environment we hope to avoid the oversimplification of reality that comes from limiting ourselves to what the human mind unaided can grasp. The fact is, however, that many more qualities of human life can be quantified or formulated for computer handling than our casual thinking has yet deemed possible. There are, of course, many human purposes and values that are not subject to quantification.

Among the scientists, the mathematician's data are most exact, the physicist's next. Useful scientific experiment by the biologist is much more difficult; he has many more variables to control. For the social scientists and planners, the variables seem limitless. And if we seriously want to involve the people themselves in creating their own environment, the entire approach of science to creating the environment will be changed.

Still, wanting to be responsible but not rigid, we have proposed that it is possible to organize thinking and research toward optimum environment in such a way as to maximize the contribution of all the sciences and professional planners. An example of the sort of result to expect in this effort might be a redefinition of privacy (one of the variables in the matrix tables; see Appendix A). Human privacy seems to need closer

---

* This organizing concept was the framework for the Portland conference and the basis of the U. S. Public Health Service commission for the conference to the University of California (Berkeley). John W. Dyckman reports on the University of California study in Chapter 3 of this volume. Its mission was "to organize knowledge of human behavior, disease and health, in interaction with a metropolitan regional environment for purposes of physical and social planning in a form suitable for use by practitioners; and to locate such lacunae in that knowledge as may be susceptible to further investigation at the present time."

attention than we have given it, particularly if we are moving toward a period of higher population density. Perhaps privacy needs a definition broad enough to encompass the effects of particular cultures. Thus privacy, instead of being as defined by Webster "the state of being apart from company or observation" might become "that condition in which the individual can control his response to signals from his environment and is not unknowingly observed."

Functions of the Environment

To begin the development of the matrix approach we list as basic functions of the environment: (1) home life; (2) school; (3) shopping; (4) commuting; (5) work; (6) re-creation (spirit); (7) leisure and recreation; (8) experiences of nature; (9) healing.

Given this list of functions of the environment, we must then consider the means to develop priorities. For example, would some people be willing to live in smaller or otherwise less desirable quarters than they would otherwise choose, if they had a magnificent view? What functional limitations will suburban people accept in exchange for easy commuting within the city?

Variables of the Environment

In order to set up priorities that would result in an optimum environment, we must first understand the effects of the variables that we can control.

For controllable variables in the matrix we list: (1) climate; (2) air; (3) water; (4) solid wastes; (5) noise; (6) supplementary food intake (includes alcohol, drugs, etc.); (7) safety; (8) privacy; also the following, which may apply to traffic, people, sound, housing, etc.: (9) gross number; (10) density; (11) duration; (12) frequency.

The Relationship of Environmental Variables to Each Other

Variables in the environment are not truly independent, but are associated with one another. The strength of the association, either measured or estimated, between parts of variables may be recorded. If there are enough observations, a correlation coefficient between pairs can be calculated. (See Matrix of Controllable Variables in Appendix A.)

The Relation between Functions and Variables

The relation between the functions and the variables of the environment is expressed by technological and production functions, "the state of the arts." These relations summarize the current state of a *dynamic* process. This is a big (and possible) step involving mathematical analysis as well as extensive controlled experimentation. (We call it the Technological Functions Matrix; see Appendix A.)

Whereas the listings of functions and variables of the environment seemed innocent enough, it may now appear that we regard human environment as reducible to a mathematical equation. This is distinctly not the case. We do not propose to reduce reality to an equation and leave it up to the experts to determine our fate. On the contrary, we are seeking a more accurate definition of reality.

We must not be content with an oversimplified definition of the realities of environment simply because that is all that our unaided minds can grasp. The human mind is incapable of sorting and relating the many variables of the environment and their myriad of combinations simultaneously. But creating real human environments on the scale we shall be doing it in this country and in the world over the next fifty years requires exactly this information. The capacity of computers is called for. The matrix is a way of communicating with the computer.

Relationship of Function to Function

How much of one function or several functions—as modified or described by combinations of controllable variables—are we willing to trade for another (or others)? This is what is sought by the environmental matrix approach.

We are now at the stage of a Functions Trade-Off Matrix which conceivably *can* be managed. With this Trade-Off Matrix we can evolve optimum (or near optimum) solutions under liberal combinations of constraints, and the entire procedure can be replicated for various age groups, cultural characteristics, or other important factors. It is important to remember that all the numbers that might be used in these matrices are to be derived from specific study of the environment; each of them must be well tested and well understood before the expert mathematician is allowed to make use of them.

The Individual, Science, and the Future

For those who fear that the structured use of science and the professions here proposed may indicate an elitist approach to creating the future environment, I would refer you to the papers in this book. They afford ample evidence that professional planners and members of related professions are deeply concerned to bring the people into the decision-making process, to enable them to participate in creating their own individual destinies. But science *is* coming into this process.

As Joachim Woyl has said, "The biggest discovery we need in the next fifty years is how to integrate science with society."

This book represents a beginning.

II

René Jules Dubos
Microbiologist, Rockefeller University

Man Adapting:
His Limitations and Potentialities

In a cave not far from here archeologists have discovered a group of sandals 11,000 years old. These sandals, which were made by Stone Age people, could nevertheless fit twentieth-century human beings. They symbolize the unbroken continuity of human life.

On the other hand, the phrase "Man as the Measure" implies that human beings prize their individuality above everything else. Admittedly, the large agglomerations of the modern world can be likened to anthills or beehives; each person in them has a limited function and returns to rest at a particular place in the evening—as if he were but an anonymous and interchangeable unit in an immense colony. In fact, however, no two human beings are entirely alike.

We find it easy to believe that we have much in common because we come from lands and cultures that have been in contact for many thousand years. But we really never forget that we differ in geographical origin, in physical and mental attributes, in social and religious allegiances. Almost unconsciously we thus give a dual meaning to the abstract word "man." We use it to symbolize a paradox inherent in the human species—the biological unity of mankind and the experiential diversity of human life.

Irrespective of origin, all men are fundamentally similar in structure, requirements, and mental attributes; yet individual human beings and human civilizations differ profoundly from place to place and from time to time. Social planning—whether for the next fifty years or fifty thousand years—must take into account these two complementary aspects of man's nature: biological unity and experiential diversity.

The Unchanging Attributes of Homo sapiens

The prehistoric and historic events of the human adventure in the Americas provide convincing evidence of the unity of mankind.

As far as can be judged, various populations of ancient man began to move into the American continent during the late paleolithic period—some 20,000 years ago. After their initial penetration, they rapidly spread over the whole continent, but they remained almost completely isolated from the rest of mankind until the seventeenth century. During that period of isolation, they progressively developed several great cultures, exquisitely adapted to particular aspects of American nature. The Incas in the Peruvian Andes; the Mayas in the tropical forests of Central America; the Pueblos in the semi-desertic Southwest; the Plains and Forest Indians of North America; the Eskimos in the frozen North, all developed cultures that were completely independent of the earlier and contemporary ones in Africa, Asia, and Europe. Yet the achievements of the American aborigines—their temples, sculptures, pottery, basketwork, and even more remarkably their love songs and their legends of creation—are very meaningful to all of us who come from cultures originating from outside the Americas. Obviously, the most fundamental and universal characteristics of the human mind were fully developed by the time ancient man first penetrated the American continent.

During the past five centuries, many waves of immigration

brought other human races into intimate contact with the various tribes of American aborigines. Interbreeding resulted in many varied and highly successful racial mixtures. The genetic and physiological compatibility between races that had been separated for so many thousand years confirms the cultural evidence that all human beings originally derive from the same evolutionary stock.

In several parts of the world, there still exist today small tribes who have had no significant contact with modern civilization and whose ways of life have hardly changed since the Stone Age. Yet experience has repeatedly shown that the members of these tribes, born and raised under extremely primitive conditions, adapt rapidly to modern life. An infant born from a culturally backward people, but adopted very early in life by a more advanced cultural group, rapidly takes on the behavioral characteristics of his foster society and commonly rejects the culture of his natural parents.

Cro-Magnon man, who lived as a hunter 30,000 years ago, long before the emergence of agriculture and of village life, was probably indistinguishable from modern man mentally as well as biologically. He stood upright like us, had the same body shape, and his cranial size was at least as large as ours; the implements he made still fit our hands; the urges that shaped his familial activities and his tribal organization are still operative in us; his paintings, sculptures, and other artifacts deeply move us, symbolically and esthetically.

These anthropological findings are of great importance for the social planner because they prove that modern man retains many biological and mental characteristics of his remote ancestors. His physiological needs and drives, his responses to environmental stimuli, his potentialities and limitations, are still determined by the 20,000 pairs of genes that governed human life when ancient man was a paleolithic hunter or a neolithic farmer. Two examples will suffice to illustrate how pro-

foundly the physiological and behavioral responses of modern
man are still conditioned by the genetic endowment that defines the species *Homo sapiens.*

Ancient man naturally lived in intimate contact with nature
and his activities were therefore governed by natural rhythms,
such as the daily change from light to darkness and the recurrence of the seasons. As a result, his bodily and mental functions exhibited diurnal, lunar, and seasonal cycles linked to
those of the cosmic order. Remarkably enough, these biological
cycles persist in modern man even where the physical environment has been rendered almost uniform and constant by technological control. Rapid changes of latitude during jet air travel
cause physiological disturbances because the body cannot adapt
rapidly enough to the new day-night rhythms. These disturbances of jet travel are not subjective; they originate from the
fact that the secretion of hormones proceeds according to a
biological time clock which remains geared—for a variable period of time—on the day-night rhythm of the place of usual
residence. Similarly, modern life may create physiological disturbances when it carries the day into the night with electric
illumination and maintains the same temperature and food supply throughout the year. The urban environment continuously
changes but man's body machine continues to function in accordance with the cosmic events under which evolution took
place.

The so-called fight and flight response is another type of
innate and subconscious activity which is governed by very
ancient emotional and physiological forces still at work in
modern man. When prehistoric man encountered a human
stranger or a wild beast, certain hormonal processes placed his
body in readiness for combat or for escape. Today, the same
physiological processes are still set in motion under circumstances that modern man symbolizes as a threat, for example
in the course of personal conflicts at the office or at a cocktail

party. In most cases, such responses are no longer useful and may even be deleterious; but they persist nevertheless, as do numerous other mechanisms and structures originating from the evolutionary past.

Admittedly, the fact that modern man is constantly moving into new environments seems to indicate that he has enlarged the range of his biological adaptability and is escaping from the bondage of his past. But this is only an appearance. Wherever he goes, and whatever he does, man is successful only to the extent that he functions under environmental conditions not drastically different from the ones under which he evolved. He can climb Mount Everest and fly at high altitudes only because he has learned to protect himself against cold and to carry an adequate oxygen supply. He moves in outer space and at the bottom of the sea only if he remains within enclosures that duplicate certain physicochemical characteristics of the terrestrial environment. Even the Eskimos, who appear so well adapted to the Arctic winter, in reality cannot long resist intense cold. Sheltered in their igloos or clothed in their parkas, they live almost a tropical life!

Thus man does not really "master" the environment. What he does is to create sheltered environments within which he controls local conditions. Such control has been achieved for temperature, food, water, and oxygen tension, and a few other obvious physicochemical requirements. But human life is affected by many other factors that are poorly understood, and often not controllable at all. For example, the biological cycles mentioned earlier became inextricably woven in the human fabric during evolutionary times, and they still link modern man to cosmic events. The dissociation of modern life from these natural cycles is likely to exert some deleterious effects on the human organism. In fact, man is likely to suffer from many of the new environmental forces he has set in motion because he has not encountered them in his evolutionary past.

He may develop some tolerance against environmental pollution, severe crowding, constant exposure to intense sensory stimuli, and the regimentation of life in a completely mechanized world. But one can anticipate that this tolerance will have deleterious consequences for the human race in the long run.

In brief, the genetic endowment of *Homo sapiens* has changed only in minor details since the Stone Age, and there is no chance that it can be significantly or usefully modified in the foreseeable future. This genetic stability defines the potentialities and requirements of man's nature. It also determines the physiological limits beyond which human life cannot be safely altered by social and technological innovations. The frontiers of technology are in final analysis less significant for the life of man than his own frontiers, which are determined by the genetic constitution he acquired during his evolutionary past.

The Potentialities of Man

While the fundamental traits of *Homo sapiens* are permanent and universal, man's ways of life and the structures of his societies differ from one area to another and change endlessly with time. The biological evolution of man's body and mind almost came to a standstill some 50,000 years ago, but his sociocultural evolution now transforms human life at an accelerated rate.

Civilizations have their primary origin in the various responses to environmental stimuli. This versatility of response, in turn, is a consequence of the wide range of differences that exist among human beings. Except for identical twins, no two individual persons are genetically alike. Furthermore, the physical and psychic character of each person is profoundly influenced by environmental forces. From nutrition to education, from the topography of the land to urban design, countless influences play a role in determining the expression of the genetic endowment and thus in shaping the body and the mind of man.

Sociocultural forces are ultimately derived of course from man's biological nature, but through a feedback process they continuously alter his body, his mind, and his social patterns. This feedback accounts for the paradox that experiential man and his ways of life are continuously changing even though his genetic make-up is so remarkably stable.

Contrary to popular belief, genes do not determine the traits of a person; they merely govern his responses to the physical and social environment. Furthermore, not all the genes of a person are active at all times. Through complex mechanisms that are only now being recognized, environmental stimuli determine which parts of the genetic equipment are repressed and which parts are activated. Thus each individual person is as much the product of the environment as of his genetic endowment. Human beings perceive the world, and respond to it, not through the whole spectrum of their potentialities, but only through the areas of this spectrum that have been made functional by environmental stimulation. The life experiences determine what parts of the genetic endowment are converted into functional attributes.

The conditioning of the physical and mental personality by the environment has of course long been recognized. Winston Churchill was aware of its importance for human life when he urged that the House of Commons, damaged by German bombs during the war, be rebuilt as exactly as possible in its original form instead of being replaced by a modern and more efficient building. He feared that changing the physical appearance and organization of the House might alter the character of parliamentary debates and therefore of English democracy. In his words, "We shape our buildings and then they shape us."

The environment and ways of life determine in fact not only the conditions under which men function, but also the kind of persons their descendants will become. In fact, environmental factors have their most profound and most lasting effects when they impinge on the young organism during the formative phases of its development. Suffice it to mention as an example the acceleration in growth and in sexual development that is occurring at present in the Western world as well as in the Oriental countries that have become Westernized. Japanese teenagers are now very much taller than their parents not as a result of genetic changes, but probably because they are better protected against malnutrition and childhood infections.

The experiences of early life are of particular importance because the human body and especially the brain are incompletely differentiated at the time of birth. The infant develops his physical and mental individuality as he responds to the stimuli that impinge on him during growth. To a very large extent, the physical appearance and mental characteristics of the adult are thus the products of the responses made to the total environment during the formative years. In other words, anatomic structures and physical performance, as well as behavioral patterns, are molded by the surroundings and the conditions of life during childhood; furthermore, the effects of such early influences commonly persist throughout the whole life span. For example, a child brought up in Florence is constantly exposed to the sights, sounds, and smells characteristic of this beautiful city; his development is conditioned by the stimuli derived from palaces, churches, and parks. He may not be aware of the responses aroused in him by these repeated experiences. But they become part of his biological make-up and render him lastingly different from what he would have become had he developed in London, Paris, or New York.

From all points of view, the child is truly the father of the man. Most aspects of human life are governed by a kind of biological Freudianism, because socially and individually, the responses of human beings to the conditions of the present are always conditioned by the biological remembrance of things past.

Environment for Man

Each person has a wide range of innate potentialities that remain untapped. Whether physical or mental, these potentialities can become expressed only to the extent that circumstances are favorable to their existential manifestation. Society thus plays a large role in the unfolding and development of man's nature.

One can take it for granted that the latent potentialities of human beings have a better chance to become actualized when the social environment is sufficiently diversified to provide a variety of stimulating experiences, especially for the young. As more persons find the opportunity to express their biological endowment under diversified conditions, society becomes richer in experiences and civilizations continue to unfold. In contrast, if the surroundings and ways of life are highly stereotyped, the only components of man's nature that flourish are those adapted to the narrow range of prevailing conditions.

The lesson to be derived from the story of biological evolution is that man has been so successful because he is the least specialized creature on earth; he is indeed the most adaptable. He can hunt or farm, be a meat eater or a vegetarian, live in the mountains or by the seashore, be a loner or engaged in teamwork, function in a free democracy or in a totalitarian state.

History shows, however, that societies which were once efficient because they were highly specialized rapidly collapsed when conditions changed. A highly specialized society is rarely adaptable. Adaptability is essential for social as well as for biological success. Therein lies the danger of the standardization and regimentation so prevalent in modern life. We must shun uniformity of environment as much as absolute conformity in behavior.

At the present time, unfortunately, the creeping monotony of our technological culture goes hand in hand with the monotony of our behavior, taste, patterns of education and of mass communication. And yet it is certain that we can exploit the richness of man's nature only if we make a deliberate effort to create as many diversified environments as possible. This may result in some loss of efficiency, but the more important goal is to provide the many kinds of soil that will permit the germination of the seeds now dormant in man's nature. Diversity of social environment constitutes in fact a crucial aspect of functionalism, whether in the planning of cities, the design of dwellings, or the management of life. So far as possible, the duplication of uniformity must yield to the organization of diversity.

Irrespective of genetic endowment, a child who grows in a city slum will differ as an adult from one who has spent most of his life within the sheltering cocoon of a modern apartment house, or from one who has participated in the chores of a family farm. Unfortunately, awareness of the fact that surroundings exert a profound effect on human life is based largely on untutored observations and has not yet been converted into scientific knowledge.

Environmental factors obviously condition all aspects of human life, but nobody really knows which factors are influential or how they work. The problem, however, is not hopeless. Experiments have revealed that in animals, also, early influences condition growth, longevity, behavior, resistance to stress, and learning ability. The effects exerted on human life by early influences can therefore be studied through the use of experimental models, much as is being done for other types of biological problem. The knowledge thus acquired will certainly help in the rational management of society.

The population avalanche and the universal trend toward urbanization will, needless to say, affect all aspects of future life. By the end of this century, most human beings will be born, will live, and will reproduce within the confines of megalopolis. Until now, cities have constantly grown and renewed themselves through the influx of people originating from rural areas or from primitive countries. Very soon, however, and for the first time in history, this transfusion of new blood will come to an end; the human race will reproduce itself almost exclusively out of persons city-born and city-bred. To a very large extent, the future will therefore depend upon our ability to create urban environments having the proper biological qualities.

One of the most important unknowns in this regard is the effect of population pressure. There is no immediate danger that the United States will experience famine or even a decrease in the standard of living as a result of population pressure. We suffer from overpopulation, nevertheless, because human life is affected by determinants that transcend technology and economics.

Unwittingly we tend to regard ourselves and our fellow men as things, rather than as human beings. We do not recognize any danger in crowding as long as we can produce enough food for physical growth, and enough goods for economic growth. Yet overpopulation can destroy the quality of human life through many mechanisms such as traffic jams, water shortages, and environmental pollution; spreading urban and suburban blight; deterioration in professional and social services; destruction of beaches, parks, and other recreational facilities; restrictions on personal freedom owing to the increased need for central controls; the narrowing of horizons as classes and ethnic groups become more segregated, with the attendant deepening of racial tensions.

Paradoxically the dangers of overpopulation will be increased by the extreme adaptability of the human race. Human beings can become adapted to almost anything—polluted air, treeless avenues, starless skies, aggressive behavior, the rat-race of overcompetitive societies, even life in concentration camps. But in one way or another, we have to pay later for the adjustment we make to undesirable conditions. The cost includes for example increase in chronic diseases and decadence of human values. Congested environments, even though polluted, ugly, and heartless, are compatible with economic growth and with political power. But they damage the physical and spiritual aspects of human life.

The adaptability of human beings to environments that are compatible with organic life, but destructive of human values, creates difficult problems for community planning. We have to determine simultaneously on the one hand the kind and intensity of stimulation required for individual and social development; on the other hand, the levels of stimulation and adaptation that are potentially dangerous for the future.

In brief, it is obvious that the technological factors, such as supplies of food, power, or natural resources, that are required for the operation of the body machine and of the industrial establishment are not the only factors to be considered in determining optimum population size. Just as important for maintaining *human* life is an environment in which it is possible to satisfy the longing for quiet, privacy, independence, initiative, and open space. These are not frills or luxuries but constitute real biological necessities. They will be in short supply long before there is a critical shortage of the sources of energy and materials that keep the human machine going and industry expanding.

A Science of Environmental Biomedicine

The contributions of science to human welfare and especially to the future of mankind will be severely restricted until a systematic effort is made to study the biological effects of the environmental factors that affect life in the modern world, for example the varied aspects of biological and chemical pollution; the constant and unavoidable exposure to the stimuli of urban and industrial civilization; the emotional trauma and often the solitude of life in congested cities; the monotony and tensions of regimented life; the boredom arising from automated work and indeed from compulsory leisure.

Unfortunately, such a science of environmental biomedicine does not yet exist. Its development might be initiated through the study of a few specific problems. The following can serve as illustrations of such environmental problems having a direct relevance to human life and amenable to scientific analysis.

a. The lasting effects of early influences, i.e., of the effects exerted on the organism during the formative stages of its development.

b. The delayed and indirect effects of environmental pollutants.

c. The distant consequences of exposure to subcritical levels of potentially injurious substances and stimuli.

d. The effects of crowding on hormonal activities, on resistance to stresses, and on behavioral patterns.

e. The range of adaptive potentialities.

f. The effects of housing conditions on the development of sense organs and of various physiological processes.

For any one of these problems, it is possible to imagine experimental models duplicating one aspect or another of actual human situations. It must be emphasized, however, that unusual research facilities will be required for the development and use of such experimental models. The following items immediately come to mind.

a. Experimental animals of known genetic structure and of controlled experiential past.

b. Quarters for maintaining animals under a wide range of conditions throughout their whole life span and indeed for several generations.

c. Large enclosures for maintaining animal populations of various sizes and densities, exposed to different types of stimuli.

d. Equipment (using telemetry) for observing and measuring responses without disturbing the experimental system.

e. Equipment for recording, retrieving, and analyzing the complex data to be derived from the study of large populations and multifactorial systems.

The mere listing of these facilities points to the need for new types of institution with a special organization of highly integrated personnel. What is required is nothing less than a bold imaginative departure to create a new science of environmental biomedicine.

Conclusions

A scientific philosophy of mankind can be derived from the knowledge that man's nature encompasses two aspects that are radically different, yet complementary. On the one hand, *Homo sapiens* has existed as a species with a well-defined genetic endowment for some 50,000 years. On the other hand, man has continued to unfold his latent potentialities ever since that time. This ancient lineage accounts for the biological limitations of mankind and also for its immense phenotypic diversity.

The biological limitations inherent in the human species create a collective responsibility for directing technological development in such a manner as to make it compatible with human survival and welfare. The wide range of phenotypic potentialities gives to each person the chance to select or create his surroundings and way of life and thus to develop along the lines he chooses.

The existentialist faith that "man makes himself" implies of course the willingness to decide and the courage to be. But it also demands that action be guided by a deep scientific knowledge of man's nature. For this reason, we must create a new science of environmental biomedicine that will help in predicting and hopefully in controlling man's responses to the environmental conditions prevailing in the modern world.

New kinds of scientific institution must be developed to study the effects that surroundings and ways of life exert on physical and mental development, especially during the formative years of life.

The characteristics of individual persons, and of societies, are largely determined by feedback reactions between man's nature and environmental forces. Since man has much freedom in selecting and creating his environment, as well as his ways of life, he can determine by such decisions what he and his descendants will become. In this light, man can truly "make himself" consciously and willfully. He has the privilege of responsible choice for his destiny—probably the noblest, and a unique, attribute of the human condition.

Comment on

Dubos

C. DAVID LOEKS
President, American Institute of Planners

Dr. Dubos comes as a dispeller of myths—myths about man's unity and diversity which have tended to cloud our ability to think clearly about man and his environment. For example, he has dispelled the myth which states: "Man has an infinite capacity to adapt to a changing environment." As you know, this is an unstated assumption underlying much of contemporary planning, particularly in rapid growth situations.

Although man has great capacity to adapt, he has warned us that there are limits beyond which man does not go without paying a price. The bigger is not necessarily the better. He has charged us to try to understand these limits if we are to participate effectively in the creation of an optimum environment. Moreover, his message establishes that man must be the measure of these environmental limits.

Another myth which he has dispelled relates to the other end of the unity-diversity spectrum. This myth states: "There is a single end-state environment that is optimum." But Dr. Dubos tells us that man's adaptive capacity permits, indeed, requires, immense diversity in the environment if his full potential as a biological and spiritual being is to be approached. Man simply cannot be designed into environmental boxes whether they be the little ones that Pete Seeger sings about or the more grandly scaled products of some of our urban design efforts.

The second role discharged so elegantly by Dr. Dubos is that of dismantler of fences which have arbitrarily divided the roles and contributions of environmental disciplines. He has pointed out the kind of research and conceptual attack which is needed if these false dichotomies are to be dismantled. I suppose that each of us has his own definition of his proposed science of environmental biology. To me, what he is talking about is a comprehensive, man-centered approach to the optimum development of man and his environment in which all relevant disciplines have an integrated role.

He has said that such a multidisciplinary approach does not exist, and has established that such an approach is essential if man as a biological entity is not to be overwhelmed by the impact of technology on the environment. And he has sketched out the elements of such an approach. This is exactly what we wanted from him. Our purpose here is not to define an optimum environment but to design a conceptual approach to its definition. The keynote has been struck for the AIP's entire two-year consultation.

III

John W. Dyckman

Center for Planning and Development Research
University of California, Berkeley

City Planning
and the
Treasury of Science*

The expectations which city planners have for science are exceedingly high. In fact, they resemble the expectations which an earlier generation of scientists had for science. We may liken them, in a way, to the renowned Dr. Ehrlich's search for the magic bullet to shoot down the deadly spirochetes. The magic bullets of city planning are as yet undiscovered, but there have been times when the planners thought they had found them in the form of scientific "standards" produced by rigorous investigation into the relatively deterministic laws of environmental physics, or the biology of survival, or the social behavior of masses. A major part of our undertaking has been to evaluate the weight which may be safely given to these generalizations.

* In these remarks I am greatly indebted to the U.S. Public Health Service, to our consultants—Janet Abu-Lughod, Bennett Berger, Daniel Carson, Maynard Hufschmidt, Richard Meier, and Peter Senn—and to our own staff at the University of California Center for Planning and Development Research, particularly to Allan Blackman and Francis Ventre, whose scholarly diligence and critical faculties have provided much of the nourishment for my judgments.

As a result, much of the science which is useful in the practical art of improving our environmental adaptation and control is social or behavioral science. The practical planner, facing a seemingly straightforward design problem, soon finds this to be the case. Climatology is of little use to the designer of a building if he does not know the behavioral patterns of the users, from the types and levels of activity to the diurnal pattern of that activity.

The problem of the use of environmental facts in city planning is, of course, much more complex than that in building design. The contemporary city planner faces not only the complexity of the modern metropolis, but also the exploding discretionary range of behavior made available by abundance. At times he must envy the planner in the poorer or more desperate situation, who is working closer to the margin at which "hard" scientific knowledge is useful. When the elimination of hunger is the planning problem, a planner can use the finding of nutritionists that individuals of given size and level of activity need 2,000 calories a day more easily than his counterpart can use social survey findings on the aspirations of middle-class families for status neighborhoods or consumer goods. But despite the bands of air around these "facts" we must face the reality that nutritional limits may be less important to contemporary American city planners than somewhat more fuzzy status variables.

In an era of abundance, in which extreme physical deprivation is becoming increasingly rare, it is ironic that a major portion of our research on physical response to environment has been concerned with extremes of temperature, noise, light, and inconvenience. After an extensive search of the physiological studies of behavioral response, including performance on difficult tasks, to environmental variation, Francis Ventre reported to our project that:

> The relative wealth of knowledge about extreme environments derives from the fact that the bulk of environmental

physiology research is underwritten by the armed forces, civil defense and space agencies for whom the limits of human physical endurance have some operational significance. But the environments which concern architects and city planners have little of the extreme about them; gauges of well-being, health or comfort—all in the middle range—are the every-day interests of the environmental design crafts.

Daniel Carson, one of the consultants to our study, estimated in a report of the Michigan project on environmental evaluations in education that physical environmental factors accounted for only about one-quarter of learning performance.

Some Cautions for Practitioners of Planning

Before undertaking any direct review of the substantive findings of interest to planners it is only fair to make clear certain of my own very strong impressions.

1. There is very little directly usable scientific research in or for city planning. It is a major exercise of creative imagination and scientific judgment to bring the findings of the scientific community to bear on contemporary American city planning problems.

2. The usefulness of science is determined as much by the questions put to it by the planners, and the scope of activity open to them, as it is by the choice of the scientists or the character of their findings. It is because of the questions now being put by city planners in the United States that the behavioral sciences, and even some of the "softer" social sciences, seem more directly applicable than the traditionally "hard" physical sciences.

3. The beliefs of city planners, which are extremely favorable to and optimistic about the work of the scientific community, pose a certain danger in the use of these materials, because there is a tendency for city planners to stretch scientific findings to cover policy issues for which there is inadequate evidence,

and which may be only marginally relevant. This danger is especially great when it leads to the free use of analogies to cover situations for which actual research findings are not available.

4. The kinds of scientific research which are most useful to city planning are still in their infancy, but are growing rapidly. These include, in particular, the studies of complex systems, and related multivariate analysis techniques, as well as the behavioral studies of decision-making in individual and social environments.

These points deserve a very brief elaboration. In scientific activity there is no answer without a prior question, and the formulation of the question is often the most difficult part of the activity. In city planning we are still groping to correctly formulate important questions, and until these are formulated, assembly of scientific "facts" is an evasion. All the policy sciences have this difficulty. My colleague Allan Blackman, who has been studying pedestrian safety in cities, wryly observes that: "Safety engineers used to say: given the car on the road, what can science and engineering tell us about improving safety? The question now being asked is: given the driver and the pedestrian, what can science and engineering tell us about improving safety? Both questions can lead to scientific investigations, conclusions and action programs; but the questions will produce different answers."

The same principle seems to hold for the use of scientific findings in city planning, since the original investigations leading to those findings are rarely planned to answer a specific city planning question. The widespread predilection of city planners to seize upon studies containing recognizable environmental variables has led to many abuses, particularly in the housing field, where the defense of housing policies has sometimes rested on the relatively trivial role of the housing variable in a social psychological study generated by questions having nothing to do with housing policy.

On a few occasions, scientific researches have been designed to make city planning variables directly testable. One such case was the study by Daniel Wilner and his associates of the impact of housing environment on selected characteristics of family life.[1] This study showed that, in a Baltimore environment at least, improved housing did make a difference in family behavior. If the findings of the study were disappointingly meager to city planners in terms of a direct policy implication, the planners may have been unreasonable. Only the accumulation of a great many direct tests, exploration of a large number of variables, painstaking replication with suitable alteration of environments or variables—in short, only a sustained large-scale effort over a period of time can produce the cumulative insight necessary for moving with scientific confidence in policy fields. We have barely begun to support the studies needed for the questions placed in city planning, and we have yet to sort these questions in terms of either their priority for policy or their suitability for research.

The Interpretation of Scientific Facts by Policy Makers

Further, the "facts" handed the planner by scientific work are at various levels of verifiability, as well as usefulness. Consider the problem of interpretation of these scientific facts. The planner must transfer the finding from a research environment into a practical working environment. The environments of the scientist are designed by him and by the questions which his field chooses to address. What he cannot control is environmental noise.

To take an example, in attempting to conceptualize the problem of environmental stress, Howard and Scott proposed a paradigm of four environments: the biochemical environment, the physical environment, the psychological environment, and the sociocultural environment.[2] These four kinds of environment, chosen to accord with the practices of different disciplines, constitute a spectrum in which environment is directly controlled at one end, as in much biochemical and physical research, and is considered to be virtually uncontrollable, except by statistical randomization, at the other end (sociocultural). In between is the field of psychology, which has perhaps struggled most with the problem of environment, both physical and psychological.[3]

In addition to the problem of constructing a composite environment, the policy uses of science also face the difficulty that a large share of behavioral science must be interpreted by analogy. Some of the potentially most intriguing studies for city planning have been conducted on rats and pigeons by Calhoun[4] and by Skinner.[5] But the adaptive behavior of humans may be expected to differ markedly from that of rats or pigeons.

If we call the first of these difficulties the E or environment problem, and the second the P or personification problem, there is also a third—the C or conceptual problem. In science, a fact has to have a realm. That is, it must fit into a general scheme of other facts, or a theory. In practice this sometimes causes difficulty, especially when we are unwilling to accept the related body of facts into which some directly observable phenomenon is imbedded. It is a fact, to any jury of professionals or laymen, that education of Negro school children in the United States is inferior to that of white school children. But a fact which emerges from social history, as this does, comes from a tangled skein of social causes which, once unraveled, could begin to pull apart the structure of a society. The courts, as Weinberg has observed in great detail,[6] have shunted the fact, which might itself call for redress, onto the process which produced it, and which can now be more easily defended.

Finally, the time span necessary to observe a "fact" may be extremely long. The influence of air pollution on pulmonary disease, reported by René Dubos,[7] is necessarily somewhat speculative, because it requires a long period for the effect to accumulate to the critically observable point. Many of the environmental stresses suggested by an analogy with the work of Calhoun and others would be of this nature—that is, they would result in a markedly or an easily observable pathological condition only after prolonged cumulative effect. Indeed, the prevalence of cumulative effects, and of varying rates of accumulation, have led to great dispute about the impact of environmental insults on humans, these disputes being especially hot in the fields of radiation, insecticide residuals, and air pollution. Where generations would be needed to develop the pathology fully, as in the case of the influence of atomic radiation on genetic mutations, the time lag is clear. It is sometimes overlooked in the case of cumulative effects on the individual in his lifetime.

Some Administrative Uses of Scientific Facts: "Standards" and "Needs"

Let us now turn to those factual ingredients, the findings of science, which form the inputs to those planning judgments called standards. Remember, too, that the standards are complex judgments, formed from some determination of "requirements" plus some normative statement, usually a dominant social value. The scientific input presumably is focused on the requirement portion of the statement, since science proposes to say very little about values. If the standard is made up of "need" and "intention," the scientific findings will more frequently be adduced as evidence for the "need."

This is not to suggest that "need" is a simple and unequivocal concept. Economists have long since abandoned the notion, for practical purposes, and think in terms of production functions which are highly relative. And planners, too, are aware of the transformation of "needs" as technologies change. For example, I have been fond of pointing out to a generation of students what has happened to school building requirements with changing educational technology. When I entered city planning, 10-foot ceilings were requirements in many state school building codes. But the 10-foot ceiling, a "need" for much school building of the time, was found, on examination, to rest upon a simple performance requirement, the production of adequate lighting in the classroom, under the constraints of average class size and classroom dimensions, and under the constraint that pupils needed the advantage of natural light for effective classwork. Given the dimensions of the classroom, the need to provide for at least thirty desks, and the requirement of natural light, high ceilings and correspondingly high windows were required to assure adequate light penetration during school hours. With decreasing attention to window lighting and greater emphasis on artificial light at higher illumination standards, this requirement has become transformed, or even abandoned.

The scientific facts of the angle of penetration of light rays, and the foot candles or "lumens" of illumination necessary at each pupil's desk, were not changed, but the possibility of producing adequate light with different production combinations was able to revise the instrumental requirement.

Of course the human biological equipment, such as the visual equipment of the reader, changes much more slowly than the technological possibilities of producing light. It is this practical fact which has caused many students of man, such as the psychologist A. H. Maslow, to argue for the existence of a *hierarchy of needs*.[8] In Maslow's classification the more basic needs form the base of this need pyramid. Thus he moves from physiological needs, such as hunger, through the need for physical and mental security, for belongingness and love and esteem, to a need for "self-actualization." For Maslow, the hierarchy of needs is more important than the description of the individual needs. He argues that some need must be satisfied before man can proceed to the higher levels. This is a doctrine of *prepotency*.

If one takes Maslow's classification seriously, one is disposed to concentrate on physiological satisfaction and security before planning for the more complex satisfactions. We have previously observed, however, that American society has, on the whole, been quite successful in providing for satisfaction of physiological needs, leaving planners the residuum of the more difficult and complicated aspirations. Even more important for planning is the problem of balancing needs, for any effort to construct a schedule of needs quickly comes upon the realization that needs must be balanced at various levels, and the unilateral pursuit of a single need leads to the destruction of the system. In an analogous way, the pursuit of a single standard, or any other unilateral objective, is recognized by city planners to spell destruction of a plan, or a capital program. Standards, then, must be viewed as a part of a system. This common-sense feasibility constraint has been recognized by physicians, public health officials, city managers, and all practitioners who attempt to accommodate the facts of scientific findings to complex, balanced systems. The physiologist's notion of homeostasis, the ecologist's notion of balance, and the manager's or planner's notion of feasibility are all related recognitions of this condition.

In using the findings of science, therefore, the planner must keep in mind the allocative complexity of the system to which these findings are applied. Indeed, the high cost of these trade-offs makes many scientific findings difficult to use to any advantage in human affairs.

Some Man-Made Problems of Environment

A brief review of what science has to tell us about the design of the environment for urban living will make this point clear. First, scientists agree that cities, and the technologies of work, transport, communication, heating, and lighting which make them possible, place a number of stresses on the human physiological organism. In the earlier forms of industrial cities, particularly from the mid-seventeenth through the mid-nineteenth century, the principal dangers were in industrial safety and public health. While these have by no means been abolished as

sources of damage to human life, they have been greatly reduced in importance in the technically more advanced portions
of the world. Today, the emphasis has shifted to other directions
—to the impact of scale and density, with its concomitant communication and transportation technology and consumption requirements, upon the psychosomatic responses of individuals,
and to the threat which the collective technology, taken with
our methods of management, may pose for such fixed resources
as the world air and water supply, particularly in the course of
the disposal of the wastes of our technology.

Let us start to assemble our scientific inputs to planning
standards as close to the basic physiological level as our evidence permits. Because of the complexity and indeterminate-
ness of the findings, when physical, biological, and social influences are filtered through the human agent, their vectors of
influence become extremely difficult to trace. We can only offer
an array of findings, without any special pretense to "proof."

Our physiological models of man are such as to lead us to
believe, deductively, that the impact of certain technologies,
certain densities, and a whole variety of urban by-products is
harmful to man. The task is to establish the *ranges* of acceptable
damage, and levels of tolerance of the society for these insults.
When a relativistic, system-wide view is taken, our findings of
these environmental insults are much more liberal and permis-
sive than when they are viewed singly. Thus the Environmental
Pollution Panel of the President's Science Advisory Committee,
reporting in 1965, found almost no serious pollution threats,
at least by comparison with the more alarmist reports of individual researchers and investigating teams in the respective
areas.[9] For example, the Committee reported no clear-cut adverse effects on health from small accumulations of DDT in the
fatty tissues of humans, a finding not only at variance with earlier reports on the danger of DDT from pesticides, but one
which might be given another interpretation if we were to look

at the level of DDT concentration in body fat as an absolute danger, and were to view the United States in comparison with other countries. Thus, in reporting to our panel, Carson and Driver noted a study by Rudd (1964) which observed that DDT concentration in body fat in the United States had increased from 6 parts per million in 1958 to 12 parts per million in 1963, a level approaching that of Hungary, and two-thirds that of Israel, nations notoriously high in DDT residues.

Similarly, the President's Science Advisory Committee failed to find evidence that chronic illness was directly related to air pollution. Yet studies of the impact of air pollution on tissues are less equivocal. In the same report, Carson and Driver cited a number of studies demonstrating the relationship of increased concentrations of sulfur dioxide to the incidence of respiratory symptoms, particularly on asthmatics.[10] But they also report that the question of damage or alteration of lung tissue is still in doubt.

The differences in environments in which air pollution takes place are significant for the effects of air pollution on physiological conditions. The situation of a city such as Los Angeles, where the air pollution is typically accompanied by high temperature and high ozone concentration, is a case in point. Sudden or unexpected temperature extremes, and temperature extreme for which there has been inadequate acclimatization, are themselves factors in physiological and performance deterioration. Where air pollution arises in situations of high temperature, as in the case of Los Angeles, it may be difficult to separate the effect of air pollution from the effect of the temperature. But taken in concert, these constitute a dangerous combination.

These physiological studies of man's response to the contemporary urban environment have permitted us to make important beginnings in drawing up an accurate cost sheet in the balancing of benefits and costs of particular technological solutions. Thus, to take the automobile, we have also learned from a study by

Surti and Gervais,[11] reported by our consultants, that freeways may have costs that have escaped the traffic experts. This study came to the interesting conclusion that driver stress on freeways, particularly at the on-ramps, during rush hours was greatly increased over the corresponding rush hour stress on surface streets. At present, of course, there is no way to measure the comparative gain in comfort and safety of the freeway at nonrush hours when compared with the condition at rush hours. We would welcome an equation which included, in its variables, considerations of stress which could be as well quantified as the time savings and accident rates now widely used in evaluating the comparative benefits of freeways and other road systems.

Part of our great debt to men like Mumford comes from their clear recognition of these aspects of technology: first, that every technology brings with it its own set of problems, and second, that the continuing problem of city planning is the mastering of these technologies so as to reduce these unwanted by-products, and turn the technology to the preparation of even more effective social techniques. The air pollution from automobiles, the liver damage from pesticides, the noise and vibrations from urban machinery, are all examples of such unwanted technological by-products. Man can learn to live with them, but the costs are high. And the gains from the primary technologists which bring about these frictions and costs are indisputable. We would not abolish the automobile to eliminate air pollution from automobiles, at least within the present range of the latter danger. The range, flexibility, and freedom of choice which that vehicle offers have enhanced "welfare," as we know it. But when the cost of auto exhaust exceeds a range still to be defined, but now in sight, and as scientific studies make more clear the true nature of those costs, we may be prompted to become more restrictive in our management of the use of the automobile, or seek more assiduously to replace the present internal combustion engine. I wish I could report more authoritatively what those ranges are, but we are still waiting for the studies which can offer some hope of generalizing this knowledge.

Aspirations for "Optimal" Environments

The city planner, equally with the consumer in our time, is characterized by rising expectations. Confronted with the evidence of these physiological studies, he might once have been disposed to concentrate on the seemingly more manageable portions of the problem. Thus, for a long time, air pollution control was directed at industrial emissions, because the technology of control of these emissions, and the leverage of social pressure, were relatively well known.

The spirit of this conference, however, has been so bold as to raise the question of "optimum" environment. There is a strong intimation here that the environment can be shaped to man's taste. In such a perspective, it would seem reasonable to attach not only industrial emissions, but the socially complex problem of automobile pollutants as well, and further, to attach not only air pollution, but the problem of excessive temperatures. But we have had occasion to taste some of the benefits of man-made environments. The recent heat wave on the East coast caused hundreds of "excess" deaths. But the number was undoubtedly far less than would have resulted had there not been a well-developed apparatus of air conditioning. Indeed, one need only conjecture what might have happened in hospitals, old people's homes, and similar establishments under these conditions without benefit of air conditioning. Or, similarly, what would have happened had the air conditioning failed during this heat wave. The problem of minimizing extreme heat stress in our cities has become an economic problem, with the technology well known. We need only ask the question, "Are we rich enough as a nation to build central air conditioning systems as reserves for the control of temperature extremes in our cities?

Can we accept such temperature control as the 'standard' condition for our housing in urban living?"

In moving from the *safe* environment to the optimum environment in our planning targets, we have greatly complicated our calculations. We have made it particularly difficult by introducing variables which are less measurable by the extreme values. Thus, *comfort* is a less precise notion than certain other elements in minimum adequate standards. Yet the performance of modern man in his urban environment is a function of his level of comfort in that environment, as well as of his level of safety, and perhaps even physical health.

Some Environmental Insults

Increasingly, therefore, our city planning attention will be turned to intrusions on that comfort, and to minimizing the possible dangers of the technology which we develop to further insure the comfort and performance of men in cities. Urban noises, for example, undoubtedly do some damage to hearing. But the damage to hearing is less grave a concern than the interference, annoyance, and stress created by that noise, and the obstacles to comfort and composure which it creates. In another study reported by Carson and Driver, this by von Gierke,[12] an effort was made to measure the startle response, the vasoconstriction, and the endocrine secretion effects on the somatic-autonomic nervous system resulting from sharp noise levels. A study such as this does nothing to measure relative comfort, but it begins to provide us with some understanding of the physical mechanisms through which noises may affect human beings. The importance of these studies might be likened to the importance of bacteriology in epidemiology, without which early epidemiologists repeatedly mistook the vector for the agent.

In the case of noise, a large number of studies have attempted to measure the impact of airport noise on residential communities up to four to six miles from the airport. In the study by Cohen and Ayer,[13] reported by our consultants, measurements were made in residences with windows open and closed under conditions of both jet- and prop-driven-aircraft noise. To quote Carson and Driver,

> In virtually all the octave bands, the noise generated inside the house with all windows closed was in excess of that recommended for sleeping and also in excess of that produced by air conditioning units.

These noises were substantially less intrusive, of course, than that caused by sonic booms. In the period of supersonic jet transport, we must expect a more serious planning challenge with respect to the location of the jet ports and adjacent uses. It is not enough that people can learn to accommodate to and live with jet noises; if we are to perform our professional task effectively, we must make clear what the cost, in physiological, psychic, and other performance terms will be for the persons affected.

Future Problems: Technology and Scale

Further, we should begin now to prepare studies of the possibly deleterious by-products of technologies not yet adopted. The failure of planners (with the exception of a few prophets) to anticipate consequences of technical changes has meant that they have been placed in the almost impossible position of attempting to undo the powerful impact of technical changes to which people have already accommodated, at whatever cost. The task of relocating cities, or airports, or even residential areas around airports, is beyond the present power of city planning in the United States. It is only appropriate, therefore, that the present wave of scientific studies to serve city planning address themselves to the technologies still to be adopted.

Among these are not only the supersonic transport, but the

communications technology utilizing lasers. Some studies of the possible thermal and radiation damage from lasers have already been reported by our consultants, though they are still in an early stage of exploration.[14]

The very technology whose by-products are the subject of concern to planners has made possible the development of cities of our present size. To some observers, the size itself is one of the most dangerous by-products. For these critics, the very prophecies of the urbanization which we have experienced are suspect, and if cities are to exist at all, they must be organized along different lines, in response to other forces. But others, who accept the urbanizing forces, fear that they may have gone too far, or that they should be limited in their extent. Many scientific analogies are invoked, calling attention to the dangers of giantism in animal organisms. So far as direct studies are concerned, however, they tend to be of two kinds.

The first of these is a consideration of scale—a search for the optimum city size, which, in the work of one of our consultants,[15] is a "community size maximizing efficiency and variety while minimizing the unavoidable concomitants of congestion and social disorganization." The implication, of course, is that larger size leads to more congestion and social disorganization, while at the other end of the scale, smaller size means sacrifice of efficiency and variety. The social science studies of this question have been largely correlational, with regression of size on lists of facilities and other service variables. The causal relations and even the mechanisms connecting facility level with size have not been satisfactorily explored. Nevertheless, there is relatively general, if rather surprising, agreement among the investigators that some city size between 250,000 and 500,000 offers the complete market basket desired by urbanites at a scale which is most manageable with respect to the frictions of size. The emergence of vast metropolitan complexes, in which cities up to 500,000 appear as satellites, or virtual suburbs, of major metropolitan centers, has clouded this analysis, however. For in these metropolitan areas, functional specialization develops which makes the package of services provided by any one city less important, and the need for a completely self-contained package a weaker basis on which to rest the normative criterion.

Defining an Optimum Urban Environment: Density and Scale

Indeed, the *welfare* implications of urban complexes, taken as wholes, have never been adequately traced. A vast literature exists comparing characteristics of urban dwellers with rural dwellers in such pathologies as psychoses, neuroses, suicide, alcoholism, etc. It is virtually impossible to assign meaning to these findings. Urbanization is a process which stands for a whole cluster of other processes, and for scores of social and economic variables. Moreover, contemporary society is so urbanized that these studies become a commentary on the kind of society we have developed, and fail to distinguish meaningful aspects of urbanization for city planning purposes.

Traditionally, city planners have been even more concerned with *density* than with size or scale. The earlier tradition in city planning reacted to the industrial city with a general pressure for lower densities. The biologically inspired arguments of Patrick Geddes and the occasionally more romantic, but equally health-and-hygiene-oriented, views of the British and American town planning movements tended to specify tolerable limits, or even optimal densities of settlement. These were often in the range of 5,000 persons per square mile, a density viewed as rather suburban today. In more recent decades, the American city planning movement has been concerned with the preservation of densities which would guarantee some degree of "urbanity." For aesthetic, commercial, or even romantic reasons, our city planners have persistently sought dense clusterings within an over-all open pattern.

The evidence of science on this score is asymmetrical. The available scientific studies say almost nothing about urbanity, they are concentrated heavily on demonstrating, either directly or by analogy, the physiological, and especially psychological, stresses that result from overcrowding, or overly dense occupancy. Studies of animal populations (particularly the rat studies by Calhoun[16]) have shown not only that overcrowding may have strong pathological consequences for the population, but that the pathology eventually results in an adjustment at a lower level of density. Specifically, through the vehicle of infertility in reduced reproduction, the population declines to a more tolerable density, even if food is plentiful. According to project consultant Richard Meier,

> Similar phenomena appeared to be common in large congested cities before the 20th Century, but the outcomes of continued *anomie* were never clear because famines and epidemics intervened. Now, however, even the densest cities, such as Hong Kong or Singapore, can pack people together in densities greater than 100,000 persons per square mile with no observable decrement in birth rate or infant survival. Modern medicine appears to be responsible for the newly acquired capacity of the cities to overcome the physiological effects of crowding.[17]

The psychological effects, of course, are not so clear. On this count, Meier reports that:

> The hypothesis that seems compatible with all evidence to date is that a feeling of individual security is sufficient to keep individuals healthy, whereas continuous exposure to others leads to stress and possible physical disablement for all concerned. The environment is relatively neutral, since it can be manipulated to help as well as allowed to be misallocated [*sic*]. Privacy, as much as it exists for animals, seems to be essential for community peace.

If this conclusion can be taken literally, one might view the present decentralization of American cities, which is certainly well marked by now, as a drive to reestablish levels of residential density more nearly optimal for the populations concerned. We have learned something of the life styles of these suburbanites from a host of studies, many appearing in popular versions, but none can be said to have thrown scientific light on the question of optimal density. Like many other scientific studies, as I mentioned at the beginning of the chapter, this set of studies has given us useful information at the extreme conditions, but has not defined the parameters of a smooth function on which an "optimum" can be located.

The Value of "Urbanity" and Scientific Views of Social Interaction

To the social scientist, the rather vague notion of "urbanity," which planners are sometimes trying to maximize, must be broken up into measurable components of social interaction. Some of these components, such as theater-going, museum attendance, and other cultural expressions, have been of relatively little interest to the social scientists, perhaps because social science theory has tended to express them as functions of class variables, such as income, college education, and professional attainment. Some sociologists, following work pioneered by William Form at Michigan State, have made some studies and measurements of shopping behavior and other forms of lower-middle-class cultural expression. And some sociologists and social psychologists have directly addressed the issue of the effect of space and numbers upon interaction.

But as our consultant Janet Abu-Lughod has noted, social scientists have tended to read physical space for what it can tell them about social space. She observes that: "Attempts to manipulate social science by means of physical variables have been rare, except by city and office planners."[18] The latter often operate with less pretense to scientific theory, and frequently with less exacting controls. It is no wonder that the most influential, and exciting, of social science studies for the city planners was one conducted more than fifteen years ago by Leon Festinger and his associates at MIT, for that study introduced explicitly controllable planning variables, such as building types, site plan, and community size as independent variables which could be used to account, in that experiment, for types and volumes of social interaction.[19]

But Festinger and his associates, equally with other social scientists, were interested not in the manipulatable ecological variables, but in the social space variables. This work was less concerned with Simmel's issue of urbanity, and much more with Lewin's notions of psychological space. Continuing work along these latter lines by social psychologists and group dynamics sociologists has not been so rewarding as the city planners might have hoped.

One reason, which is taken for granted by most social scientists, is noted by Janet Abu-Lughod. She observes that:

> Ecological parameters and forms are continuously filtered *through* the social structure, the value systems, the technological and economic conditions, shaping and modifying them as well as being in turn altered by them. These are essential intervening variables without knowledge of which effects cannot be predicted. When they are held constant, effects can be traced and outcomes anticipated within ranges; when they are varied or changing rapidly, the predictive model must anticipate *how* they will deflect or modify the response to ecological stimuli.

The notion that findings must continuously be corrected for differences in class, occupancy, ethnicity, and life cycle has been discouraging to some city planners. Fortunately, as Mrs. Abu-Lughod's report points out, techniques of social area analysis have been developed which permit, with suitable factor analysis and statistical techniques, some management of these social ecology studies in the use of city planning. Nevertheless, this is, and will be, a tedious process, involving elaborate measurement of census and survey data, suitable classifications of the data, factor analysis and data manipulation, and most important, the relation of these statistics to hypotheses developed by more controlled studies of social interaction.

The "Iron Laws" of Ecology

At this point, there may be something of a conflict between the push of the social scientists to be "scientific" and the push of the planners to manipulate the environment, using ecological guides. A degree of determinism is beguiling to the social scientist, who would be pleased to find "laws" of ecology comparable to those of astronomy or physics. The "scientistic" social scientists, including the proponents of social physics, see the development of a describable environment of social ecology as the product of impersonal forces which can themselves be generalized in relatively simple laws. (Perhaps the outstanding example of this view was the work of George K. Zipf, in his formulation of the Principle of Least Effort, by which a variety of phenomena, from city size to urban income, were describable by simple distributions.) And it is certainly true that no one, in any directly personal way, wills the distributions that result from market competition or technical engineering forces.

These forces are significant, and must be reckoned with in planning, but the idea of social determinism is rejected by planners for at least two reasons. First, and most obviously, planning must operate on the significant (to planners) changes which take place within these large force fields. In other words, the questions asked by planners are begged by such gross formulations. Planning shares this viewpoint with those social sciences which are policy-oriented. It is no accident that the policy-oriented social sciences make fewer such scientific claims, and are themselves cause for the view that social science may not be scientific. The heart of this doubt was voiced by the philosopher of science, Ernest Nagel, in a passage reported by one of our consultants.[20] In Nagel's words:

There are some grounds for doubting that the social sciences are likely to refine their current distinctions beyond a certain point —the point fixed by the general character of the problems they investigate and the level of analysis appropriate for dealing with these problems.

Most frequently, city planners are concerned with making just those small distinctions in a land use ordering, a distribution of population, accessibility, and even esthetics, which are not treated at all by the deterministic formulations.

Secondly, city planning is in relentless pursuit of betterment. It is searching for "optimum" arrangements, even though its steps in that direction are slow and incremental. The deterministic formulations point out the processes by which existing distributions have come about. They do not evaluate the desirability of those distributions. The more meddlesome planners cannot be content with merely sleuthing the accommodation to these processes. Planning is frankly interventionist.

The Prospect for Scientific Planning

Must planning, then, give up hope of being scientific? One of our consultants, Peter Senn, has quoted John Stuart Mill in arguing the contrary. For Mill, the purpose of every art was related to science in a "scientific theory of the art." In Mill's words,

> art in general consists of the truths of science, arranged in the most convenient order for practice, instead of the order which is the most convenient for thought. Science groups and arranges its truths, so as to enable us to take in at one view as much as possible of the general order of the Universe. Art, though it must assume the same general laws, follows them only into such of their detailed consequences as have led to the formation of the rules of conduct.[21]

The practicing utilitarian, Mill, further argued the "need of a set of intermediate scientific truths, derived from the higher generalities of science, and destined to serve as the generalia or first principles of the various arts," much in the spirit in which Martin Meyerson called for his famous "middle range bridge."[22]

These "generalia or first principles" of the middle range would seem to be the "standards" which planners have so often used as their provisional science, their production functions of city design. Some such provisional scientific generalizations will need to be used in the future as well. But these will not be "magic bullets" to be fired in the direction of individual scientific truths. As another member of our team, Maynard Hufschmidt, has observed,

> The techniques which environmental scientists and designers used to solve yesterday's simple, single-purpose problems are not applicable to deal with today's complex, multi-purpose problems. When epidemics and endemic water-borne diseases were the problems, suitable water-purity standards were straightforward solutions. Today, with the health problem largely in hand, the quality standards approach no longer is the appropriate solution to the subtle and diffuse issues of amenities and aesthetics.[23]

The techniques for dealing with these multivariate problems are not unknown to the city planners. For the "systems approach" they read "comprehensive planning"; for the "cost-benefit" techniques they read a weighing of public values. In developing their plans, they will draw, to the extent that they are able, on environmental scientists, "applied chemists, biologists, bacteriologists, sanitary engineers, public health scientists, and ecologists," as well as upon social scientists— "economists, political scientists, geographers, sociologists, and social psychologists."[24] The assembly of this evidence will be a collective affair, and hopefully one which will make individual planners appropriately humble.

The scientific information is but one part of the information needs of planning. Traditional scientific studies of the environment must be supplemented by behavioral studies of more subjective intentional factors, such as the attitudes of people toward risk and uncertainty, by studies of an engineering nature, of real costs of developments, and of frankly projective studies of future possibilities which are less clearly scientific in foundation. In addition, planning must conduct a major inquiry into values. In this the planners can be greatly assisted by social science techniques, but there will remain an area of value exploration which is more indirect, and which will depend upon inferences from behavior that are somewhat subjective.

Conclusion

Finally, we must recognize that this effort to assess for environmental excellence is a partial and highly selective account. I have been reserved, perhaps overly cautious, about the contribution of contemporary scientific studies to planning decisions. We should not be unmindful that our present framing of the planning problem is itself influenced by the previous successes of science, including social science. A statement of the Behavioral Sciences Subpanel of the President's Science Advisory Committee in 1962 claimed that:

> The impact of the behavioral sciences on our society is far greater than most people realize: at one level they are providing technical solutions for important human problems. But at a deeper level they are changing the conception of human nature—our fundamental ideas about human desires and human possibilities; when such conceptions change, society changes.[25]

While the ideas of evolution in progress, borrowed from science, have sufficiently penetrated our culture as to make planning, which leans on these ideas, generally acceptable, the process by which these ideas are integrated into the culture is a slow one. One must expect a substantial lag. Many other ideas of science will be as bitterly resisted as was the doctrine of evolution, and we may expect that in the social sciences, where value questions are as close to the surface as evolution was to theology, substantial struggles will take place before new ideas become part of the apparatus of social planning. In other cases, supposedly "scientific" problems will be shown to be essentially value problems. In one of our reports, Hufschmidt has pointed out the role of economic thinking in achieving this transformation of the natural resource question; in another, Bennett Berger has made a similar reduction of the problem of segregation and the preservation of ethnic subcultures.

I would hope that city planning, by raising new questions for the social and physical sciences, will have some feedback on these sciences and will help to alter some marginal scientific choices in a more productive direction. For the sciences are themselves undergoing major transitions, both of concept and of interest. Physics is at a temporary standstill, slowed down by the weight of its own applications, and increasingly a theoretical handmaiden to other studies. Computers and modern mathematics have turned psychology's attention once again to the problem of how we think. It has not, however, helped us much in exploring the nature of man—is he a playing or a working animal? In biology, vitalism is dead, but life is still not well understood, and microbiology will need new models to integrate its very substantial findings. The sociological issues are innumerable, from the manipulative to the humane and reformist. Economists, as abundance breathes hot upon their traditional concerns, are turning again to examining the ends of consumption. A host of behavioral sciences are enmeshed in concerns of motivation. Ecology is being revived at a new and more respectable level by the growing interest in systems analysis everywhere from engineering to epidemiology.

In city planning, I think we have an unrivaled opportunity to participate, if only marginally, in some of these new developments of science, both as an occasional contributor and as an avid consumer. The time is past when we were naive borrowers from science—the days of easy analogies, such as that between residential "blight" and infectious plant pathologies, is long past. We no longer believe that an apparent "scarcity" of some resource calls for an immediate increase in supply. In short, we have learned to be sophisticated about both our sources and our generalizations.

One may hope that as the sciences of the environment turn increasingly to sciences of managing the environment, we will also enrich the scientific meaning of terms such as equilibrium, stability, and balance, which are so important in management, as well as anonymity, conformity, and urbanity, and similar concepts of the urbanist. We may even be able to put useful parameters around such notions as "irreversibility" in natural resources, and "amenity" in public esthetics.

Comments on

Dyckman

W. C. LORING
U. S. Public Health Service

The Public Health Service is concerned with the effect of environment on health in the next fifty years. An important part of our mission is to provide health-related criteria for planning decisions and design solutions. The increasing population, burgeoning densities, and urban concentrations of the next five decades probably will require much creative design of new residential, industrial, workaday, and recreational environments. Dr. Dubos's remarks underline the close linkage between planners of environment and PHS's concern for environmental health.

The Public Health Service was glad to make the services of Dr. Dyckman and his team of colleagues and consultants available to the AIP program on Optimum Environment with Man as the Measure. Our purpose was to develop a quick review of the state of knowledge available to planners from the basic scientific disciplines. Mr. William R. Ewald, Jr., in developing the programs for the AIP's two-year consultation, had conceived the idea of such a review. He envisioned the development of an ordered framework for the many factors bearing on planning the environment, including a matrix model suitable for the use of many disciplines. The matrix was to provide the possibility of entering some metrics in many of the matrix cells, and to help develop specific recommendations on priorities for future research and experiments.

The Office of Urban Environmental Health Planning in the Division of Environmental Engineering and Food Protection became most interested in assisting this project. With the assistance of the National Institute of Mental Health and the Division of Air Pollution, a contract was undertaken with the Center for Planning and Development Research, University of California, Berkeley. Malcolm C. Hope, Acting Chief, Division of Environmental Engineering and Food Protection, stated that the purpose of the PHS interest in this collaboration with the AIP is not only to reveal the present useful knowledge in a systematic review, but also to discover the gaps in knowledge which researchers in the several sciences should be encouraged to fill. It is the hope of the Public Health Service to encourage, through this undertaking, a flow of research grant applications to the interested Divisions of the Service and to private foundations.

It is evident from Professor Dyckman's report that all the facts needed by planning practitioners are not yet available in useful form from some of the basic science. Only parts of the several systems or matrices can now be filled in. Apparently the social sciences report definitive grist for the planners' mill mainly on *extreme* conditions, and do not as yet offer much that affords criteria for guidance in planning decisions within the average or normal range of conditions and behaviors which typify ordinary American communities. So here we have much need of research collaboration between planners, health and behavioral researchers.

Present trends point toward an overdensity in urban areas. How dense can we get without adverse effects on health, creativity, and

culture, and on economic productivity? These are questions to which
the PHS is giving a great deal of attention. The AIP theme for these
meetings shows that planners are concerned. I take it from discussion today that some of our corporate giants are concerned.

René Dubos said that in his opinion animal studies were relevant.
Dr. Dyckman mentioned Dr. John B. Calhoun's study of animals.
Calhoun, at the National Institute of Health, has done fascinating
studies on what can happen to animals when density gets out of
control in well-planned environments. I strongly urge that you read
Calhoun's "Population Density and Social Pathology"[1] and John J.
Christian's "Phenomena Associated with Population Density."[2]
Calhoun's animals were in a well-planned environment. They did
all right for the first two generations; but by the third generation,
by misuse of their physical environment, they "culturally" conditioned themselves to seek food in only one of the four "neighborhoods" of their environment. Because of this, they brought on themselves the curse of a tremendous overload of contacts or interactions,
which they could not stand. Withdrawal or psychosocial isolation
was frequently observed as a behavior developing when the overcrowding of activities got unbearable. They not only broke down in
mental health, but also in physical health to the point where the females could not continue reproductive processes to a fruitful end.
Christian also reports systemic malfunction and endocrine problems
associated with overcrowding.

Now is this kind of animal study pertinent to man? Should we
heed this evidence and its pertinence to human health and behavior
in constructing studies to gain guidance in planning our future residential environments? I think so, because we have certain indications
coming out of studies of human beings by epidemiologists and social
scientists which suggest that they cannot protect themselves from
the health consequences of overdensity without careful physical and
social planning.

The epidemiologists look for controllable variables of a health
problem in host, agent, or environment. Before the advent of the
germ theory of disease, public health people hoped to be able to
reduce the incidence of communicable disease by controlling an associated environmental factor—overcrowding. Dr. Allan Martin, Sen-

ior Medical Officer, Ministry of Health, United Kingdom, wrote a good review of this period for the World Health Organization, "Environment, Housing and Health,"[3] which shows how control through attacks on host or agent became more important than control of density. He goes on to say, however, that there begin to be a lot of indications that environment and mental health are so linked, without any germ, agent, or host link available to help correct the problem, and that environmental planning is the resource we shall have to use to reduce the impact of overcrowding and density on mental health.

There are a number of exploratory or pilot studies that indicate the nature of the problem. In summary, it seems that a lot of health problems stem not from mere physical crowding, but from activity overcrowding, role overdensity and possible subsequent withdrawal into psychosocial isolation, and from faulty communication related to environmental "noise." On the one hand, the Office of Civilian Defense has done an exhaustive review of space occupancy and health consequences of the more notable recorded cases of sheer physical crowding in slave ships, prisons, concentration camps, and shelters; most people subjected to such experiences survived and recovered rapidly if during their ordeal they allowed their systems to adjust by accepting the situation, reducing interaction and energy expenditure. On the other hand, the concentration of many types of ill health in crowded areas has long been noted. Controlled research studies in this country and Europe in the mid-1950's reported: (a) that the only housing or neighborhood characteristic associated with social disorganization is overdensity;[4] (b) that high first mental hospital admission rates for psychoses among elderly, and others, occur *regardless of socioeconomic status* in center-city high-density areas typified by high concentrations of multiple family dwellings;[5] (c) that tension build-up in an urban household, leading to the probable appearance of abnormal social behavior by the end of a day, relates to the amount of habitable space per person in the dwelling, and that pertinent threshold limits in any culture can be ascertained for setting standards;[6] (d) that the presence of immediately accessible common spaces, private or public, that can be alternated with the dwelling unit as the place for activity during the crowded hours of the dwelling (after school and work) may prevent tension build-up to abnormal behavior.[7] In all this evidence it appears that the standards of design and provision of physical spaces and circulation, and the cultural patterns of use of such physical facilities, are equally pertinent controllable variables for planner and health official to learn to employ.

Epidemiologist Ido de Groot, working with the Office of Urban Environmental Health Planning on criteria for residential environment hygiene, points out that both the animal and the human behavioral studies at present suggest that interaction under overcrowded environmental conditions is a source of stress which can lead to systemic malfunctionings, especially those mediated by higher brain functioning, i.e. those expressing themselves as mental disorder, heart disease, and endocrine deficiencies. Here we see the need for an important research collaboration between the health and planning professions and basic scientific disciplines. The coming increased densities of urban life, which we must learn how to make healthful, set the urgency and size of this task in planning the optimum environment for urban man.

DANIEL CARSON
Department of Psychology, University of Michigan

The planner works on complex problems in a real world and has great need for scientific knowledge and systematic methodology relevant to the solution of these problems. Until now, knowledge and methodology coming from the sciences have been limited and the planner has developed his own bag of tricks to conjure up solutions.

Because I have worked as a planner in the past, I do not envy him in this task. The laboratory scientist, for example, has a much easier bag of tricks to handle, since he can define and restrict his problem much more readily. Moreover, he can bring to bear on that restricted problem a conventional set of techniques and thus grind out easily communicable answers in the jargon of his science.

One of the implications of Dyckman's paper is that science still has little to offer planners who must meet everyday exigencies in the real world. Part of the reason for this stems from the fact that scientists seldom deal with the real world in its full complexity. Another part of it stems from their inability or unwillingness to communicate in terms appropriate to the planner's problems the results of their investigations.

We might summarize this situation by saying that the scientist does not look where the object is lost, but rather, where the light is best. He then behaves somewhat like T. S. Eliot's Prufrock when he tries to answer the planner's questions, and is likely to get from the planner the same response Prufrock got: "That is not it at all, / That is not what I meant at all!"

However, it should be said in defense of the scientists that it may be unfair to ask them for solutions to the very broad, multivariate problems which face the planner each day. Scientists typically do not bring along with them the equipment to meet such requests. I would suggest that the growth and development of a science of the environment which can generate data and methods for use by the planner will come from within the planning profession itself. It will train its own scientists, who will direct their skills toward problems encountered in the environment.

A second point touched upon by Dyckman in his paper deals with awareness. In speaking to this point, I should like to emphasize that I am not speaking of the awareness of the planner, or of the environmental scientist, but rather of that of the public.

Because of his profession, the planner is much more aware of problems in the environment than the average citizen. It may also be difficult or impractical for him to communicate these problems to the public, so that each citizen becomes aware of them. Yet in some instances, it is imperative that he increase individual awareness.

Awareness is a slippery variable. In its measurement, we can think of two things that we might use. The first of these is simply questioning about a situation, and the second is performance based on what we assume to be awareness in the situation. Often these two measures do not agree.

If we ask an individual whether he has a specific vitamin deficiency, it is doubtful whether he could tell us. In the case of vitamin A deficiency, there is evidence in the literature that individuals suffering a vitamin A deficiency may not be aware of it because they are not equipped to detect it. But even in the case of vitamin B deficiency, where there are specific detectors, individuals may still not be able to state that they are aware of it. In the two instances, their behavior in the selection of foods can tell the investigator that they are "aware" of the vitamin B deficiency but not "aware" of the vitamin A deficiency.[1] Moreover, the experiments on such deficiency further suggest that the detectors for vitamin A deficiency may be there, but that under certain nonwild conditions, e.g., the animal in a laboratory environment, this detector may be reduced in its efficiency. If it is possible for an animal to lack effective detection of such basic physiological needs, we may conjecture that less basic needs will also lack awareness.

We may consider an individual's awareness of an environmental hazard as an example at a more general level of environment. By asking individuals whether they are aware of such hazards as smog, air traffic noise, brush fire, flood, or earth slide, we can obtain a detection matrix about the accuracy of perceiving a hazard. Such a matrix will tell us, at the level of questioning, whether the individuals do or do not perceive the hazard. Such a detection matrix can often show that individuals do have very poor awareness.[2] In addition, there is the observation of what action is taken based on awareness of hazard, or at the performance level. The studies by Nixon[3] and Borsky[4] demonstrate that although aware of a hazard such as sonic boom, residents typically do not react with some attempt to remove this hazard.

There is the final problem that awareness may not be an unmixed blessing. Verwoerdt and Douvenmuehle[5] suggest that an increased awareness of heart illness introduces further stress and depression. Apparently this awareness adds to the stress of helplessness.

In dealing with awareness, the planner has a complex problem to consider. He must first decide for specific factors of the environment whether awareness is going to restrict the choice of behavior or increase it. After he has made that decision, he must then decide in what ways he can design the environment to increase or decrease

awareness of these factors, basing his judgment on whether awareness aids or hinders performance.

To state it simply, he can assume the position of caretaker, where
he conditions the individuals with or without their awareness. Or he
can assume the position of educator, where he creates environments
to teach individuals and make them more aware. Before he can
decide which position to take with respect to a specific environmental
variable, he must first develop tools of measurement and analysis
appropriate to the science of environment and human behavior.

Christopher Alexander

Department of Architecture and
Center for Planning and Development Research
University of California, Berkeley

The City as a Mechanism
for Sustaining
Human Contact

People come to cities for contact. That's what cities are:
meeting places. Yet the people who live in cities are often con-
tactless and alienated. A few of them are physically lonely:
almost all of them live in a state of endless inner loneliness.
They have thousands of contacts, but the contacts are empty
and unsatisfying.

What physical organization must an urban area have, to func-
tion as a mechanism for sustaining deeper contacts?

Before we can answer this question, we must first define exactly what we mean by "contact" and we must try to understand just what it is about existing cities that prevents the deepest contacts from maturing. Once we have done that, we can
define a set of characteristics which an urban area requires to
sustain the contacts. This chapter therefore has four parts:

In the first part I shall define the most basic and most urgently
needed kind of contact, *intimate contact.*

In the second part, I shall present a body of evidence which
strongly suggests that the social pathologies associated with

urban areas—delinquency and mental disorder—follow inevitably from the lack of intimate contact.

In the third part, I shall describe the interplay of phenomena which causes the lack of intimate contact in urban areas today. These phenomena are facets of a single complex syndrome: *the autonomy-withdrawal syndrome.* I shall try to show that this syndrome is an inevitable by-product of urbanization, and that society can recreate intimate contacts among its members only if they overcome this syndrome.

In the fourth part, I shall show that in order to overcome the autonomy-withdrawal syndrome a city's housing must have twelve specific geometric characteristics, and I shall describe an arrangement of houses which has these characteristics.

1. Intimate Contact

Modern urban society has more contact and communication in it than any other society in human history. People who would never have been in contact in a preindustrial society are in contact today. There are more contacts per person, and there are more kinds of contact. Individuals are in touch with a larger world than they ever were before. As metropolitan areas grow, society will become even more differentiated, and the number and variety of contacts will increase even more. This is something that has never happened before, in the whole of human history, and it is very beautiful: Durkheim said so long ago, in the *Division of Labor in Society.*[1] Melvin Webber and Marshall McLuhan and Richard Meier are saying it eloquently today.[2]

But as the individual's world expands, the number of contacts increases, and the quality of contact goes down. A person only has twenty-four hours in his day. As the total number of his contacts increases, his contacts with any one given person become shorter, and less frequent, and less deep. In the end, from a human point of view, they become altogether trivial. It is not surprising that in just those urban centers where the greatest expansion of human contacts has taken place men have begun to feel their alienation and aloneness more sharply than in any preindustrial society. People who live in cities may think that they have lots of friends; but the word friend has changed its meaning. Compared with friendships of the past, most of these new friendships are trivial.

Intimate contact in the deepest sense is very rare. *Intimate contact is that close contact between two individuals in which they reveal themselves in all their weakness, without fear.* It is a relationship in which the barriers which normally surround the self are down. It is the relationship which characterizes the best marriages, and all true friendships. We often call it love. It is hard to give an operational definition of this kind of intimate contact: but we can make it reasonably concrete, by naming two essential preconditions without which it can't mature.

These conditions are: (1) The people concerned must see each other very often, almost every day, though not necessarily for very long at a time. (2) They must see each other under informal conditions, without the special overlay of role or situation which they usually wear in public.

In more detail: (1) If people don't meet almost every day—even if they meet once a week, say—they never get around to showing themselves; there are too many other things to talk about: the latest news, the war, the taxes, what mutual acquaintances have been doing lately. These things can easily fill an evening once a week. Unless people meet more often, they never have a chance to peel the outer layers of the self away, and show what lies inside. (2) Many people meet every day at work. But here the specific role relationship provides clear rules about the kinds of things they talk about, and also defines the bounds of the relationship—again there is little chance that the people will penetrate each other, or reveal themselves. The same thing is true if they meet under "social" circumstances, where the rules of what is proper make deep contact impossible.

These two conditions are not sufficient—they do not guarantee intimate contact—but they are necessary. If these conditions are not met, intimate contact can't mature.[3]

It may help to keep in mind an even more concrete criterion of intimacy. If two people are in intimate contact, then we can be sure that they sometimes talk about the ultimate meaning of one another's lives; and if two people do sometimes talk about the ultimate meaning of their lives, then we are fairly safe in calling their contact an intimate contact. If they do not talk about these things, then they are not really reaching each other, and their contact is superficial.

By this definition, it is clear that most so-called "friendly" contacts are not intimate. Indeed, it is obvious that the most common "friendly" occasions provide no opportunity for this kind of contact to mature. Friends who come around to dinner once a month ("Honey, why don't we have them round to dinner sometime?"), or the acquaintances who meet for an occasional drink together, clearly do not satisfy the two conditions which I have defined. At these occasions people neither reach each other, nor do they reveal themselves. Let us, therefore, begin by asking what social mechanism is required to make contacts intimate.

In preindustrial society, intimate contacts were sustained by primary groups. "A primary group is a small group of people characterised by intimate face to face association and cooperation."[4] The three most universal primary groups are the family, the neighborhood group of elders, and the children's playgroup. These three primary groups have existed in virtually every human society, and they have been primary in forming the social nature and ideals of the individual. It is clear that the contacts which these primary groups created do meet the two conditions I have named. The members of a primary group meet often—almost daily; and they meet under unspecialized conditions, where behavior is not prescribed by role, so that they meet as individuals, man to man. It is therefore clear that in a society where primary groups exist, the primary groups do serve as mechanisms which sustain intimate contact.

Because intimacy is so important, and because primary groups have, so far, always been the vehicles for intimate contact, many anthropologists and sociologists have taken the view that man cannot live without the primary groups.[5]

Here are two typical statements: First Homans, writing in 1950:

> In the old society, man was linked to man; in the new agglomeration—it cannot be called a society—he is alone. . . . All the evidence of psychiatry shows that membership in a group sustains a man, enables him to maintain his equilibrium under the ordinary shocks of life, and helps him to bring up children who will in turn be happy and resilient. If his group is shattered around him, if he leaves a group in which he was a valued member, and if, above all, he finds no new group to which he can relate himself, he will, under stress, develop disorders of thought, feeling, and behavior. His thinking will be obsessive, elaborated without sufficient reference to reality; he will be anxious or angry, destructive to himself or to others; his behavior will be compulsive, not controlled; and, if the process of education that makes a man easily able to relate himself to others is itself social, he will, as a lonely man, bring up children who have a lowered social capacity. The cycle is vicious; loss of group membership in one generation may make men less capable of group membership in the next. The civilization that, by its very process of growth, shatters small group life will leave men and women lonely and unhappy.[6]

Second—Linton:

> Although the disintegration of local groups in our society may progress even further than it has, the author is inclined to regard it as a transitory phenomenon. The sudden rise of the machine and of applied science has shattered Western civiliza-

tion and reduced Western society to something approaching chaos. However, unless all past experience is at fault, the society will once more reduce itself to order. What the new order will be no one can forecast, but the potentialities of the local group, both for the control of individuals and for the satisfaction of their psychological needs are so great that it seems unlikely that this unit will be dispensed with.[7]

Linton wrote those words in 1936. In the years since then, many architects and planners have tried to recreate the local primary group artificially, by means of the neighborhood idea. They have hoped that if people would only live in small physical groups, round modern village greens, the social groups would follow the same pattern; and that these artificial groups would then once more provide the intimate contact which is in such short supply in urban areas today.[8] But this idea of recreating primary groups by artificial means is unrealistic and reactionary: it fails to recognize the truth about the open society. The open society is no longer centered around place-based groups; and the very slight acquaintances that do form round an artificial neighborhood are once again trivial: they are not based on genuine desire.[9] Though these pseudogroups may serve certain ancillary purposes (neighbors may look after one another's houses while they are away), there is no possible hope that they could sustain truly intimate contact, as I have defined it.

The only vestige of the primary groups which still remains is the nuclear family. The family still functions as a mechanism for sustaining intimate contact. But where the extended family of preindustrial society contained many adults, and gave them many opportunities for intimate contact, the modern nuclear family contains only two adults. This means that each of these adults has at most *one* intimate contact within his family. (Although the contact between parent and child is, in a colloquial sense, an intimate one, it is not the kind of contact which I am discussing here; it is essentially one-sided; there can be no mutual revealing of the self between adults and children.) Furthermore, one-third of all households in urban areas contain only one adult (either unmarried, widowed or divorced[10]). These adults have *no* intimate contacts at all, at home.

As ways of providing intimate contact, it seems that primary groups are doomed. Modern urban social structure is chiefly based on secondary contacts—contacts in which people are related by a single role relationship: buyer and seller, disc-jockey and fan, lawyer and client.[11] Not surprisingly, the people who find themselves in this dismal condition try madly to make friends. Urban Americans are world-famous as an outgoing, friendly people. They are able to make friends very fast; and they join associations more than almost any other people. It is not hard to see that this is an inevitable consequence of urbanization and mobility, and will ultimately happen everywhere, as urban society spreads around the world. In a society where people move about a lot, the individuals who are moving must learn to strike up acquaintances quickly—it is essential for them, since they very often find themselves in situations where they don't know anybody. By the same token, since deep-seated, old, associations are uncommon, people rush to join new associations and affiliations, to fill the gap they feel. Instant friendship is well adapted to the circumstances which the average American urban dweller faces. But the very life stuff of social organization—true participation among people who learn to penetrate each other—is missing. Outward friendliness adds nothing to the need for deeper contact; it trivializes contact.

People may not be ready to admit that most of their contacts are trivial; but they admit it by implication, in their widespread nostalgia for college days, and for army days. What is it that makes the college reunions so powerful? Why do grown men and women at reunions pretend to be boys and girls again? Because at college, they had an experience which many of them never have again: they had many intimate friends; intimate contact was commonplace. The same is true of army days. However grisly war may be, it is a fact that the vast majority of men never forget their army days. They remember the close comradeship, the feelings of mutual dependence, and they regret that later life never quite recreates this wonderful experience again.

All the recent studies of dissatisfaction when slum dwellers are forced to move say essentially the same.[12] So far these studies have been used to demonstrate the poor quality of new towns and urban renewal; but this is really incidental. No one has been bold enough to face the larger fact. These people are moving from a traditional place-based society into the larger urban society where place-based community means nothing. When they make the move they lose their intimate contacts. This is not because the places they go to are badly designed in some obvious sense which could be easily improved. Nor is it because they are temporarily uprooted, and have only to wait for the roots of community to grow again. The awful fact is that modern urban society, as a whole, has found no way of sustaining intimate contacts.

Some people believe that this view is nothing but nostalgia for an imaginary past, and that what looks like alienation is really just the pain of parting from traditional society, and the birth pang of a new society.[13]

I do not believe it. I believe that intimate contacts are essential for human survival, and, indeed, that each person requires not one, but several intimate contacts at any given time. I believe that the primary groups which sustained intimate contact were an essential functional part of traditional social systems, and that since they are now obsolete, it is essential that we invent new social mechanisms, consistent with the direction that society is taking, and yet able to sustain the intimate contacts which we need.

Expressed in formal terms, this belief becomes a fundamental hypothesis about man and society:

An individual can be healthy and happy only when his life

*contains three or four intimate contacts. A society can be a
healthy one only if each of its individual members has three or
four intimate contacts at every stage of his existence.*[14]

Every society known to man, except our own, has provided
conditions which allow people to sustain three or four intimate
contacts. Western industrial society is the first society in human
history where man is being forced to live without them. If the
hypothesis is correct, the very roots of our society are
threatened. Let us therefore examine the evidence for the
hypothesis.

2. Evidence

Unfortunately, the only available evidence is very indirect.
Individual health is hard to define; social health is even harder.
We have no indices for low-grade misery or sickness: we have
no indices for fading social vitality. In the same way, the relative
intimacy of different contacts is hard to define and has never
explicitly been studied. The evidence we really need, showing
a correlation between the intimacy of people's contacts and the
general health and happiness of their individual and social
lives, does not exist.

In a strictly scientific sense, it is therefore possible only to
examine a very extreme version of the hypothesis: namely, that
extreme lack of contact causes *extreme* and well-defined social
pathologies like schizophrenia and delinquency. Several large-
scale studies do support this extreme form of the hypothesis.

Faris and Dunham studied the distribution of mental disorders in Chicago in the 1930's. They found that paranoid and
hebephrenic schizophrenias have their highest rates of incidence
among hotel residents and lodgers, and among the people who
live in the rooming house districts of the city. They are highest,
in other words, among those people who are most alone.[15]

Faris and Dunham also found that the incidence of schizophrenia among whites was highest among those whites living

in predominantly Negro areas, and that the incidence for Negroes was highest among those Negroes living in predominantly non-Negro areas.[16] Here again, the incidence is highest among those who are isolated.

Alexander Leighton and his collaborators have spent ten years in Stirling County, Nova Scotia, studying the effect of social disintegration on mental disorders.[17] To stress the fact that people in a disintegrated society exist as isolated individuals, without any kind of emotional bonds between them, he calls the disintegrated society a collection. In a collection there are numbers of individuals occupying the same geographical area, having nonpatterned encounters with each other. They have no personal contacts of any sort; they have no voluntary associations with one another—let alone any kind of intimate contact between households.[18] They are suspicious about making friends, and try to keep clear of all involvements with people.[19] These people have substantially higher rates of psychophysiological, psychoneurotic, and sociopathic disorders than people who live in a closely knit traditional community.[20]

Langner and Michael, studying the incidence of mental disorders in Manhattan, find that people who report fewer than four friends have a substantially higher chance of mental disorder than those who report more than four friends.[21] What is more, their findings suggest that this effect may even be partly responsible for the well-known correlation between low socioeconomic status and high rates of mental disorder and delinquency.[22] Langner and Michael find that people in the lowest socioeconomic groups tend to have fewer friends than the people in the highest socioeconomic groups. Thus in the lowest group, 12.7 per cent report no friends; in the highest group, only 1.8 per cent report no friends.[23] This may seem surprising to those readers who have an image of the lower socioeconomic groups as urban villagers, with widespread webs of friendship and kinship. Although the people who live in depressed areas of cities do occasionally still have such a traditional society, and many friends, most of them live in conditions of extreme social disorganization. They do lack intimate friends; and it is very possible that this lack of intimate friends plays a substantial part in the correlation between poverty and mental disorder. Langner and Michael show, finally, that membership in formal organizations and clubs, and contact with neighbors, have relatively slight effect on mental health—thus supporting the idea the contacts must be intimate before they do much good.[24]

Many minor studies support the same conclusion. Most important among them are the widely known correlations between age and mental health, and between marital status and mental health. Various studies have shown that the highest incidence of mental disorders, for males and females, occurs above age 65, and, indeed, that the highest of all occurs above 75.[25] Other studies have shown that the incidence rates for single, separated, widowed and divorced persons are higher than the rates for married persons. Rates per thousand, for single persons, are about one and a half times as high as the rates for married persons, while rates for divorced and widowed persons are between two and three times as high.[26]

Of course the disorders among old people may be partly organic, but there is no getting away from the fact that old people are almost always more lonely than the young, and that it is usually hard for them to sustain substantial contacts with other people. In the same way, although the disorders among divorced and single people could actually be the sources of their isolation, not the causes of it, the fact that the rate is equally high for widowers and widows makes this very unlikely. In both cases we are dealing with populations of individuals who are exceptionally prone to isolation. The simplest possible explanation, once again, is that the loss of intimate contact causes the disorders.

So far we have discussed only cases of adult isolation. It is very likely that the effects of social isolation on children are even more acute; but here the published evidence is thinner.

The most dramatic available results come from Harlow's work on monkeys. Harlow has shown that monkeys isolated from other infant monkeys during the first six months of life are incapable of normal social, sexual, or play relations with other monkeys in their later lives:

> "They exhibit abnormalities of behavior rarely seen in animals born in the wild. They sit in their cages and stare fixedly into space, circle their cages in a repetitively stereotyped manner, and clasp their heads in their hands or arms and rock for long periods of time . . . . the animal may chew and tear at its body until it bleeds . . . . similar symptoms of emotional pathology are observed in deprived children in orphanages and in withdrawn adolescents and adults in mental hospitals.[27]

It is well known that infant monkeys—like infant human beings—have these defects if brought up without a mother or a mother surrogate. It is not well known that the effects of separation from other infant monkeys are even stronger than the effects of maternal deprivation. Indeed, Harlow showed that although monkeys can be raised successfully without a mother, provided that they have other infant monkeys to play with, they cannot be raised successfully by a mother alone, without other infant monkeys, even if the mother is entirely normal. He concludes: "It seems possible that the infant-mother affectional system is dispensable, whereas the infant-infant system is a sine-qua-non for later adjustment in all spheres of monkey life."[28]

In Harlow's experiments, the first six months of life were critical. The first six months of a rhesus monkey's life correspond to the first three years of a child's life. Although there is no formal evidence to show that lack of contact during these first three years damages human children—and as far as I know, it has never been studied—there is very strong evidence for the effect of isolation between the ages of four to ten. There is also an informal account by Anna Freud, which shows how powerful the effect of contact among tiny children can be on the emotional development of the children.

Anna Freud describes five young German children who lost their parents during infancy in a concentration camp, and then looked after one another inside the camp until the war ended, at which point they were brought to England.[29] She describes the beautiful social and emotional maturity of these tiny children. Reading the account, one feels that these children, at the age of three, were more aware of each other and more sensitive to each other's needs than many people ever are.

The most telling study is that by Herman Lantz.[30] Lantz questioned a random sample of 1,000 men in the United States Army, who had been referred to a mental hygiene clinic because of emotional difficulties. Army psychiatrists classified each of the men as normal, suffering from mild psychoneurosis, severe psychoneurosis, or psychosis.

Lantz then put each man into one of three categories: those who reported having five friends or more at any typical moment when they were between four and ten years old, those who reported an average of about two friends, and those who reported having no friends at that time. The following table shows the relative percentages in each of the three friendship categories separately. The results are astounding:

	5 or More Friends	About 2 Friends	No Friends
Normal	39.5	7.2	0.0
Mild psychoneurosis	22.0	16.4	5.0
Severe psychoneurosis	27.0	54.6	47.5
Psychosis	0.8	3.1	37.5
Other	10.7	18.7	10.0
	100.0	100.0	100.0

Among people who have five friends or more as children, 61.5 per cent have mild cases, while 27.8 per cent have severe cases. Among people who had no friends, only 5 per cent have mild cases, and 85 per cent have severe cases.

It is almost certain then, that lack of contact, when it is extreme, has extreme effects on people. There is a considerable body of literature beyond which I have quoted.[31] Even so, the evidence is sparse. We cannot be sure that the effect is causal, and we have found evidence only for those relatively extreme cases which can be counted unambiguously. From a strictly scientific point of view, it is clearly necessary to undertake a special, extensive study to test the hypothesis in the exact form that I have stated it.

However, just because the scientific literature doesn't happen to contain the relevant evidence, that doesn't mean that we don't know whether the hypothesis is true or not. From our own lives we know that intimate contact is essential to life; and that the whole meaning of life shows itself only in the process of our intimate contacts.[32] The loss of intimate contacts touches each one of us—each one of you who reads this book. The evidence I have quoted happens to concern only people who are suffering from some form of extreme social isolation. But the loss of intimate contacts is not restricted to these people. It applies equally to the man who is happily married, a father of four children and a member of numerous local groups. This man may seem to have many contacts—indeed, he does—but the way that our society works today, he is still most likely lacking intimate contact as I have defined it, and therefore, if my hypothesis is right, even this lucky man is still suffering from disorders which are different only in degree from the extreme disorders I have mentioned. The way of life we lead today makes it impossible for us to be as close to our friends as we really want to be. The feeling of alienation, and the modern sense of the "meaninglessness" of life, are direct expressions of the loss of intimate contact.

3. The Autonomy-Withdrawal Syndrome

As far as we can judge, then, people need three or four intimate contacts at every moment of their lives, in order to survive. If they don't have these contacts they undergo progressive deterioration and disintegration. It is therefore clear that every human society must provide social mechanisms which sustain these intimate contacts, in order to survive as a society. Yet as we know, the historic mechanisms which once performed this function for our own society are breaking down.

I shall now try to show that we are faced not merely with the collapse of one or two social mechanisms, but rather with a massive syndrome, a huge net of cause and effect in which the breakdown of primary groups, the breakdown of intimacy itself, the growth of individualism, and the withdrawal from the stress of urbanized society are all interwoven. I shall call this syndrome *the autonomy-withdrawal syndrome.*

To study the syndrome, let us begin with the most obvious mechanical reasons for the breakdown of intimate contacts. I have already named them. In preindustrial societies the two institutions which sustained intimate contacts between adults were the extended family and the local neighborhood community. These two primary groups have almost entirely disappeared. The family has shrunk; friends have scattered.

The modern metropolis is therefore a collection of many scattered households, each one small. In the future, individual households will probably be even smaller, and the average size of urban areas even larger.[33] Under these circumstances the three or four intimate contacts which each individual needs are no longer available in his immediate physical surroundings: not in his shrunken family, nor in his neighborhood. We must therefore ask how, in a society of scattered, mobile individuals, these individuals can maintain intimate contact with one another.

Let us go back to the two conditions which intimate contact requires: (1) the people concerned must see each other very often, almost daily; and (2) they must see each other under informal conditions, not controlled by single role relationships or social rules. How can a society of scattered, mobile individuals meet these two conditions?

The first answer which comes to mind is this: since friendships in modern society are mostly based on some community of interest, we should expect the institutions which create such friendships—workplace, golf club, ski resort, precinct headquarters—to provide the necessary meeting ground. It sounds good; but it doesn't work. Though people do meet each other in such groups, the meetings are too infrequent, and the situation too clearly prescribed. People achieve neither the frequency nor the informality which intimacy requires. Further, *people can reach the true intimacy and mutual trust required for self-revelation only when they are in private.*

Frequent, private, almost daily meeting between individuals, under conditions of extreme informality, unencumbered by role prescriptions or social rules, will take place only if the people visit one another in their own homes. It is true that occasional meetings in public places may also be very intimate: but the regular, constant meetings which are required to build up the possibility of intimacy cannot happen in public places. In a society of scattered mobile individuals people will therefore be able to maintain intimate contacts with one another only if they are in the habit of constant informal visiting or "dropping-in."

In modern American society dropping-in is thought of as a peculiarly European custom. Yet in fact, it is a normal part of life in every preindustrial society. In part it has to be, because there are no telephones. But dropping-in is not merely the preindustrial version of what we do by phone. The very notion of friendship demands that people be almost totally exposed to one another. To be friends, they must have nothing to hide; and for this reason, informal dropping-in is a natural and essential part of friendship. This is so fundamental that we may even treat it as a definition of true friendship. If two people feel free to drop in on each other knowing that they will be welcome, no matter what is happening, we can be sure that they are intimate friends; if two people feel inhibited about dropping in on each other, we can be sure they are not truly intimate. Why is dropping-in so rare in mobile urban society?

The first reason, of course, is still mechanical. Two people will not sustain a pattern of daily dropping-in unless they live within a few minutes of each other, ten minutes at the most. Although the car has enormously enlarged the number of people within ten minutes' distance of any given household, most of the people in the metropolis are still outside this distance. If we remember that we are concerned with the half dozen individuals who are potentially most intimate with any given individual, we must face the fact that in a metropolis these individuals are very likely to live as much as half an hour or an hour apart. At this distance, intimate contact can't develop. They see each other very rarely—at most once or twice a month for dinner —and when they do meet, it is after careful invitation, worked out in advance. These kinds of evening contact have neither the frequency, nor the informality, which intimacy requires.

However, distance alone, though it is a serious obstacle, does not fully explain the loss of intimacy. There is another reason for it, far more devastating, and far more profound: when people get home, they want to get away from all the stress outside. They feel more private than they used to feel. They treasure their quiet moments. A visitor who drops in unasked, at such a moment, even if he is a friend, is an intruder. People do not want to be perpetually exposed; they often want to be withdrawn. But withdrawal soon becomes a habit. People reach a point where they are permanently withdrawn, they lose the habit of showing themselves to others as they really are, and become unable and unwilling to let other people into their own world.

At this stage people don't like others dropping in on them, because they don't want to be caught when they aren't ready: the housewife who doesn't like anyone coming around except when she has carefully straightened out her house; the family who don't like to mix their friends, and entertain their friends one couple at a time in case the couples shouldn't get along. Truly intimate contact is not possible to such people. They live behind a social facade. Afraid of showing themselves as they really are, they never reach a truly intimate degree of contact with others.

This fear is partly caused by stress. The man who lives in modern urban society is exposed to innumerable stresses: danger, noise, too many strangers, too much information, and above all, the need to make decisions about the complexities of personal life without the help of traditional mores. These stresses are often too much to bear; so he withdraws from them. He draws a cloak of impenetrability around him, to ward off the too many strangers he meets in the street; he locks his door; he lives buried beneath a system of elaborated social and behavioral defenses against unwelcome and unbidden intrusions from outside. The houses of a century ago were outward-looking; the porch had people on it; the front garden was occupied. Today only the slum-dwellers—who sit on the stoop because it is too grim inside—face toward the city. Everyone else has turned away. Even when they are in public, people behave as though the other people who surround them were not there. A man walks down the street with a glazed look, not looking at people's eyes, but focused determinedly on nothing. A woman cheerfully wears curlers in the street because, although she is curling her hair for people who are real to her, the people who surround her don't exist: she has shut them out.

In its extreme form, this withdrawal turns into schizophrenia: that total withdrawal into the self which takes place when the outside world is so confusing, or so hard to deal with, that the organism finally cannot cope with it and turns away.[34] In the process of withdrawing into the self, the schizophrenic loses sight, entirely, of his dependence on other people. Schizophrenics are completely individualistic: the world they live in is their own world; they do not perceive themselves as dependent on the outside world in any way, nor do they perceive any interaction between themselves and the outside world. Nor indeed, do they enter into any interaction with the world outside.[35]

The stress of urban life has not yet had this extreme and catastrophic effect on many people. Nevertheless, what is nowadays considered "normal" urban behavior is strikingly like schizophrenia: it is also marked by extreme withdrawal from stress, and this withdrawal has also led to unrealistic belief in individualism and the self-sufficiency of individuals.

Any objective observer comparing urban life with rural or preindustrial life must be struck by the extreme individualism of the people who live in cities.[36] This individualism has reached its most extreme form in the urban areas of the United States. Though it has often been criticized by non-Americans as a peculiarity of American culture, I believe this view mistaken. Individualism of an extreme kind is an inevitable by-product of urbanization—it occurs as part of the withdrawal from stress. This individualism is very different from healthy democratic respect for the individual's rights. It is a pathological over-belief in the self-sufficiency and independence of the individual and the individual family, and a refusal to permit dependence of any emotional weight to form. Where contact with others reaches very high proportions—beyond the capacity of the individual organism—the organism is forced to shut these contacts out, and therefore to maintain an unreal belief in its own powers of self-sufficiency.[37]

An obvious expression of individualism is the huge amount of space which people need around them in the United States. Edward Hall has shown that each person carries an inviolable "bubble" of personal space around with him and that the size of the bubble varies according to the intimacy of the situation which the person is involved in.[38] He has also shown that the size of bubble required varies from culture to culture. It is remarkable that people need a larger bubble in the United States, for any given situation, than in any other country; this is clearly associated with the fear of bodily contact, and with the fact that people view themselves as isolated atoms, separate from everybody else.

This isolation of the individual is also expressed clearly by the love of private property in the United States, and the wealth of laws and institutions which keep people's private property inviolate.

Another recent, and extreme, form of this worship of the individual exists in certain communities on the west coast of the United States, like Canyon, east of Oakland. The people in Canyon have a cult of honesty—about their individual wants— which leads to total disregard for others. Each one of them eats when he chooses to—in order to be "honest"—which means that groups no longer eat communally around a table. They are highly unresponsive to one another: when they meet, instead of moving physically toward each other as normal people do, they merely incline their heads, or nod with their eyelids. Each individual comes and goes as he pleases: there is no mutuality, no interplay of reaction and response.

Another form of extreme individualism, which threatens the development of intimate contacts, is the exaggerated accent on the nuclear family. In modern urban society it is assumed that the needs for intimate contact which any one individual has can be completely met in marriage. This concentration of all our emotional eggs in one basket has gone so far that true intimacy between any friends except man and wife is regarded with extreme suspicion. As Camus says: in Greece a man and his friend walk down the street holding hands—in Paris people would snigger at the sight.

Perhaps the most vivid of all expressions of individualism is the song *People who need people are the luckiest people in the world*, top of the U.S. hit parade in 1964. A society where this statement needs to be made explicitly has reached a low ebb indeed.

Where has this exaggerated arrogant view of the individual's strength come from? It is true that it is a withdrawal from stress. But it could never have happened if it weren't for the fact that urbanization makes individuals autonomous. The extreme differentiation of society in an urban area means that literally any service can be bought, by anyone. In material terms, any individual is able to survive alone. Women can make a living on their own; teenagers no longer need their families; old people can fend for themselves; men are able to get meals from the local automat, or from the freezer in the supermarket. Insurance is not provided by the extended family, but by the insurance companies. Autonomous trailer houses can exist in the wilderness without community facilities.

Of course these isolated, apparently autonomous individuals are in fact highly dependent on society—but only through the medium of money. A man in a less differentiated rural economy is constantly reminded of his dependence on society, and of the fact that his very being is totally intertwined with the being of the social order, and the being of his fellows. The individual who is technically autonomous, whose dependencies are all expressed in money terms, can easily make the mistake of thinking that he, or he and his family, are self-sufficient.

Now, naturally, people who believe that they are self-sufficient create a world which reinforces individualism and withdrawal. In central cities, this is reflected in the concept of apartments. Though collected together at high densities, these apartments are in fact, like the people themselves, totally turned inward. High density makes it necessary to insulate each apartment from the world outside; the actual dwelling is remote from the street; it is virtually impossible to drop in on someone who lives in an apartment block. Not surprisingly, recent studies report that people who live in apartments feel more isolated than people who live in any other kinds of dwelling.[39]

But autonomy and withdrawal, and the pathological belief in individual families as self-sufficient units, can be seen most vividly in the physical pattern of suburban tract development. This is Durkheim's dust-heap in the flesh. The houses stand alone: a collection of isolated, disconnected islands. There is no communal land, and no sign of any functional connection between different houses.

If it seems far-fetched to call this aspect of the suburb pathological, let us examine the results of a study undertaken in Vienna in 1956. The city planning department gave a questionnaire to a random sample of 4,000 Viennese, to find out what their housing preferences were. Most of them, when asked whether they would rather live in apartments or in single-family houses, said that they preferred apartments, because they wanted to be near the center where everything was happening.[40]

A Viennese psychiatrist then gave the same questionnaire to 100 neurotic patients in his clinic. He found that a much higher majority of these patients wanted to live in one-family houses, that they wanted larger houses relative to the size of their families, that they wanted more space per person, and that more of them wanted their houses to be situated in woods and trees. In other words, they wanted the suburban dream. As he says: "The neurotic patients are marked by a strong desire to shun reality and to isolate themselves."[41]

Most people who move to suburbs are not sick in any literal sense. However, there can be no question that their move is a withdrawal. The four main reasons which people give for moving to the suburbs are: (1) Open space for children, because children can't play safely in central urban areas.[42] (2) Wanting more space inside the house than they can afford in the central city.[43] (3) Wanting to own a house of their own.[44] Ownership protects the owner from the uncertainties of tenancy, from reliance on others, and from the dangers of the future. It creates the illusion that the owner and his family have a world of their own, where nobody can touch them. (4) Wanting more grass and trees.[45]

Each of these is a withdrawal from stress. The withdrawal is understandable; but the suburb formed by this withdrawal undermines the formation of intimate contacts in a devastating way. It virtually destroys the children's play-group.

As we saw earlier, the intimate contacts in preindustrial society were maintained by three primary groups: the extended family, the neighborhood group, and the children's play-group. The first two, those which maintain intimate contacts between adults, are obsolete, and need to be replaced. But the third primary group—the children's play-group—is not obsolete at all. Little children, unlike adults, do choose their friends from the children next door. It is perfectly possible for children's play-groups to exist in modern society, just as they always have; and indeed, it is essential. The children's play-group sets the whole style of life for later years. Children brought up in extensive play-groups will be emotionally prepared for intimate contacts in later life; children brought up without play-groups will be prone to individualism and withdrawal.

On the face of it, the suburb ought to be a very good place for children's play-groups. People move to a suburb specifically for the sake of their children. It has open space, and safety, and good schools. Yet, paradoxically, this children's paradise is not a paradise at all for little children. Children begin to seek other children at about ten months.[46] Remembering that Harlow's monkeys required play with other monkeys during the first six months of life in order to be normal, and that these first six months correspond to the first three years in the life of a human child, let us ask: "How well does a suburban subdivision cater for the play-groups of the one and two and three-year-olds?"

If you drive through a subdivision, watching children play, you will see that children who are old enough to have school friends do have local play-groups of a sort. (Even these groups are sparse; in summer many of the children have to be sent off to summer camp.) But what happens to the smallest children? If you look carefully, you see them squatting forlornly outside their houses—occasionally playing with an elder brother or sister, and occasionally in groups of two or three, but most often alone. Compare this with the situation in a primitive village, or with a crowded urban slum: there the little children are out on the street fending for themselves as soon as they can walk; heaps of children are playing and falling and rolling over one another.

The need for preschool play-groups is so desperate and urgent that many mothers try to get their children into nursery school.[47] But even nursery school lasts only 15 hours a week. For a child the week is 100 waking hours long. The 15 hours of nursery school do little to relieve the damage of the other 85 hours.

Why are suburban play-groups small? There are several different reasons. First of all, suburban density is low and little children can't walk very far. Even if every house has children in it, the number of two and three-year-olds that a given two-year-old can reach is very small. Secondly, even though the suburb is safer than the central city, the streets still aren't entirely safe. Mothers keep their two and three-year-olds off the street, inside the individual yards, where they can keep an eye on them. This cuts the children's freedom to meet other children. Further, many suburbs have no common land at all in them, not even sidewalks. There isn't any natural place where children go to find each other: they have to go and look for each other in one another's houses. For a child this is a much more formidable enterprise than simply running out to see who's on the street. It also makes the children hard to find, and keeps the size of play-groups down, especially since many parents won't allow large groups of children in the house. And finally, when children play in one another's yards, parents can control the playmates they consider suitable: "Johnny isn't nice, you mustn't play with him." One young mother told me that her son, four years old, had to be driven to the nearest child he was allowed to play with, and had to come home by taxi.

It is small wonder that children who grow up in these conditions learn to be self-reliant in the pathological sense I have described. As they become adults they are even less able than their parents to live lives with intimate contacts; they seek even more exaggerated forms of individualism and withdrawal. As adults who suffer from withdrawal they create a world which creates children who are even more prone to suffer from withdrawal, and more prone to create such worlds. This closes the cycle of the syndrome, and makes it self-perpetuating.

We may summarize the syndrome briefly. Stress forces people to withdraw into themselves; autonomy allows them to. Pushed by stress, pulled by autonomy, people have withdrawn into a private world where they believe that they are self-sufficient. They create a way of life, and an environment, which reflects this belief; and this way of life, and this environment, then propagate the same illusion. It creates more people who believe in self-sufficiency as an ideal, it makes intimate contact seem less necessary, and it makes it more and more difficult to achieve in practice.

The autonomy-withdrawal syndrome is not a unique American phenomenon. It is true that it is, so far, more acute in the United States than in any other country; but this is merely because urbanization is more advanced in the United States than

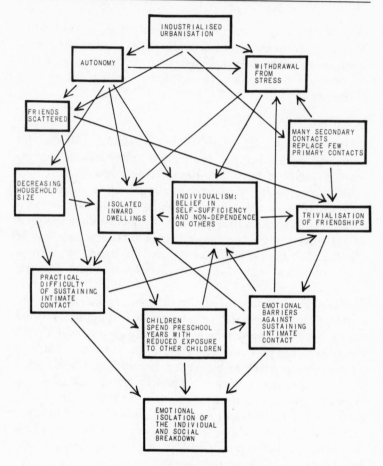

The autonomy-withdrawal syndrome

anywhere else. As massive urbanization spreads, the syndrome will spread with it. I believe this syndrome is the greatest threat to social human nature which we face in this century. We have already seen that it can create misery and madness. But in the long run its effects are far more devastating. An individual human organism becomes a self only in the process of intimate contacts with other selves. Unless we overcome the syndrome, the loss of intimate contacts may break down human nature altogether.

4. Solution

How can cities help to overcome the syndrome? If the city is to be a mechanism for sustaining intimate human contact, what geometric pattern does the mechanism need?

Of course, no amount of geometric pattern in the environment can overcome the syndrome on its own. The syndrome is a social and psychological problem of massive dimensions: it will be solved only when people decide to change their way of life. But the physical environment needs changing too. People can change their way of life only if the environment supports their efforts.

There are two fundamentally different approaches to the problem. On the one hand, we may decide that intimate contact can be sustained properly only by primary groups, as it always has been in the past; we shall then try to create new kinds of primary group which might work in our society. On the other hand, we may decide that adult primary groups are gone forever, and that it is unrealistic to try to recreate them in any form whatever in modern society; in this case we must try a more radical approach, and create a social mechanism which is able to sustain informal, daily contact between people without the support of a primary group.

It may be that the first of these approaches is the more hopeful one. This is what T-groups try to do, it is the idea behind the groups of families which Aldous Huxley describes in *Island,* and above all, it is the idea behind group work. If work can be reorganized so that people band together in small work groups of about a dozen, and each group is directed toward a single concentrated socially valuable objective, then the dedication and effort which develop in the group are capable of creating great intimacy, which goes far beyond the working day.

However, so far none of these methods has met with any great success. So far the forces which are breaking primary groups apart have been stronger than the efforts to construct artificial primary groups. I shall, therefore, assume that much more radical steps will have to be taken: that although children's play-groups can be saved, adult primary groups are doomed, and adults will have to sustain their intimate contacts in a new way, by frequent casual visiting. I shall now describe the re-organization of the housing pattern which is required by this approach.

At present, people have two main kinds of housing open to them: either they live in apartments, or they live in single-family houses. Neither helps them overcome the autonomy-withdrawal syndrome. I shall now try to show that, in order for them to overcome the syndrome, the houses in a city must have twelve specific geometric characteristics, and that these twelve characteristics, when taken together, define a housing pattern different from any of those which are available today. The detailed reasons for the twelve characteristics are described in notes *a–l*, beginning on page 94. I recommend strongly that you read these reasons in detail. The characteristics themselves are these:

1 Every dwelling must be immediately next to a vehicular through street. If there are any multi-story buildings with dwellings in them—like apartments—then there must be vehicular through streets at every level where there are entrances to dwellings.[a]

2 Each dwelling must contain a transparent communal room with the following properties: on one side the room is directly adjacent to the street, on the opposite side the room is directly adjacent

to a private open air court or garden. Since the room is transparent its interior, seen against the garden, and the garden itself, are both visible from the street.[b]

3 This transparent communal room is surrounded by free-standing, self-contained enclosed pavilions, each functioning as a bed-living unit, so arranged that each person in the family, or any number of people who wish to be undisturbed, can retire to one of these pavilions and be totally private.[c]

4 The street immediately outside the dwelling must be no more than about 1,000 feet long, and connected to a major traffic artery at each end.[d]

5 There must be a continuous piece of common land, accessible and visible from every dwelling.[e]

6 This common land must be separated from the streets by houses, so that a child on the common land has to go through a house to get to the street.[f]

7 The common land, though continuous, must be broken into many small "places," not much larger than outdoor "rooms," each surfaced with a wide variety of ground surfaces, especially "soft" surfaces like earth, mud, sand, grass, bushes.[g]

8 Each house must be within 100 yards' walk of 27 other houses.[h]

Photographs of a cutaway model of a hill.
Model by Terrence Mechling

a.

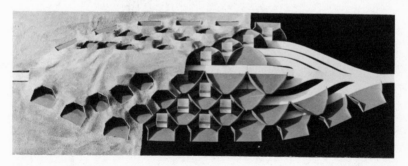

b.

c.

d. Single pad with transparent communal room and six private
pavilions

Towns, ed. Leo Kuper (London, 1953), pp. 235-64. The common land, then, must be broken up into many tiny places, which have natural earth and mud and plants in them.

h. Let us assume that there are two children per household in the areas where children live (the modal figure for suburban households), and that these children are evenly distributed, in age, from 0 to 18. Roughly speaking, a given preschool child who is x years old will play with children who are $x - 1$ or x or $x + 1$ years old. In order to have a reasonable amount of contact, and in order for play-groups to form, each child must be able to reach at least five children in this age range. Statistical analysis shows that in order for each child to have a 95 per cent chance of reaching five such potential playmates, each child must be in reach of 27 households.

(The problem may be stated as follows: In an infinite population of children, one-sixth are the right age and five-sixths are the wrong age. A group of r children is chosen at random. The probability, $P_{r,k}$ that these r children contain exactly k right-age children is given by the hypergeometric distribution. The probability that r has 5 or more right-age children in it is $1 - \sum_{k=0}^{4} P_{r,k}$. If we now ask what is the least r which makes $1 - \sum_{k=0}^{4} P_{r,k} \geq .95$, r turns out to be 54, requiring 27 households.)

If we assume that preschool children are not able, or allowed, to go more than about 100 yards in search of playmates, this means that each house must be within 100 yards of 27 other houses. To achieve this density in a conventional suburban layout, house lots would have to be less than 40 feet wide, about half the width and twice the density they are today.

i. There is a second reason why residential densities must be higher than today. Informal daily dropping-in will not take place between two households that are more than about ten minutes apart. Since average door-to-door speeds in urban areas are about 15 mph, ten minutes is about 2½ miles, thus putting each person in reach of about twenty square miles, or about 100,000 people at current metropolitan densities. This is a tiny fraction of the population of a metropolitan area—a twentieth of a small one, a hundredth of a large one. Since we have started out with the axiom that a person's best friends may live anywhere in the metropolitan area, this means that people are within dropping-in distance of no more than a twentieth of their potentially closest friends.

Obviously vehicle speeds and streets can be improved. But it seems unlikely that average door-to-door speeds will more than double in this century. This means that people in the largest metropolitan areas will still be within informal distance of less than one-twentieth of the population. While transportation must clearly be improved, it is clear that over-all mean densities must *also* be raised as far as they can be.

Many planners believe that high density is bad for man. This is based on the fact that high density is often correlated with the incidence of crime, delinquency, ill health, and insanity. If this belief were justified, any attempt to increase the density of population would obviously be ill advised. However, though the belief has a long history, the evidence available today does not support it.

Let us try to disentangle the evidence. First of all, there seems little doubt that overcrowding—too little living space per person—does cause damage. Calhoun has shown this dramatically for rats. J. B. Calhoun, "Population Density and Social Pathology," *Scientific American*, 206 (Feb., 1962), pp. 139-46. Loring, Chombard de Lauwe, and Lander have shown that it is true for humans. William C. Loring, "Housing Characteristics and Social Disorganization," *Social Problems* (Jan., 1956); Chombard de Lauwe, *Famille et habitation* (Paris: Editions du Centre National de la Recherche Scientifique, 1959); B. Lander, *Towards an Understanding of Juvenile Delinquency* (New York: Columbia University Press, 1954). This finding makes it clear that people who are now forced to live in crowded conditions either need more income, or need ways of reducing the square foot costs of living space. But it does not imply that the density of population per square mile should be reduced. Even dwellings which are individually very large can still be arranged at very high population densities without overcrowding.

What evidence is there that high population density itself causes ill effects? It is true that there is often a positive correlation between high population density and various indices of social disorder, like crime, delinquency, ill health, and insanity rates. Robert C. Schmitt, "Delinquency and Crime in Honolulu," *Sociology and Social Re-*

search, 41 (Mar.-Apr., 1957), pp. 274-76, and "Population Densities and Mental Disorders in Honolulu," *Hawaii Medical Journal,* 16 (Mar.-Apr., 1957), pp. 396-97. However, it seems almost certain that these effects are caused by intervening variables, and are not directly caused by density. There are places—Boston's North End and Hong Kong, for instance—which have exceptionally high densities and exceptionally low indices of social disorder. Jane Jacobs, *The Death and Life of Great American Cities* (New York, 1961), pp. 10 and 206; Robert C. Schmitt, "Implications of Density in Hong Kong," *AIP Journal,* 29 (1963), pp. 210-17. Unless we assume that Italian-Americans and Chinese are organically different from other people, this means that density, as such, cannot be the source of trouble in the cases where a correlation does exist.

The following hypothesis fully explains all the observed correlations: Those social disorders apparently caused by density are in fact caused by low income, poor education, and social isolation. It is known that people who are poor and badly educated tend to live in high density areas. It is also known that people who are socially isolated tend to live in high density areas. Both variables are associated with high indices of social disorder. Although some published studies of density have controlled for one or the other of these variables, no study has controlled them both. Lander (p. 46) has shown that the correlation between *overcrowding* and delinquency, when controlled for these two variables, vanishes altogether. Schmitt has published a table showing that the correlations persist when income-education is controlled, but also showing a strong negative correlation between household size and social disorder (large households are less prone to social disorders), which suggests strongly that social isolation may be responsible for the persistent correlation. Robert C. Schmitt, "Density, Health and Social Disorganization," *AIP Journal,* 32 (Jan., 1966), pp. 38-40. The fact that there are very few social disorders in Boston's North End and in Hong Kong is clearly due to the existence of close-knit extended families: the lack of social isolation. I predict that the partial correlation between density and social disorder, when controlled for income-education *and* for social isolation, will disappear altogether.

This hypothesis explains all the available data. Although it is untested, there is no published evidence which contradicts it. As far as we can tell, the high density characteristics called for by the need for contact are perfectly safe.

j. We cannot expect people to live at high density, just because it has certain social benefits. The low density of suburban tracts is not due to chance; it has been created by a number of insatiable demands, far more important to consumers than the point of view I have presented. These demands are so basic, and play such a basic role in the operation of the urban land market, that low residential density is a universal feature of emerging metropolitan areas throughout the world. Unless these demands can be satisfied equally well at higher densities, there is not the slightest hope that over-all densities will ever be increased. There are five main demands: (1) People seek more open space for their children than they can find in central urban areas. (2) People want to live in a house which is their very own property. (3) People seek more space per person than they can afford in central areas. (4) People want a house which is different from the next man's—not simply one of hundreds of identical apartments. (5) People seek grass and trees as symbols of stability and peace.

All of these demands lead to the same basic tendency: the desire for land. The pattern of density in an urban region is created by the conflict between this one basic tendency and another equally basic tendency: the desire for easy access to central areas. For a given income, each person can choose less land at the center, or more land further from the center. When a population of individuals tries to resolve this conflict for themselves, a characteristic pattern of density comes into being: density declines exponentially with distance from the center according to the equation: $d_r = d_o e^{-br}$. Brian J. L. Berry, James W. Simmons, and Robert J. Tennant, "Urban Population Densities: Structure and Change," *Geographical Review*, 53 (1963), pp. 389-405; John Q. Stewart and William Warntz, "Physics of Population Distribution," *Journal of Regional Science*, Vol. I (1958), pp. 99-123. This relation holds for cities all over the world. Colin Clark, "Urban Population Densities," *Journal of the Royal Statistical Society*, Series A, 114 (1951), Part 4, pp. 490-96; Berry, cited. What is even more surprising, the relation is almost entirely fixed by absolute population, and by the age of the city. This means that in a free market, neither the over-all mean density of a city nor the densities at different distances from the center can be controlled by planning action.

They can, however, be controlled indirectly. The density pattern comes into being as a result of millions of peoples' efforts to resolve the conflict between their desire for access and their desire for land. If we can make land more useful, so that a person can get a given level of satisfaction from a smaller piece of land than he needs to get that satisfaction now, then the desire for access will balance differently against the desire for land, and densities will increase.

Land is valuable for two basic reasons. First of all, it is the prime building surface. Secondly, it provides open space. The first is replaceable. The second is not. It is easy to create artificial building surfaces at many levels. But the area of open space cannot be increased beyond the area of the land. This is a basic natural resource. Yet this resource is almost entirely wasted and destroyed in urban areas today. Fifty per cent is wasted on roads and parking lots, which really don't require it: 25 per cent is wasted on roofs, which get no benefit from it at all. The 25 per cent of open space left over is chopped up and useless.

If a city were built so as to conserve this resource, with all roofs covered with grass and trees, and all roads roofed over, so that the total exterior surface of the city was a parkland of grass and flowers and bushes and trees, people could have the very same amenities they have today, at far higher densities.

How much useful open land does a family in a suburban tract command? At a gross density of 5,000 persons per square mile, each family has a lot about 70' by 100', 7,000 square feet in all. Of this, 2,000 square feet go to the house, and another 1,000 square feet to the driveway, leaving about 4,000 square feet of open land, or about 1,000 square feet per person. If the entire exterior surface of the city were artificial open land, it would be possible to house 25,000 people per square mile, and still give them the same 1,000 square feet of open land per person.

To make it work, the surface must undulate like a range of rolling hills, so that windows in the hillsides can get daylight to the houses under the surface.

k. So that people can get the same feeling of ownership, and the same opportunity to build what they want and the same private open space that they get in the suburbs, the houses under the hillside must be built on individual artificial lots. To avoid the half-hearted feeling of ownership which condominium apartments offer, each lot must be totally separate from the other lots, and so made that the owner can build what he wants to on his own lot. Each lot is an individual load-bearing pad, large enough to hold a 2,000-square-foot house with a private garden.

l. Since density will still vary with distance from urban centers, even if the land-access equation changes, the hills must vary in height and slope. The highest and steepest hills, whose density is greatest, will be near the urban centers; the low flat hills at the periphery.

Comments on

Alexander

H. PETER OBERLANDER
*Program of Community and Regional Planning,
University of British Columbia*

How does Mr. Alexander's insight help us to achieve a start in defining our notion of optimum environment? I have had the benefit of reading some of the things that Mr. Alexander has written before, and I will discuss what he has done and what still needs to be done.

In his book, *Notes on the Synthesis of Form,*[*] he distinguishes between form and context. Let me quote: "The ultimate object of design is form." He explains this by using the old example of iron shavings placed in a magnetic field, where they are obviously responding to these forces and creating a form. He then goes on to say, "Every design problem begins with an effort to achieve fitness between two entities; the form in question and its context. The form is a solution to the problem; the context defines the problem. When we speak of design, the real object is not the form alone but the

[*] Cambridge: Harvard University Press, 1964.

assembly comprising the form and its context. Good fit is a desired property of this assembly which relates to a particular division of this assembly into form and context." There is a wide variety of assemblies which we can talk about like this; the ecological example is very clear in our minds since Dr. Dubos outlined this notion.

"In the pursuit of urbanism," Alexander continues, "the assembly which confronts us is the city and its habits. Here the human background, which defines the needs for new buildings, and the physical environment provided for the available sites make a context for the form of the city's growth. In an extreme case of this kind, we may even speak of a culture which is in itself an assembly where the various factions and artifacts which develop are slowly fitted into the rest."

Density by itself, Alexander suggests, has no real impact one way or the other. I entirely agree, on the basis of my own studies and analyses. My concern is with space and its human usefulness as the basic, and perhaps most critical, component of our urban fabric.

If we look at the city from any vantage point we see that space is created by default, not by design. It is what's left over after people have built buildings and put them on the ground. Not only is that critical space negatively created, but it is created and enforced by law. This is the point I wish to stress. We are surrounded by and operate within a context of restraints which have the force of law. The basis of that, as we well know, is arbitrary. These are absolute measurements without real functional standards. The setback, the side yard, the front yard are all rule of thumb. What's magic about a 5-foot side yard? A 35-foot setback? Why not 34½ or 33⅓? Having studied building and zoning laws across the country this past five years, we have found a surprising similarity of these "magic" numbers. We have found that these are arbitrary and, I submit, based on an irrational notion of what space is and of its utility and on an entire negation of its utility for those who are supposed to use it, and above all, for those who own it. These standards of space are rigid and resistant to change, for they are enforced by law.

What are we trying to achieve in trying to make sure everyone has a setback, a side yard, a front yard, particularly in the most critical component of the urban environment, the residential sector? Why are we trying to separate buildings by force of law, and what are we trying to achieve when we in fact impose space and, in effect, make people give up their land without compensation? The 35-foot setback in the city of Vancouver is, to my mind, a flagrant taking away of the usefulness of land without compensation.

We have to develop a system of space objectives. This can be paralleled with a system of space coordinates. These together could result in a matrix of space requirements which would be both rational and systematic and subject to both description and measurement. I am talking about performance standards which are responsive to changing needs and which can achieve the notion of the utility of space above and beyond the notion of density. Our studies are restricted to residential areas because that is where the problem seems to be the most critical.

Space as an essential component of human life, of human action and interaction, in the residential segment is subject to specific analysis. In the history of building standards and zoning by-laws you will find that they all started with a crisis. In the middle of the seventeenth century, the city of London was destroyed by fire. It was because of that fire threat that men began to insist on separation of buildings. So we looked at fire as a real measure of space and its utility. We then looked at daylight. We looked at noise and at the notion of privacy. As regards noise, science can tell us what man can stand and what he needs; as regards daylight, what he needs and what he does not need. It is possible to relate the findings of science in a systematic way and it is our hope to achieve a kind of matrix of space requirements which reflect scientific knowledge and the rational use of human space.

PHILIP THIEL

College of Architecture and Urban Planning,
University of Washington

Professor Alexander has presented us with a provocative example of social engineering, in which the environment is consciously arranged to produce a social effect. In describing the rationale with which he arrives at his proposed arrangement of the environment he cites a number of studies of correlations of mental health with urban form and types of social interaction, and implies therewith a causation. This is as if to conclude that since many umbrellas are carried on rainy days, the carrying of many umbrellas is what causes it to rain. How can he be sure that other (genetic?) factors are not in fact causal?

Aside from this point of interpretation, however, is the question of drawing all one's data from studies in pathology. Since our interest is in promoting optimums, it would seem more appropriate to involve the insights provided by studies on the creative, self-realized personality, such as those by Professor Maslow at Brandeis and Professor McKinnon at Berkeley. My impression is that the occurrence of this type of personality does _not_ correlate with the type and degree of human contact and physical environment that Professor Alexander concludes to be essential, and that is to be produced by the forms he proposes. To generalize, would it not be even better to base causative conclusions on studies of broader groups, rather than on those which tend to come to the attention of the authorities?

But given his goals, one wonders at his requirement for people to drive past and peer into each residence's public zone. If the intention is to really promote a "frequent, informal, relaxed confrontation," analogous to that of the traditional extended family group in the local neighborhood, could not this be done better in our age with the closed-circuit television-phone, rather than with an enlargement of the picture windows on the public highway?

ROBERT F. WEHRLI
Department of Architecture, University of Utah

The environmental designer—urban planner and architect—has come face to face with technology. Should he take up the computer as a design tool? Should he adopt design methodology? Should he apply to design findings from the life and behavioral sciences? All of these issues are interlocking, for the use of the computer is not only itself a method but places demands for rigorous method upon its users. The added burden of dealing with information from the life and behavioral sciences compels method; and the life and behavioral disciplines bring to the designer not only a backlog of scientific data and theory but scientific methodology as well.

Christopher Alexander is wrestling with these issues of technology. In his *Notes on the Synthesis of Form* he outlined a comprehensive method of stating design requirements, grouping the requirements according to sets, and resolving the sets by computerized mathematics. He substantiated his rationale for this set theory method with a great number of readings from many disciplines. In his presentation at this conference, Alexander revealed a novel solution to the problem of housing. As near as one can tell, the housing scheme was arrived at, not by his set theory method, but by the traditional method of concept getting, with the important difference that Alexander made a scholarly attempt to support his design concepts with theories from psychology, sociology, and the like.

Before discussing these two methods—set theory and concept getting—it might be well to say a few words about method generally, for it is a topic that has long been distasteful to the environmental designer, who views it as a threat to his role as a conservator of historic human values, as a champion of esthetics, and especially, as an intuitive artist trying desperately to make a lasting, personal impact upon society. Distaste for method is a carryover from the rebellion, now nearly won, against the beaux-arts system, which was concerned, however, not essentially with process, but with product. That is, its primary concern was not the thought process by which a scheme for a building or city was attained, but rather that the scheme should adhere to certain "laws" of order and proportion, or even that it be composed of historic forms adapted more or less directly. If we can be assured, as I think we can, that the present interest in method is process-oriented rather than product-oriented we should welcome it, for it ought not to delimit our schemes, but to give us a greater and more widespread capability for attaining them.

After all, every designer has a method. It is only that it remains a modus operandi until he directs his attention to it and talks and writes about it. For most designers the modus operandi is a set of habits and techniques learned in a studio situation where assigned projects are periodically criticized and eventually judged by professionals trained in the same fashion. Again, the primary emphasis in the studio has been upon the product—a scheme at any state of completion—rather than upon the process of thinking and doing. Meanwhile human factors engineers, systems engineers, industrial engineers, and computer scientists have made progress in reducing design to method, while psychologists explore the relationships between language, imagery, and thought.

The bulwark of studio situation teaching is the getting of single, dominant concepts, which subsequently serve to guide secondary design decisions. Concept getting is a powerful method in capable hands and produces forms clearly related to a deep understanding and a comprehensive consideration of needs. Unfortunately, our lack of interest in method has resulted in a predicament where neither the teaching nor the use of concept getting is well understood, so that students and professionals repeatedly adopt concepts of form which are not so much appropriate as simply expedient or fashionable. This is a grievous situation when, as is presently true, needs are constantly changing, and when we may wish to state those needs in the terminology of the life and behavioral scientist but have no sure guide for converting from problem statement to form.

Alexander's set theory method aims at a comprehensive listing and logical resolution of needs. The method is sufficiently complete to be called a theory of design comparable to a scientific theory in that it is testable and original; it has already proved to be heuristic; and, it is reasonably explicit, simple, and self-consistent. The disadvantages are that it is verbal and mathematical rather than visual, and therefore not attractive to visual-minded architects and planners, and further, it has not been shown to produce a scheme in sufficient detail to be converted to working drawings and subsequently built.

In *Notes on the Synthesis of Form* Alexander used the design of a water kettle to illustrate his method, but he did not design or produce a water kettle. In the spring of 1966 Robert Nestor, a fifth-year student in architecture at the University of Utah, undertook to test Alexander's method by designing a water kettle as six week's credit for a two-hour course under my direction. Simply stated, the question was: "Can an upper-class architectural student, aided only by Alexander's master set theory method, design a simple object?" Working diligently but without benefit of a competent mathematician, it is not surprising that Nestor got no further than a listing of requirements, a delineation of their interactions, and a few crude graphs. On the other hand, thirteen members of the same class produced sketches of a water kettle in twenty minutes by traditional methods.

These studies are by no means conclusive but suggest that architects and planners as presently trained will not find a ready use for set theory method as developed to date. To justify the necessary training in mathematics, the merits of the method must be proved for schemes brought at least to the working drawing stage, and these schemes must be shown to be superior to those produced by conventional means.

It appears that the basic fault of the set theory method is that the problem requirements, however exhaustively stated, elegantly clustered, and nicely resolved, are never really converted to form. Form, after all, is the sum of the attributes of a thing, and we name as many attributes as we wish to make decisions about. Certainly we need such elementary attributes as dimension, shape, color, light and shadow, location, and arrangement. The effect of technology is to name more and more attributes like heat loss, reflectivity, sound absorption, flame resistance, and the like. But Alexander stated requirements which do not seem to refer to or guide decisions about elementary attributes, much less technological ones. For many of his requirements it would be necessary to make some intermediary inference in order to make a reasonable reference to some attribute of form. This explains why Alexander's illustrative city is a collection of diagrams rather than a definitive design.

It appears that Alexander, when confronted with producing a definitive design—that of the housing presented at this conference—abandoned set theory design in favor of concept getting. Whereas set theory suffers from an inability to convert from verbal statement to constructed form, concept getting suffers from an inadequately broad statement of requirements, and thereafter from an unreasoning subservience to the central concept. No designer would deny

REMINDER

Be careful of semantics.

Example: alley: a narrow street   alley: an ugly word

How many of these alleys are ugly?

What are the scope and dimensions of beauty in environment?

What is the raw material
of environment?

Is it raw stuff such as this

plus imagination and creativity

plus all the arts and all
the disciplines

plus the family, and faith
of any creed?

Psychic influences on perception

claustrophobia

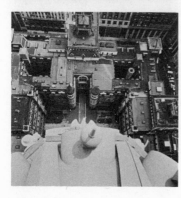

agoraphobia

illusion

REMINDER
Spatial perception has more than three dimensions

Each individual perceives differently and reacts differently to
what he sees

What is *psychological perception?*

Man's thoughts probe
complex space

How much do they probe the
simple act of a small child?

Here's a man with a positive
set of values—I know him well;
his name is Tom

He's familiar with the geography
of loneliness

Here's a stranger to me—surely
her set of values is as
positive as Tom's

Does environment mean the
same to everyone? Does it ever
mean the same to children
and adults?

REMINDER
Each man is an individual

His genetic number—family—education—personal values—forever
set him apart

And now—*sociological perception*

Children

Family groups—emotions
openly expressed

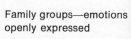

Random groups—involvement in the scene

Special groups—sharing a new experience

Here are 100,00 people— cheering

Can't you feel the surging millions of a big city at night?

122

Is environment a daytime thing?

Excitement—turmoil—sound—
action—interaction

REMINDER

We plan for people and their interaction in diverse groups—and with variable concentrations

But remember, we also design our environment with life, not with statistics

Let's think for a moment about history and change

Romantic

Old-fashioned?

Curved lines—are these out of date?

123

Or do we need straight lines?
Are these up to date?

Art museum—is this out
of date?

Is this addition to the same
museum up to date?

Monticello—is this *really*
out of date?

Motel—up to date of course!

Transportation—out of date

REMINDER

Perhaps in a few years the automobile will be out of date—and gone
forever—like the horse

Now, what is a pedestrian?

Someone who dodges traffic?

Are there two classes of
pedestrian—

those who don't walk

127

and those who do?

Or is a pedestrian

a little girl on the way to
the zoo?

REMINDER
Perhaps the pedestrian should be given a higher priority when we set
the warp and woof of our urban matrix

Let's consider now space and
geopolitics

Rivers separate states,
generating problems and port
authorities

State borders zig and zag at Lake Tahoe, and two jurisdictions split a community of common interests

We're running out of urban space in my part of the country— with myriads of overlapping jurisdictions

How can we keep people, space, and resources in equilibrium?

For instance, here's an island that ran out of space— inelegantly

In our largest state— a university running out of space to expand logically

129

In our second largest state—
running out of space in the
middle of square miles of
real estate

In another day (long since gone)
—integrated design—quiet
growth—equilibrium

Is this integrated design in
our day? Do those monuments
against the horizon indicate
our aspirations?

Or do they recall other
monuments against the sky?

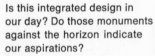

inspired by the wide reaches
of nature

the great culture of all
our cities

the subtleties of the
countryside

combined with the fabric of
cityscape

searching for beauty   and simplicity

creating a finer environment
for all our children

creating greater cities for
all our people

Let us leave a full, rich
legacy of accomplishment in
the next fifty years

using a total perspective
seen from the vantage point
of all disciplines

V I

Bertram M. Gross
National Planning Studies Program
Maxwell School, Syracuse University

The City of Man:
A Social Systems Reckoning

While the present is indeed a period of unprecedented change, let us keep in mind that social change takes place today—as it always has—at differential rates. While some things move with the speed of our mechanized idiots, the computers, others move like our idiotic central-city traffic jams. Indeed, relative to the speed of scientific and technological change in the United States, many American ideas, traditions, and institutions are more backward and rigid than the caste system is in the Indian environment, the therapeutics of the Ubangi medicine men in Africa, or the Catholic clergy in Latin America. Some of the backwardness comes from the narrow provincialism of the affluent and the powerful. Some of the rigidity comes from the hyperspecialization of our scientoids and technopols.

Among those involved in urban planning, fortunately, there is a new and thrilling ferment. There are more and more people pressing, probing, testing, and willing to see—even if not to state publicly—that some kings have been going around with no clothes on. The ideas in this paper are merely an effort to package this ferment and stimulate more significant explorations.

The new wave of creative ideas on urban planning is taking us, I believe, toward a deeper awareness of (1) the revolution-

The Rise of the Megalopolitans

Another myth still haunting us is the idea that we can understand and deal with urbanism merely by shifting our attention from the city to the metropolitan area.

The metropolitan approach is now the safe and sanitary, smooth and easy conventional wisdom. It allows urban planners —some still transfixed by the mirage of metropolitan government —to ignore the emergence of *much larger urban regions* extending beyond any possible boundaries of local government and often transcending the boundaries of states and nations.

Let me quote an analysis of census statistics—joined in by Richard Scammon, until recently Census Director—which may bring some discomfort to those still jealously guarding their vested interests in municipal or metropolitan planning:

> We can now see the beginnings of other megalopoli in different areas. One is clearly forming along the southwestern end of Lake Michigan, comprised of Gary-Hammond-East Chicago, Chicago, Kenosha, Racine and Milwaukee; another smaller megalopolis is growing from Miami north to Fort Lauderdale and beyond; still another megalopolis may one day connect Los Angeles and San Francisco-Oakland (with Fresno in the middle) but this will take a long time in the coming; and a fifth urban belt may eventually link Detroit and Cleveland with Toledo in the middle, or Cleveland and Pittsburgh with Youngstown in between.[3]

One may dispute the exact location and composition of these future megalopoli. One may even disagree with Wattenberg and Scammon on the exact number. Yet the framework of the debate will certainly be within the 3-to-5 range. In other words, it seems certain that the United States will soon become a multi-megalopolitan nation. When one realizes that a megalopolis is a huge concentration not merely of people but of wealth, science, influence, and prestige, this may be seen as one of the most significant facts in the distribution of power throughout the world. After all, there are very few other countries—probably only the Soviet Union, China, and India—that can be expected to attain multimegalopolitan rank. Only some will be unimegalopolitan or demimegalopolitan ("demi" refers to the status of such countries as the Netherlands and Belgium, which will become parts of a huge transnational megalopolis). Most will be nonmegalopolitan.[4]

All the megalopoli of the future—in this country and elsewhere—will transcend national boundaries in many ways. They will provide the home bases and regional offices of organizations engaging in operations that encircle the world. They will become the major "reference points" (this term being used in a sense similar to that of "reference groups") in the minds of elites from nonmegalopolitan areas throughout the world, serving both as the "staging ground" on which they will be trained for leadership and as the stage on which they hope to play a major role. Around the megalopoli will develop a megalopolitan culture much broader and more diverse than the cosmopolitan culture which developed in the large cities of the past. The elites based in one megalopolis will develop intimate associations with people and organizations in many other megalopoli. They will get to know foreign megalopoli much better than the hinterlands in their own country—and I suspect this is already true of many people.

By the time many nations have learned to cope with the internal problems of these huge polynuclear subnational territorial entities, most megalopoli themselves will be obsolete. They will be rendered obsolescent by the "mobiletics" of the coming decades: the wide availability of low-cost, instantaneous transmission of information and energy in many forms and the supersonic movement of people and things at speeds approaching that of our space-ship earth. Thus the planet itself will

become a single polynuclear supermegalopolis, with new conflicts among unneighborly neighbors.

The Birth Pangs of a World Society

In the past twenty years more nation-states have come into
being than in all previous centuries of recorded history. We
therefore still tend to think of the people of this planet in terms
of separate nations alone. This outdated idea blinds many of us
to *the* central fact of our time: *The painful birth pangs—un-
heralded, unanticipated, and to many people unseen—of a new
world society of interdependent nations.*

This world society is brought increasingly together by (a)
worldwide interest in simple survival; (b) worldwide aspirations that cannot be even partially fulfilled without collabora-
tive actions and transactions; (c) the "mobiletic" revolution
that is shrinking the earth to small proportions by contracting
the time needed to move people, things, information, and energy across space; (d) techniques of "informal penetration" and
"infusive diplomacy" that make it impossible to divide the
world into old-fashioned spheres of influence and that create
spheres of mutual interest even among adversaries; and (e) the
growing influence of world-oriented megalopolitans.

To recognize the world society is to face some difficult facts.

The emerging One World hardly conforms to the visions of the
utopians—any more than does the giant organization to "classical" ideas of administration, the megalopolis to the models of
city planners or the great societies to Keynesian theory. The
world society includes a bewildering variety of subsystems increasingly locked together in conflict-cooperation relationships.
The world polity is characterized by polycentric conflict, inter-
secting coalitions, continuing outbreaks of localized violence,
many possibilities of escalation, and spreading capacities for
nuclear destruction. The political instrumentalities of conflict
resolution and regional and world integration operate—as in nations, states and cities—in an atmosphere of pressure and power

politics, behind-the-scene lobbying, rotten borough representation, moralistic double-talk, deception and self-deception. The world culture, on the one hand, tends to submerge national characteristics and values in a homogenizing flood of material goods and international styles. On the other hand, it includes vast value differences and sharp value conflicts. Like Megalopolis, the world society is a territorial entity without a government. It is an all-inclusive complex macro-system with remarkably complicated and unpredictable—although increasingly structured—mechanisms of mutual adjustment.[5]

Watchmen, What about Man?

With the world shrinking in space-time, will people themselves shrink—as Durkheim suggested—into anonymous specks in a cloud of dust?

Will postindustrialism mean posthumanity, with "cybernetic deities" leading to human dessication and stultification?

Will the sprawling giantism of megalopolis—as presented in the Mumford nightmares—lead to bureaucratic hell and psychosis?

If we had to rely entirely on the vision of most current city planners, I'm afraid that Mumford nightmares might come to pass. The model of some city planners is still the City of Things. When people enter the model, it's in dehumanized, unorganized form. It's as though educational planners should turn things over to gym teachers—the experts in physical education.

The idea of city planning as physical planning alone has been riddled with bullets on the streets of Watts and Harlem. The body stinks. Let's bury it quickly.

The old hard good techniques of zoning, building regulation, subdivision control, and capital budgeting are not enough to cope with the pressing urban problems of postindustrial America in the emerging world society. They have but little bearing on economic growth, civil rights, education, poverty, ugliness, air and water pollution, and traffic congestion. They do not

people are interrelated with such nonmachine components as land, various things in it and on it, money, and even air. Perhaps a better term is "man-resource system" or—following the fruitful vocabulary of the Tavistock Institute of Human Relations—"sociotechnical system." So long as we are clear that nonhuman resources and technology are included, perhaps the simplest term is "social system."

If we are really to put men in our models, we must be bold enough to cope with the following five aspects of social systems (each one of which has already been contemplated by the authors of recent articles in the AIP journal): (1) individuals and groups—not money, land, roads, roles, or disembodied benefits—as the central elements and actors in the structure of a social system; (2) the satisfaction or frustration of individual and group interests or needs as the most important dimensions in the performance of a social system; (3) continuing processes of conflict as well as cooperation between a social system and its environment, and among and within its subsystems (including the smallest subsystem, the individual personality); (4) complexity based not only on many interrelated subsystems but on being contained in larger systems and crisscrossed by many overlapping systems, and (5) system looseness, with many "black boxes" that are partially autonomous, imperfectly coordinated, only partially controllable, and never fully knowable.[7]

One way to sum up these points is simply to state that a useful social system model—whether used in a fully general sense or spelled out to become a "special model" of a nation or a city, or a "unique model" of, let us say, Portland in 1966 or the U.S.A. in 2017—*must include qualitative as well as quantitative information.* While a social system model can help provide for the fuller exploitation of operations research, linear programming and nonlinear programming within their spheres of relevance, it cannot as yet be presented (except for selected segments or cross-sections) in the language of present-day, thing-oriented mathematics.

Urban Areas as Open System Clusters

Every city, town and village in the modern world is "wide open." I'm not talking just about openness to gambling, prostitution, pollution, and nuclear fall-out. Nor am I using the words "city" or "village" in the narrow sense of "city government" or "physical lay-out." Few towns, villages, or neighborhoods are self-contained social systems. Rather, they are spatially concentrated aggregates of individuals, families, associations, and organizations that often operate outside its boundaries. Their parts—particularly local branches of far-reaching families, corporations, and government agencies—are themselves parts of much larger systems. These smaller territorial entities—with few or no home offices of large collectivities—are the remote-controlled town and cities. Many of the critical decisions are—and must be—made elsewhere.

As urban areas become more densely populated, some of them include the home offices of large organizations that are decision centers for operations across the nation and world. But here the decisions are not made primarily in the frame of reference of the territorial entity. They are—and must be—made in a much broader framework. The aggregation of these ships that pass in the night, this localized intertwining of nonlocalized systems, this overlapping within certain physical boundaries of boundary-transcending systems—all this gives us the fragmented metropolis and the randomly polynucleated megalopolis.

The best way to misunderstand such unsystematic systems is to think of urban areas as organisms with some inner-directed pattern of growth.

The only way to understand the forces affecting the growth of any urban area is to look first at its subsystems and their interrelations: (1) people as individuals, (2) families, and (3) the more formally organized entities: corporations, pressure groups, political parties, and government agencies.[8]

With government agencies, as with corporations, moreover, understanding cannot stop at the boundary, political or otherwise. One must understand and deal with the local and higher offices of county, state and national agencies and of quasi-independent public authorities. We must think much less of "local government" and much more of "governments at the local level." The elected and appointed officials of local government, particularly, must think in these terms.

Thus one of the simplest but most widely neglected principles of urban planning is that: "Local coordination depends on the interaction of many subnational, national (and perhaps international) forces."

So let's keep the fingers of our other hand crossed until we know that we're not fouled up by closed system models. Every city is a part of a nation and a port to the world.

Many years ago Elton Mayo retorted to Tawney's comment on the "sickness of an acquisitive society." He suggested that the problem of industrial civilization, rather, is "the acquisitiveness of a sick society."[9]

Similarly, to get perspective on moral and physical ugliness in the cities of our postindustrializing society perhaps we should look at the sicknesses of our city-centered world.

So let's keep the fingers of our other hand crossed until we can develop useful operational models of urban areas not as autonomous organisms but as open systems in the national and world environment.

State of the Area Reckonings

A few centuries ago in an earlier incarnation—1945 and 1946, to be exact—I held the pencil for the Senators and Representatives who drafted the Employment Act. Section 2 of that act, which provided for the annual Economic Report of the President, was a real "sleeper." Few people at that time realized the tremendous power of ordered information presented at regular intervals by an elected tribune of the people.

But the very success of the Economic Reports in raising the level of economic literacy has created two new problems: (1) the new economic philistinism that presumes to measure the quality of life in monetary terms, and (2) "aggregatics," a form of mental acrobatics in which nonspatial, macro-guesstimates are juggled in the air without reaching the ground in any territorial entity smaller than the nation itself.

The remedy for the first problem: Social Reports of the President to supplement the Economic Reports and Budget Messages.[10]

The remedy for the second problem: State-of-the-City reports by our mayors. These could be as broad as the metropolitan areas, in fact. They would go far beyond the traditional practice of reporting on government activities. They would report, rather, on *the condition of man in the metropolitan area.*

An annual reckoning of this type could provide a means of bringing the information of many specialists together into some meaningful whole, helping the key leaders of organized groups to interrelate with each other, helping political leaders find out where they are and formulate better programs of where they might go, helping individuals to find out about the urban area and participate more fully in planning processes, and facilitating interaction among local, regional, and national forces affecting the area.

Let me state the proposition more formally: in a system characterized by multiple communication channels and a serious information overload, the annual "system state review" could become a strategic catalyst in the essential processes of multiple feedback without too much "lead" or "lag." In simpler terms, it could become one of the more important new techniques in the urban planning of the 1970's. Here is where we could use some initiative and experimentation by the mayors of our largest cities and their large staffs of physical, social, economic, and budgetary planners.

A word of warning. One must reckon with some unpleasant consequences of regular reckonings on the "State of the Metropolis."

Thus Professor Phillip Hauser, the former Census Director, has helped launch a University of Chicago study on the relation between socioeconomic status and mortality.[11] His global figures already prove that the poor—and the illiterate—die young. Dealing only with the white population of the country as a whole, he compares the 1960 mortality indices of male family members between the ages of 25 and 64. He finds that for those with less than $2,000 annual family income the mortality index (198) was 2.5 times as high as the index (76) for those families with more than $10,000 income. In due course this information will be available for the Negro population also.

And then—watch out—it may be broken down (and associated with other indicators of health and well-being) for Harlem, Watts, and the Negro ghettos beside the University of Chicago.

Any good social reckoning must be able to cope with the co-existence—in William Blake's words—of "joy and woe." We'll get information on the second and third order consequences whereby the extensions of man conflict with the intentions of men.

3. Anthropolis Unbound

Like Oliver Wendell Holmes, I have no faith in panaceas and almost none in sudden ruin. But I'm fascinated by the story of the man who jumped off the Empire State building. "What a view!" he exclaimed as he passed the 80th floor. And then, at the 40th floor: "Let's get all America moving again!" At the 20th floor: "Say, I just had an idea. What about a Great Society?" And at the 10th floor: "Doing pretty well so far—." The moral of this story, according to Sir Geoffrey Vickers, is that we're reaching the end of "free fall" and must get "some parachute operation to break up the abruptness of the change."[12]

If we're going to use up-and-down imagery, I prefer to stand Darwin on his head and talk about not the descent but the ascent of man. The paleontologists, I'm told, have just discovered the missing link between the apes and civilized man: *it's us.*

The problem today is not so much whether God has died. It's whether man will be born. We can always create more gods in our own image. This is a time to proclaim that the Age of Things is over. As Frank Manuel, the historian, has recently written, "The Age of Heroes, like the Age of the Gods, is dead. It is time that the Age of Men began."[13] Let this be the generation that shall start building the City of Man. I suspect we are overly wedded to such words as metropolis and megalopolis, which refer mainly to size and numbers. Perhaps for a new age we need a new word: Anthropolis.

But what are the characteristics of Anthropolis? How will the City of Man differ from the City of Things? Let me attempt the kind of answers that amount to a partial reformulation of the question.

First, there can be no *one* ideal Anthropolis. We need many different kinds and styles of our new cities of man. By "optimum environment" let us be perfectly clear that we are thinking of *a variety of ever-changing optimum environments.* That letter "s" is tremendously important. While it is legitimate to drop it off for the sake of rhetorical effect, we must bring it back when we start thinking in specific operational terms. May God and man protect us from the terrors of any standardized urban environment with only man in the abstract (rather than the varied and diverse interest of many children, women, and men) as "*the* measure"!

Second, the essence of Anthropolitan ideals is that there be not *fewer* things but *more things that truly serve human interests.* True affluence is not conspicuous consumption through which a minority acquire privileged status and the power to push others around. We shall be a truly affluent society only when most of us enjoy houses designed to facilitate personal and family life, schools designed to promote learning processes, transportation systems that take us quickly and pleasantly where we want to go (even to and from airports), and air that we can breathe without yearning for a gas mask.

Third, the age of Anthropolis must be one in which minimum living standards are available to all except a small percentage of "frictionally poor." This means that *in absolute terms* we must put a floor under living standards—a floor with no holes in it and one that rises in conformance with our rising productive capacity. A floor under income is not enough. Our anti-poverty program must be four-dimensional, aiming at combating not only (1) income deprivation but also (2) asset deprivation, (3) public service deprivation, and (4) the deprivation of opportunities to participate in social decision-making.

Fourth, our Anthropolitan urban areas must be geared to the new and higher interests of people in the age of postindustrialism and the world society. In addition to providing the minimum facilities needed for urban subsystems (individuals, families, and organizations) they must be *dynamic centers of culture, education, science, and technology.* Let's sweep aside the dry rot of the city planning textbooks that cannot cope with—and often do not even mention—culture, art, and the things of the mind and spirit. If we want to build new Jerusalems let us go not to the professional city planners of Israel. Let us go, rather, to the inspired politicians and artists[14] who built the great new Bezalel Museum and the Billy Rose statuary garden on the rolling hills of Judea.

Finally, perhaps we may humanize and modernize the Augustinian vision of the City of God. For St. Augustine the City of God had two aspects, intellectually but not physically separable: the City Triumphant and the City of Pilgrims. In neo-

Augustinian terms, perhaps we may say that Anthropolis Triumphant occurs whenever people and groups have achieved security, brotherhood, friendship, self-respect, respect for others, and the substance of power to affect in some way the lives of themselves and others. Above all, it is the triumph over sheer materialism—a triumph impossible until basic material needs are met. It is the vigor and beauty of those who are leading self-actualizing, self-fulfilling, or self-developing lives.

For Augustine, the City of Pilgrims referred to those still struggling in the Slough of Despond. Anthropolis, too, must be a City of Pilgrims—of people wanting to arrive, not those who have already arrived, a divine discontent and creative dissonance rather than the dull statics of the old-fashioned master plan.

In Anthropolis, because it is the City of Man, there will still be the forgetting man and the forgotten man. Indeed, there must even be poverty—in the sense of differential deprivation above the level of rising minimum standards; since equity and justice will not be sacrificed on the altar of equalization. There will be conflict and struggle, release from apathy, satiety, and purposelessness. Only thus can the true creative powers of people be unleashed. Only thus can we achieve Anthropolis Unbound.

4. Power and Planning

The five-letter word POWER is something that shouldn't be mentioned among gentlemen—particularly among city planners. It's like sex used to be; almost everybody wants it, but why go around talking about it in public? Did you read Galbraith's analysis of the "convention which outlaws ostensible pursuit of power and which leads to a constant search for euphemisms to disguise its possession"?

We city planners don't usually have to stay up nights worrying about disguising its possession. Our problem, rather, is how to get it. Some of us, of course, are not exactly sure what we want. It's not just that we stand foursquare for motherhood and against sin. It's rather that at the one and the same time we're for both motherhood and virginity. Fortunately, there's a new breed of city planners more interested in building the City of Man and less interested in virginal remoteness from power politics.

Power, of course, can be a filthy business. For some planners, its pursuit has meant ending up as a well-paid "call boy" or a hired brain in an air-conditioned brothel. But without power (or "influence," if you prefer a little softer word), any plan is a useless scrap of paper. Unless oriented toward the power and capacity *to get things done,* the planning process is a costly exercise in futility, self-deception, and deception of others.

Any social system—from a ladies' club or a homeowners' association to a highway department, a supermarket, or a mayor's office—is a system of power. If planners want to serve the interests of children, women, and men in our complex urban systems, they must be frankly, seriously, and persistently concerned with *the mobilization, maintenance and use of power.*

The implications of this principle are great enough to fill another book. Let me just suggest a few of these implications. (1) The planning process must be considered not as a disembodied form of rationality but rather as an effort to integrate diverse interests, both organized and unorganized. (2) The planners must attempt the factual analysis of both the manifest and the latent interests of different kinds of people and groups. (3) In the very process of plan formulation the planners must consider alternative ways of developing the kind of power base (or "activation base" or "support network")[15] without which plans cannot be implemented, even though this may imply the demolition, reconstruction, or extension of a local political machine. (4) The planners must develop technical skills in the appraisal of the various forms of persuasion and pressure that enter into an "activation mix."[16] (5) Planners must consciously cultivate the many arts of playing politics "for keeps" through the various rituals of being "bipartisan," "nonpartisan" and "above politics."

At the level of larger social systems, these implications have been suggested in some of the most recent publications concerning national planning. Thus, at this level I have already attempted to synthesize the results of empirical inquiries by setting forth a series of both descriptive[17] and prescriptive[18] principles. Similar—but more far-reaching—efforts are now urgently needed at the level of the most important subnational territorial entity, namely, the urban area.

5. The Face—and Interface—of the Planner

Rexford Guy Tugwell, I'm told, was the best looking planning commissioner of New York or any other American city. One day, the story goes, Tugwell asked the fateful question, "Mirror, mirror, on the wall, who are the best planners of them all?" Quick as a flash, the mirror came back with a three-M answer: "Robert Moses—General Marshall—General Motors."

The moral is clear: If the label "planning" is attached to your office, you probably don't do much of it. The real-life planners are the people who run limited-purpose organizations with the capacity to get things done. In these separate organizations, the value of the professional specialist in planning depends upon his linkages with administrators and top-level executives and leaders.

For a planning specialist interested in the broad lines of progress in a territorial entity—whether nation, region, metropolis, town, or village—the key problem is the whole set of his many-layered relations with political leaders, administrators, lower-level bureaucrats, business enterprises, interest groups, pressure groups, groups with little pressure, and interests not yet organized.

Instead of saving professional face, the planning specialist's role is to build an *interface* with all these other people and groups. This is the only way to get a face worth saving—in front of a mind worth having.

But let's not everyone try to become that very special form of specialist, the fellow who specializes in being the generalist who tries to knit things together.

And in our enthusiasm for comprehensive vision and general systems models, let's not denigrate the specialist in physical planning. This is an area in which we need not only more specialists, but more subspecialists and subsubspecialists. I'm still looking for the architects who can design an up-to-date library or city art center, for the city planners who can help governments design public housing projects that don't look like welfare institutions, for the budget-bouncing systems analyst capable of analyzing a transportation system, for the specialists in linking school parks, high rise buildings, and other high density areas with transportation systems. We need more planning specialization and differentiation—but with two provisos: (1) that the specialists learn something about the larger systems of which they're a part, and (2) that there be more education and training in the generalist skills of system guidance.

In Anthropolis, the toughest physical planner or highway engineer and the sharpest-eyed systems analyzing budgeteer will be able to talk and think about love and politics. And the dewiest-eyed social worker and toughest civil rights or antipoverty warrior will be able to talk and think about land acquisition, building codes, and mass transport programs.

I'm tired of hearing that progress in this direction means the transfiguration of our city planning departments. That's just a small part of the picture. It means social learning and creative adaptation on a much wider front—namely, in our departments of political science, economics, sociology, and social psychology. Above all, new concepts, new thinking, and a human approach to social systems in this period of transition to postindustrialism and the emergence of a world society.

If we want true "urban renewal" instead of merely "Negro removal," we need a little "myth removal" and a lot of "mental renewal."

But mental renewal can come only from some form of "getting where the action is," not from withdrawal. In this mood, let me end by going back to William Blake's "arrows of desire." With a little adaptation to a land less green than England, we get the following perorational text:[19]

> We shall not cease from mental fight
> Nor let the swords rest in our hands
> 'Til we have built Jerusalem
> Throughout these rich and mighty lands.

My sword is not yet sharp enough, my words have been blunt. I hope your swords are sharper, and that they will be used during the coming years.

VII

William L. C. Wheaton

Institute of Urban and Regional Development
University of California, Berkeley

Form and Structure
of the
Metropolitan Area

This is the first Catherine Bauer Wurster American Life Lecture, honoring one who made many vital contributions to American planning, housing and development. The tremendous range of her interests and activities is well known to all members of the American Institute of Planners and needs no repetition here. Three special aspects of her thought deserve mention, however: her concern with both short and long-time perspectives, her interest in both humanity and technology, and in the relations between thought and action. In each of these her expression of the best aspirations of planners engaged their interest and devotion.

Planning must necessarily be concerned with futures, usually long-range futures. In a world which heavily discounts the future, and often if not invariably sacrifices the future for some more immediate satisfaction, planners often find themselves lonely defenders of some distant welfare against the exploitations of the present. Yet the protection of that welfare usually requires some present sacrifice. In its starkest form, in the developing countries, already hungry people must go hungrier to save and invest so that later generations may have a higher standard of living. Here, Catherine Bauer Wurster, passionately dedicated to the conservation of natural resources, was

especially sensitive to the current human costs of actions which de-
ferred the satisfaction of the moment in the interest of the future.
Her lively interest in and affection for political leaders stemmed from
a recognition of how frequently they have to make difficult choices
regarding time preferences.

Planners similarly divide their attention between the human or
social and the physical and technological. Social purposes and hu-
mane concerns are deeply imbedded in both the rhetoric and the
action of planning. Often, however, the building becomes more im-
portant than the people, the new gimmick, system, or design more
interesting than its social or psychological consequences. While she
was fascinated by technology and deeply devoted to innovation,
especially in design, Catherine Bauer Wurster ruthlessly criticized
the purely technocratic or esoteric. Applauding the artistic innova-
tions of a Unité d'Habitation, she would insist that it be judged on
the grounds of whether it in fact produced a more comfortable or
pleasant home. Urging technical and design experiments, she in-
sisted that they be used as laboratories to discover that which was
better in human functional terms. She did not hesitate to ridicule a
design, however elegant, to the avant garde tastes of the moment,
which produced net inconvenience.

Finally, planners, like all of the professions, are compelled to act
in the face of uncertain knowledge. Some, obsessed by the lack of
knowledge, can turn to the scientific pursuit of better methods, so
that later planners can be more effective. Others, obsessed by the
necessity for remedial action, apply their unproven procedures and
pray that the unanticipated costs will not outweigh the unproven
benefits of their recommendations. The professional ethic imposes not
only the imperative of humility, but also the moral obligation to
record the results, especially the mistakes, and make them available
to others so that the practice can improve. Catherine Bauer Wurster
clearly preferred the life of action, the professional to the scientific.
But she scorned the unproven claims of the blind practitioner, made
significant contributions to development of scientific foundations for
planning, and perpetually insisted on visiting the site, examining the
product, and querying the people to learn their reactions.

In honoring one who was an inspiration to so many of this genera-

tion, we commit ourselves to the search for the solutions she ardently pursued.

The founders of city planning in the United States, men of enormous vision, largely failed to perceive the influences which democracy, technology, and affluence would exercise on the city of the future, its scale, its form, and its modes of expression. They failed to anticipate the influence which the automobile, the horizontal assembly line, or the widespread availability of electric power and means of communication would exercise to virtually destroy the old, compact city, draw from its central district most of the retailing and manufacturing functions which had historically sustained it, and spread the metropolitan area over countless square miles at low density. Men of vision though they were, these great leaders largely embraced design philosophies now wholly repudiated, the classic and revivalist notions of the nineteenth century, the Renaissance forms and architectural formalism. They ignored the inspirations of St. Elia, of Garner, or of Sullivan and Wright, which were more relevant to the future. Nor did these founders fully appreciate the extent to which social objectives would replace the traditional concerns of government. Though they were active participants in movements for social and political reform, the directions that those reforms would take half a century later in the search for full employment, social security, public health, mass education, and racial equality were rarely foreseen.

There is no reason for believing that our vision of the future of metropolitan areas will prove to be substantially better than those of our forebears. Perhaps because we are conscious of their frailties in forecasting, we may be more cautious. Perhaps we have a slightly better sense of historical evolution, but any of us looking at the record of the past must be exceedingly humble in looking at the future.

Today we believe that half a century from now the population of the United States will exceed 500 million people. If this proves true, we will have 500 to 1,000 metropolitan areas as now defined. The largest of these, the East Coast New York region, will contain perhaps 50 million people and will be part of a larger region exceeding 100 million people. There may be several other metropolitan areas with 25 million population. Presumably 85 to 95 per cent of the population will be urban. Further, it is now possible to foresee a day when the average family may have an income of $15,000, when ten years of productive work may yield the equivalent of a normal lifetime's work in today's terms, with all that this portends for consumption and for work. If these forecasts prove to be true, they will work vast changes in the nature of society and the functions of urban areas. Our concern today is to try to anticipate some of these changes and to suggest how they may affect the form and structure of metropolitan areas.

In approaching this broad and nebulous topic we will first discuss the functions of the city and its life styles. Then we will deal with some of the more important physical elements of the city.

Changing Functions of Metropolitan Areas

Half a century ago, Frederick Jackson Turner was noting the closing of the American frontier as a fact which would redirect the attention of society to urban development, alter the labor market in many ways, and ultimately affect the American way of life. A quarter of a century later, when the urbanization of America was already at full flood, Louis Wirth could write a seminal article on "Urbanism as *a* Way of Life."[1] But even Wirth did not anticipate the enormous rate of population growth which has subsequently occurred, its concentration into urban areas, the depopulation of the countryside as a result of increases in agricultural productivity, and thus the overwhelming urbanization which now characterizes our society. Whereas in all previous times urbanism was the way of life of a minority, and the basic population was rural or small-town, within these two generations urbanism has become *the* way of life of an overwhelming majority of the population. Whereas formerly people moved to the city to perform special or unusual functions, leaving the reservoir of population on the land, today that reservoir lives in cities, functioning or otherwise, and urban ways of life are characteristic of modern societies.

This observation should force us to reconsider the functions of the city, for the facts will compel that reconsideration in any event. If the city is to become the reservoir for population, it may have to sustain large populations who have no traditional function. Where we have traditionally dealt with the economic, political, cultural, or military functions of the city, perhaps a major function of the city of the future will be sustaining the population, enabling it to consume. We already have retirement communities and resort communities, whose chief functions are consumptive. We have poverty communities, which are distinguished largely by the fact that they are not able to consume enough. We are currently engaged in token efforts to retrain or redirect the residents of these communities toward employment, at the same time recognizing that if we were to succeed we might merely increase the number of employable unemployed.

Sociologists formerly assumed that the city was a mechanism for acculturation, that it would assimilate migrant populations, raise them in middle-class value systems, and incorporate them into the economic system. Today sociology suggests that assimilation may no longer function toward these ends. Acculturation and assimilation may not be inevitable. Instead, internally spawned heterogeneity may generate a variety of life styles, as Janet Abu-Lughod notes in a fascinating paper.[2] This tendency is already evident in our styles of work and leisure, and in the functions of the home. If we extrapolate these trends the functions of the metropolitan area of the future may be both different in nature and differently distributed.

The traditional functions of work, home, and play will remain, of course, though in changing forms and proportions. We all recognize the shifts which have occurred in the composition of employment. Agriculture has declined from the prevailing occupation in America to that of less than 10 per cent while agricultural output has multiplied. Manufacturing next became the dominant force in the economy, but in recent years output has increased steadily while employment has declined. It is not inconceivable that a small fraction of the population will, in the future, produce all of the products required by consumers. Construction remains a large employer, but its rationalization cannot be deferred indefinitely. Services are currently expanding, including government services. They offer the prospect for continued growth, but within services rationalization and mechanization proceed apace, even into hitherto backward areas like education. Many services can be largely replaced by manufacturing, as disposable clothing may someday largely eliminate laundries, or as laundromats have already shifted much of this function away from the home.

Under the circumstances, the composition of employment, its duration, and its definition are subject to radical future changes. We are already talking about the thirty and the twenty-hour work week. When incomes double, however, some of the population will prefer two twenty-hour week jobs, to keep busy and increase income. Others may prefer to work six months and play six. Still others may prefer to work very hard for ten or fifteen years so that they can retire at forty and indulge in other activities for the rest of their lives. The professions will never get any rest. The very nature of their work makes them completely dedicated to it. Finally, there are those who prefer to "work" very inefficiently, or at a leisurely pace, but for long hours. Some small shopkeepers and artists seem to fall in this class. Their "work" is in fact a way of life, engaging them for many hours, containing elements of leisure, and often producing relatively low compensation.

With "surplus" population having "surplus" time the very definition of work will change, as it is already changing. We will pay people to go to school, to keep them out of the labor market as well as to instruct them. This can be extended indefinitely, providing the individual with an exhilarating sense of accomplishment while keeping him busy. Community organization efforts, the leadership of certain recreation activities, and all kinds of rites, formerly regarded as voluntary activity, may become defined as "work" and be paid. Some of these occupations may be humble. The Parisian street sweeper receives a modest stipend to hold a broom and occasionally flush the street. He has a secure and continuing occupational and social status from this activity. Others such as artists are highly paid and honored for what is defined as work but may for others be play. We can readily redefine many activities as work, provide compensation and status for them, and in the process change the functions of the city and its subareas. When a quarter or a third of the population can produce all the essentials of life, those of the remainder who desire a function will find it, and society will support the activity in one way or another, and honor it.

Leisure is the obverse of work, as De Grazia has noted.[3] The portion of life devoted to it will increase radically. Already we can see that what we now call retirement may encompass more than half of the adult years. Much leisure activity is energetic—as in gardening or sports, the pursuit of arts or crafts, travel and exploration. These activities are socially sanctioned and rewarded. Perhaps, as the competition for space increases, we will reward space-economizing forms of leisure. There may be prizes for those who sit at home and read most, or who put in the most elapsed hours looking at TV, or acquire the most perfect tan. Neighborhood and community rites and ceremonies, which consume time and energy in socially accepted ways, may be at a premium. Dancing in the streets should become more common.

We all recognize the enormous demands for space which

will be generated by increased leisure of the active recreation types. We will need hundreds of thousands of miles of highways for leisure driving, countless square miles of beaches, lakes and rivers, parks and playgrounds, and hundreds of new forms of destinations and service places. But we will also require hundreds of new cities to accommodate these needs, quite possibly a quarter of all new urban growth. There would be cities with no visible means of support—existing solely to accommodate the lives of those who have no active productive functions as now defined.

The last of the traditional triumvirate of functions is the home. It was once the center of almost all activities. Many of its functions, e.g., education, recreation, and health, have been transferred to specialized institutions. For some of the population this trend may continue—the home may be merely a place for sleeping and the storage of personal property. For the student living in a dormitory, or a resident nurse in a hospital, or the child in a summer camp, this may be true today. Thus a home may be merely a point of departure. For many others the home may develop far more functions. It may be the center of work for those engaged in the arts or crafts, for salesmen, some professions, or neighborhood services. It may become the center of leisure for those who prefer gardening, or crafts, or for those of lowered mobility.

The most important historic function of the home, of course, has been as a place for child-rearing. This function has expanded as adolescence and education have been extended, but it has also contracted as many educational, recreational, and maintenance functions have become institutionalized. At some time in the near future all nations must adopt population policies which must have the effect of reducing the average size of child-rearing families or of reducing the proportion of such families, or both. Presumably the consequences of these efforts will be a shift toward smaller homes, and an increase in the proportion of dwellings designed, located, and priced to serve single persons and couples without children. Very similar effects have been historically associated with rising incomes and education. The two factors may reinforce each other. Leo Grebler long ago pointed out that only half of the potential number of households actually occupied their own dwellings.[4] With rising incomes this proportion should be increased steadily, too, by an increasing proportion of dwellings for single or two-person occupancy.

An increasing proportion of the population owns more than one home. Resort areas for summer occupancy have been expanding at an astonishing rate. Winter resorts and communities are burgeoning. An increasing number of families have country homes and city apartments. Many station their families in the country, suburbia, or a small town house to which the breadwinner commutes for weekends, or every other day, living meanwhile in a city apartment. The redefinition of work and leisure, and the changes in their proportions, will create great incentives for extensions of these patterns of living.

Finally I should note two other features of our styles of life which will influence metropolitan form and structure. First, more people will change their style of life during their lifetime than heretofore. We are accustomed to think of youth, adulthood, and old age as the primary types, and one or two communities as the locus of life. In the future we might think of childhood at home, adolescence at college, young married at college, young adult with or without children, mature adult without children, retired and able-bodied, retired and impaired. In addition to these different periods of life we will have more families choosing suburban, urban, exurban, and rural locations. We will have families who choose to live in different regions or countries for periods of their lives. In short, the number and types of home and location a normal family may occupy will increase. Second, we may discover that people have a wide range of tolerance of change. Some may be able to tolerate frequent change, but others may require considerable locational permanence, may have a low propensity to move, despite their enhanced possibility of movement. I will return to this theme later.

Changes in Functional Areas

We now turn to the effect of these forces, intangible as they are, upon the form of the metropolitan area. Planners have traditionally described metropolitan form in terms of central cities, suburban areas, urban-rural fringe zones, greenbelts, and new towns. We have described the form of the metropolitan area in terms of contiguous growth, sprawl or noncontiguous growth, linear forms, radial forms, and satellite forms. Within the developed areas we have described central business districts, regional subcenters and neighborhood centers, and neighborhoods. We have distinguished between modes of transportation and their form-giving influence, particularly rail and automobile transportation, and we have terminology dealing with the separation or mixture of land uses in the fine grain. This has been the terminology of city planning dealing with the form of the metropolitan area.[5]

During the last half century some of this language, or the dimensions which we attribute to it, has changed notably. When Ebenezer Howard wrote about new towns he described a community of 30,000 people. When the program was adopted by the British government a new town had become 60,000 people. When those towns were finished, they included 80,000 people. In the new plans for southeast England and for Paris, they were conceived as cities of 300,000 or more. Thus the scale of the concept of a new town or a satellite community has grown with the urban population and the metropolitan area until the term means something quite different from the original concept.

Similarly, our concept of the metropolitan area is being subjected to rapid change. We have scarcely begun to analyze the meaning of the megapolitan area, much less to adapt our language to this new reality. For this reason, I propose to discuss some of the terms which we use to describe metropolitan areas, selecting those in which the most dramatic changes appear to be in prospect.

Few things are more fixed in our language than the idea of a central business district. There must be only one. It must have such a high proportion of certain types of activity that it dominates a metropolitan area. But such districts were once dominated by retail trade. Few are today. Today a central business district means an office, managerial, and financial center, which need not coincide with a retail center. New York City clearly has two central business districts on Manhattan Island. Los Angeles has grown prodigiously and prosperously without ever developing a classical central business district. The East Coast megalopolis has a dozen or more, depending upon the definition that we choose. It seems clear that in a city of 50 million there will be numerous high-density zones of a character quite different from the central business district as it is now known.

High Density

These high-density zones will probably ultimately consist of single or linked structures containing residential, office, and retail facilities for several hundred thousand people. We already have buildings housing 10,000 or more employees. We already have 100-story structures containing both offices and apartments. We already have examples of employment densities and residential densities exceeding 10,000 persons per acre and in the range of ¼ to ½ million persons per square mile. If these conditions exist today and are accepted as tolerable in places like Manhattan, Chicago, and Hong Kong, it is not unreasonable to suppose that as the urban population triples and as the size of the largest metropolitan areas moves into the 25 to 50 million range, we will see many such high-density zones.

Constitution Plaza, Penn Center, the Shinjuku district of Tokyo, are crude or primitive expressions of this kind of zone. It is regrettable that we do not have anywhere in the world a good example of a planned building complex for 100,000 people capable of accommodating the daily movements of goods and people which would be necessary in such a complex. No one will question that such a complex is technically possible, or that it could be designed and built to be an exceedingly attractive, exciting, and economically efficient place in which to live and work. In a four-block length of Sixth Avenue in New York City the equivalent of such a complex has been built within the last five years in the most primitive form imaginable. It consists of eight skyscraper office buildings and hotels. If that complex had been built on top of a ten-story parking lot with aerial ramps to the surrounding freeway system, mechanical walkways between buildings at the 20th and 40th-story levels, and mechanical circulation from the underground subway serving it, we would today have the kind of high-density zone of which we will have many examples in the future.

Note that in describing this type of zone, I am not using the traditional terminology of central business district, because I am describing both a residential and a work place and one which may contain all of the other service facilities of a very large city of several hundred thousand people. Further, such high-density zones may have specialized functions. In any event, we must open our eyes to the possibilities that densities will reach far beyond anything we have heretofore considered acceptable and that when attained, such high densities will be of a different character from those which we have heretofore known or described.

Other Activity Zones

Aside from these zones of ultra-high density, other types of activity zones of moderately high density appear to be emerging. Typically they contain mixed uses, and do not fit neatly into our descriptions of either industrial districts or regional centers. At the Valley Forge Interchange there is emerging a huge development accommodating 25,000 industrial employees, a million square feet of retail space, a thousand acres of parking lots, expressways, and thoroughfares, and not a single dwelling. The Los Angeles airport is rapidly becoming the largest office building and hotel district on the West Coast, far more convenient for business meetings than any other place in the western million square miles of the country. Airports will doubtless be major metropolitan area form givers in the future because of their propensity to generate these and other activities.

We are seeing the emergence of other activity centers of a city building scale. Man-made resort, recreation, and convention centers are now beginning to burgeon at an unprecedented rate. As the natural recreation sites diminish in number, wholly man-made resort cities will emerge: Disneyland and Las Vegas are illustrations. There will doubtless be some permanent World's Fairs. The two most important types of activity center now on the horizon, however, are institutions of higher education and hospitals. The proportion of the population that participates in higher education is rising sharply. With increased college attendance and continuing increases in vocational and nonvocational education, the number of major centers of educational activity in our metropolitan areas will double and double again. A metropolitan area of a million population may well expect to have several new educational complexes of the 15,000-25,000 student size. Each can generate a population of two or three times the student population.

There will be a similar explosion in health facilities. With increased longevity, the launching of medical insurance, and the expansion of our concepts of health and treatment, community and metropolitan health centers of much larger size, accompanied by specialized housing, specialized retailing, recuperative, and recreation facilities of new types will undoubtedly become major activity centers. We may expect, then, a major increase in the types of activity center and in their number, size, and complexity, and in the types of urban areas which they generate.

Low-Density Origin Zones

At the other end of the scale many forces seem to reinforce the development and maintenance of very low-density, mixed-use zones which may eventually be the characteristic form of land use in megalopolitan areas, filling a large part of the space between higher-density zones. In planner terminology it is called sprawl or scattered development. It consists of low-density residential uses mixed with minor retail facilities, planned industrial districts, and scattered, inoffensive industry. I cannot envisage that the traditional concepts of separation of land use over large areas will apply to such low-density zones. They rarely do today. The detailed separation of land use at the street scale will prevail so that industrial and commercial traffic does not penetrate and impair residential areas. But otherwise the forces of the market, the adoption of performance standards, the need to reduce journeys to work and shopping, and the changes in our concepts of home and work place are likely to alter so that we will accept a much higher degree of mixture of uses than we have been accustomed to in the past.

For this reason, maybe we shouldn't call these low-density zones "neighborhoods" or "residential areas" at all, but instead adopt some more neutral terminology like "origin zones." Such a terminology would recognize that many residential areas could include attractive places for work and local retail areas, that a large proportion of any population is locally employed in service industry, that under some circumstances it may be easier to bring work to people rather than to take people to work, and that especially as the volume of movement out of origin zones builds up in major metropolitan areas, it will become desirable to maintain the highest possible degree of residence, work, and recreation within the origin zone.

Within these zones, of course, we will have neighborhoods of varied types. During the last half century we have accumulated a vast amount of knowledge of the human ecology of the city. Hundreds of studies have portrayed the social structure, geographic distribution, behavior, and values of different populations in different areas.[6] This literature reveals the immense and growing variety of life styles in our society. We have some who live out their lives within a neighborhood in the heart of a metropolis, scarcely ever moving outside a small orbit. Herbert Gans has aptly called them the urban villagers. At the other end of the scale we have cosmopolitan and jet-set types who breakfast in New York, lunch in Los Angeles, and dine in Chicago almost weekly, who may live in Washington but have more friends in San Francisco or Boston.

In the face of this knowledge our traditional concept of the neighborhood is fatally deficient and is in the process of being replaced. Traditionally, we have considered high, low and medium-density areas, and single or mixed dwelling type areas, and little else that is relevant. Surely the work of the sociologists and anthropologists tells us more. We need neighborhoods for the villager and the cosmopolitan, for youth, for the aged, and for mixed age groups, neighborhoods of high and low density, of single and mixed dwelling type, socially homogeneous and mixed, economically stratified and economically mixed, central, suburban and rural, stable and changing, historic and contemporary neighborhoods for those who prefer anonymity and for those who like community, for the poor as well as the rich, for the mobile and the stable.

Thus there are at least a dozen dimensions by which we could characterize a neighborhood, and there are several hundred possible types of neighborhood. Further, we have the analytical and diagnostic techniques by which we can measure, approximately, the composition of the population with respect to its desire or need for each of these characteristics.[7] From such an analysis we could plan for the far richer and more diverse types of neighborhood which the future metropolis will require, and future affluence demand.

More is at stake here than merely meeting market demand. The pace of change is such that many in the population cannot bear it with equanimity.[8] They need the stability and continuity of an environment which will persist at least a generation. Some require the social security of a stratified neighborhood, the comfort and ease that come with living with like people. This may be true of many middle-class families who have just made it to suburbia, and also true of many low-income families among minority groups. Others may desire change and diversity. Their needs may be easier to meet. The very stability of social life requires that we take a new look at the neighborhood, and try to plan to meet a wider range of needs. Such a reexamination will surely reveal that the classic "mixed" neighborhood was at best an obscure ideal with many internal contradictions. At worst, as Isaacs has noted, it was an excuse for some form of segregation. Perhaps it is fortunate that there has been such an enormous gap between the planners' traditional ideal and its realization.[9]

Among the types of neighborhood there are several that demand special attention because of their novelty or seeming difficulty. We have both new and old neighborhoods, even whole cities, composed almost exclusively of elderly adults—a forbidding prospect, but a reality. We have neighborhoods consisting almost wholly of youths—around colleges. In the future we may have whole cities of youths built around new universities. We seem to be building whole neighborhoods around hospitals and health facilities—neighborhoods for the sick, the recuperating, and their caretakers. We are getting seasonal or second-home neighborhoods, whole communities which are inhabited part of the year. We shall have many more, enough perhaps for a quarter of the population. We need new neighborhoods with built-in employment opportunities, for urban villagers of all types. If some of these types sound unfamiliar or repulsive, they are nevertheless here, and will surely multiply in the future as urban society becomes larger, more heterogeneous, and more affluent.

On the fringes of the metropolitan area another phenomenon is emerging—the unfarmed zone. Recently a ranch containing 80,000 acres has been subdivided in southern California into such an area. Some of it is divided into conventional 2½-acre lots. Still more is in 20 to 40-acre farmlots, including an area zoned for small, highly mechanized dairy farms and another for uneconomic orchards. The largest area is being sold off in lots of 40 to 200 acres, for country estates, horse raising, and other gentleman farmer pursuits. Sales are brisk. Soon the buyers will qualify for federal subsidies not to plant their farms, not to market their cattle. Most will have farm losses to write off against income taxes, and all will wait for future capital gains, when this area, an hour and a half from Los Angeles, is further subdivided for higher density urban uses. In the affluent world of the future there will be millions of families seeking such places—as a refuge from the city, as a tax gimmick, and as a long-range, self-supporting speculation.

New Towns

New towns or new cities have a vital role to play in this new kind of metropolitan area. The present lively and growing interest in new communities has yet to produce anything approximating the classical idea of a new community, or any approximation of the many new cities of Europe. The present projects under private sponsorship are necessarily limited by the housing market and density preferences which prevail in their local areas. They are limited by the restrictions imposed upon them by local governments. They are limited in their financial capacity to install overhead investment in advance of development. They are limited by their inability to control or directly influence the provision of transportation facilities to nearby or central employment centers. Despite these limitations, one or two may make significant contributions in urban design and amenity. One or two may make significant advances in the provision of community facilities, or in the range of dwelling types offered, or other features. None, of course, can market to a very wide spectrum of incomes, especially in the lower-middle income ranges. Despite these limitations, these pilot projects deserve support because they help to awaken the American people to new possibilities and standards.

The United States alone among the major nations of the world has failed to adopt and implement some sort of new towns policy. As a consequence, we have no examples of the convenience, amenity, and economy characteristic of the high-quality new city design performance found in the Scandinavian countries. We particularly need planned new cities to set design standards for a population which has come to accept scattered, unorganized growth as the norm. We have few distinguished examples of how beautiful an urban area can be. Thus we urgently need 50 to 100 standard-setting models. With even a dozen demonstration new cities in the next decade we might logically expect the merit of those performances to attract the national support required to create a national policy. Such a policy would attract a moderate share of all future building, to ease the pressure for scattered development, to provide substantially better environments, often at higher densities than can otherwise be provided, and to permit some real tests of the economies of planned cities.

Despite these hopes, here, as abroad, the expansion of existing communities will continue to account for most metropolitan growth. Further, we will see great variety in the size, composition, and location of new cities. Some will emerge as wholly new cities, based upon new recreation or retirement markets, new technologies, new exploitable resources. A half-dozen new cities in these forms have developed in the postwar years. Most new cities will occur as satellites to existing metropolitan areas, some at moderately great distances from the center and many nearly contiguous to it, separated from the area by natural landmarks, parks, or other relatively narrow open space zones. Certainly there is no single pattern which we can point to as a natural prototype for the United States.

Open Space

In the terminology for describing the metropolitan area we also need a category which might be labeled "zone separators." Open space performs many functions in the metropolitan region which we are only beginning to treat. It provides corridors for movement, scenic beauty, agriculture, climatic or thermal protection, hydrological functions, recreation space, and reserve space for future urbanization. In no area of planning have we so miserably failed to develop a full set of concepts and to devise the means for regulation and control. The two failures are undoubtedly related. Until we can distinguish the purposes of open space, we will probably fail to secure public consent to regulation.

All too often we have taken refuge in the traditional idea of the greenbelt. If it made some sense to Ebenezer Howard in the nineteenth century, it makes very little today. While we can readily get along without abstract notions about greenbelts, we must at the same time recognize that important ecological functions are performed by open space and that we have long neglected the study of urban physical ecology. The bays, the river valleys and the hilltops, the forests and the fields, perform essential hydrological, climatic, and other functions which we have scarcely begun to define and measure. They maintain and control the flow of water essential to the civilization of the urban area. In many areas they moderate the climate, purify or humidify air, and in other ways maintain thermal controls in the metropolitan area. We can guess, though we cannot prove, that filling San Francisco Bay would raise the temperature of the metropolitan area by five to ten degrees and blanket it with a layer of smog which would cost tens of millions annually. But these arguments will command little support until they can be scientifically demonstrated and measured.

Another form of open space consists of public park and recreation areas. Although our methods of estimating the requirements for these may be inadequate, they constitute an essential part of the open space system of the metropolitan area. In most metropolitan areas the natural sites for regional parks were delineated many years ago. In most metropolitan areas we have failed to acquire those sites systematically. The resurgence of national interest in this subject currently offers some hope that we will now proceed to acquire them.

But public open space does not now, and probably will never comprise more than a small share of the open space required in the metropolitan region. Some of it is required to provide visual breaks in an otherwise continuous and often dreary developed region. Some of it will be required to make movement in the open space corridor more efficient, safer, and pleasanter, especially when 90 per cent of our recreation activity is recreation driving. Some of it will be required for the thermal and hydrological effects which I have mentioned. Many of these requirements can be accommodated under private ownership, but subject to both police power and other types of control.

I see no major reason why future expressways should not be used to create scenic corridors within the metropolitan region and on a two to four-mile grid. More than a generation ago, the Merritt Parkway demonstrated that a corridor 600 to 1,000 feet wide could be landscaped to create the impression of countryside, forests, and woods even while it traversed a densely developed urban area. It is ridiculous to propose the preservation of greenbelts or mile-wide scenic corridors if the purpose is to provide visual recreation. That purpose can be efficiently achieved with comparatively narrow rights of way properly landscaped. If there are those who desire to see rural land uses, cows can be stationed in the highway corridor to simulate the traditional image of the countryside without wasting useful urban land. We might even install plastic cows and sheep to create a simulation of the desired rusticity. Since the user pays or should pay for the highway facility, and is the primary beneficiary in terms of both safety and pleasure, it should be reasonable to pay for scenic expressway corridors from highway funds, and to insist that all future expressways conform to such standards.

Farm belts are another matter. Many commercial farm areas are not the pleasant state of nature that they were once considered. In fact, farm areas can be dangerous and unpleasant for urban dwellers. They contain unpleasant smells, odoriferous fertilizers, and dangerous insecticides which increasingly render them hostile or unpleasant to the nonagricultural population. Far from a pleasant refuge from city, cultivated areas are becoming areas from which nonagricultural residents should be excluded for the protection both of the agriculture and of the urban dweller.

Agricultural uses, however, virtually never pay an economic return comparable to urban uses. While there is no impending shortage of agricultural land which would justify alarmist demands for agricultural zones, the protection of the urban dweller from agricultural dangers requires the development of such zones, and the long-range protection of agricultural soils from speculative sterilization in nonagricultural uses may soon justify such zones.

The motivation for owning and holding land will increase mightily in the next two generations. As population and affluence rise and as the pace of change in an urban society increases, we may expect millions of families to desire the emotional security and the lifetime continuity of owning a place of refuge from urban tension and change. We may expect millions of families to be able to afford to indulge this desire as hundreds of thousands now do. Presumably they could readily usurp agricultural uses and sterilize millions of acres of land which might otherwise serve agricultural purposes. Under these circumstances it would be reasonable to limit nonagricultural holdings of this semirecreational type to nonagricultural areas.

Thus, between the scenic uses, the movement corridor uses, the ecological functions, the recreation uses, and the farm uses of land, we may find concepts for defining those spaces within and around the urbanized region which should be preserved at ultra-low density or in their scattered condition. Ian McHarg in Pennsylvania, Phillip Lewis in Wisconsin, and Garret Eckbo in California have begun to define metropolitan open space in these terms.[10] As studies of this type are extended and refined, I have little doubt that we will develop both the scientific basis and the legal justification for creating a network of linked open spaces which will serve to provide that minimal separation between activity zones which is justified and which will help to give form to the metropolitan area and to provide the separation necessary for identity in an otherwise urbanized landscape.

Transportation Links

The links between origin zones and activity zones are the media of transportation, communication, and goods or energy movement. Here technological developments have already reshaped the metropolitan area twice in this century, first toward higher densities and greater concentration, and more recently toward lower densities and greater dispersion. We customarily

think of the shift from rails to roads as a major dispersing element, but the automobile-generated dispersal could never have
been effective without universally available electric power, telephone, and radio, the development of household equipment to
replace services, and the like. The link modes are therefore important: rail, highway, wire, wireless, pipelines and other forms
of tubes, air, water, and ground. New classes of vehicles like
hydrofoils and hovercraft open new transportation possibilities.
New control devices present interesting prospects for vehicle
guidance and volume control.

Manifestly there are enormous possibilities for substitution
in these linkages. The automobile has replaced rails for virtually all intrametropolitan movement of persons outside of a
dozen cities. The airplane and the automobile have eliminated
intercity rail travel in most of the United States. Facsimile may
replace newspapers. Video phone and linked computers can
replace many business trips. Atomic power can replace transmission lines. Pipe lines can replace tank cars and ships. The
garbage grinder can obviate the garbage truck. It is important
to note that technology affects not only the home-work relationship but also the location of industry and employment and of
course the nature of the activities located.

Here we can consider only a few of the most important of
these potentialities, and our judgment of them may be wide of
the mark. The automobile, bus, and truck will continue to be
the major mode of movement in metropolitan areas of up to
two million population. They work now with remarkable efficiency, and could be improved substantially with better highway and parking facilities, safety devices, and pollution preven-
tion devices. The automobile will have to be further constrained
when we have 250 million cars. One would guess that the
volume and direction of automobile movement will be widely
controlled by computer and that the driver will be required to
reserve freeway space as is now done with airline reservations.

On major facilities automatic control of vehicles will prevail.

As one approaches any major high-density activity center in those areas, the degree of social control will perforce increase, the degree of individual control will be reduced, the degree of collective ownership or use will be increased, and that of individual ownership or use decreased, the proportion of mass transit will be increased. Vehicles entering major high-density zones may be equipped with homing devices so that they will go away by themselves, be stored, and reappear upon demand and after reasonable notice. Individual ownership of the vehicle will probably be much more costly, if permitted at all, than collective ownership. Payment of a rental charge would entitle the user to services on a system of collectively-owned small vehicles which were available upon demand at many points within the system and were charged on an actual utilization basis. In at least a dozen of the larger metropolitan areas only fully automatic tracking vehicles like the Starr car will be permitted. These will permit individual guidance and control at the low-density destination and mass control at high volumes in the high-density destination. The automobile is not going to disappear, in short, but it will be radically modified and controlled, pooled and rented, and, in high-density areas, supplemented by other facilities.

At present, only 2 or 3 per cent of the population flies regularly and only about 10 per cent has ever flown. Yet airports have become major shapers of the metropolitan area and major forces determining the growth or decline of whole metropolitan areas. Since it seems inevitable that within the foreseeable future the proportion of the population that flies regularly will multiply manyfold, and the proportion that has flown will increase several-fold, one would guess that the form-shaping effects of air travel have only begun to be felt. We are only at the beginning in vertical take-off craft and helicopter service, and local travel by air is therefore in its most primitive stages.

The control mechanisms for modest volumes of local flights are largely in existence in the space and defense programs and will surely be applied to permit much larger volumes of local air travel. Even though local air travel may not serve the huge volumes required by high-density zones, since both air and land modes will operate and exist side by side, it is clear that pricing, licensing, and other volume controls must be devised as technical capacity restraints become operative.

In mass transit we are beginning to see a resurgence of rail transit by means of subsidy. This has been stimulated by the belated recognition that the central city cannot survive without efficient mass transit. Japan already has a 225-kilometer-per-hour train system which functions superbly and which is planned to operate at even higher speeds. The East Coast Corridor Study is now exploring other possibilities, including the revival of the pneumatic subway, a train-like vehicle which would have center to center speeds exceeding those of air travel. Sooner or later, of course, we must solve the problems of travel to the airport to enable air travel to be competitive or even humane.

The terminals and stops on high-density, high-speed transportation systems have yet to be fully exploited. The Pan American building on top of Grand Central Station is not an accident. When the 200-mile-an-hour railroad is finally installed, it will generate many ultra-high-density activity centers, and many ultra-high-density residential centers. An interesting and unresolved enigma is whether other changes of mode points can ever achieve the volumes to justify, or the technologies to permit, high-density development.

Conclusion

The functions of the metropolitan area are changing rapidly. As the functions change, the form and structure of the metropolitan area must also change. A new technology, a new affluence, new forms of corporate and governmental organization, and changing public values—all of these acting in combination are creating metropolitan areas whose size, geographic extent, and variety exceed anything previously envisaged by man. Metropolitan areas of the future may reach 100 miles in any direction and contain populations larger than those of many nations. It would be foolish to attempt to forecast in detail the effect of these changes upon form and structure.

But further, our life styles are changing, becoming more varied and different. Read the Utopias again, the Utopias which have shaped so much of our thought about the future. In the main, they present pictures of relatively single-valued systems, of societies more monolithic than our present one, of static or closed societies, ill adapted to change and innovation.[11] If there is any virtue in the American society it is in the promise that it will remain open. Democracy, the free market, and receptivity to change have produced something here that no one could have envisaged at the turn of the century. Having embarked upon receptivity to change as a sort of national principle, we would be ill advised at this late date to seek others, especially the more fixed and stable ones of the Utopias.

American metropolitan areas are not headed toward Ebenezer Howard's tidy little new towns surrounded by countryside. While we may have several—indeed, we may hope that we could have many—the new communities we build will certainly contain populations of 100,000 and are more likely to contain populations of a quarter of a million. They will be larger than the whole metropolitan areas with which Howard was concerned. Nor will our metropolitan areas be those envisaged by Bellamy, with their solid middle-class values—everyone nice, tidy, polite, well dressed, and well ordered. They will not even be Wirth's metropolitan areas of acculturation and assimilation. Instead, they will be characterized by a wide variety of values and ways of life, hopefully organized so that each can explore its own destiny in contiguity to others, or perhaps in the same physical space. Certainly we will have many, perhaps mostly, nonspatial communities. Nor will our metropolitan areas be the cities of empire arranged in grand geometric order by Burnham. That order has already been dissolved by the free-flowing form of the expressway, by the disintegration of the ordered central business district, by the asymmetrically-centered skyscraper technology. The new centers and subcenters will have a far different order, a different rhythm, a different technology, and a different purpose.

Our metropolitan areas of the future will not even resemble the garden metropolises of Le Corbusier, of ordered skyscrapers standing in a park. We will have many pieces of Le Corbusier, as we do today, in Chicago, in New York, and in Los Angeles. But the parks envisaged are in fact a surrounding landscape of single detached houses. Similar areas of the future may reach higher densities than he envisaged and still remain only fragments of the metropolitan area—model points in a changing metropolis. Nor, finally, will our metropolitan areas be Wright's Broadacre City, though they will contain hundreds, indeed thousands, of square miles of relatively low-density urbanized area, mixing industrial, commercial, and residential uses much as he envisaged them and linked primarily by automobiles.

No, the metropolis of the future will be one of huge size, of vast extent, of great diversity, of rigid change, and to the extent that it is open to future change, of indeterminate form. Many of these forms will be new, the ultra-high-density nodes, central districts, outlying highly accessible residential districts, and outlying highly accessible specialist activity districts. These will be linked with ultra-high-speed transportation and communications systems. Both will exist in zones of relatively low density, as measured by the standards of the past. They will also be linked by networks of public and private open space sufficient, we hope, to maintain a viable natural ecology. We will have new cities, many of them representing new styles of life and some, perhaps, to replicate for those who desire it relatively fixed examples of old styles of life. Because we need both stability and change, we will have areas for conservation and areas constantly being renovated or renewed, areas for the citizen whose neighborhood is the world, and areas for the urban villager.

Our concepts of metropolitan planning have been evolving rapidly. They have been expanded, have become enriched, and are becoming more open. They still, however, fail to provide for the flexibility which must characterize the future, for the degree of local choice which will surely be maintained to preserve what is left of the tradition of local democracy. Nor do our metropolitan plans embrace the geographic scope of the metropolis of the future or its administrative form. We are embarked upon a period of very rapid evolution in professional thought to devise new methods of foreseeing the forms which the future will generate and to accommodate our present actions and our proposals to that scale of change.

Comments on

Wheaton

HENRY FAGIN
Department of Urban and Regional Planning,
University of Wisconsin

Professor Wheaton well knows the difficult challenge of the assignment he accepted. Early in his paper (and also in good academic tradition) he says about forecasting, "any of us looking at the record of the past must be exceedingly humble in looking at the future." But then with the courage, indeed zest, that we have come to expect of Wheaton, he does us all the great service of drawing on a long background of experience and study to peer with 20:20 vision a full fifty years into the urban future. Particularly lively and debunking are his observations about four topics: neighborhoods, open space, life styles, and district stereotypes.

My first question after reading Wheaton's draft was: Why should anyone be asked to describe his idea of fifty years hence? After all, planning is about what to do now—not what to do a great many years from now. Ordinarily, one would analyze possible options but leave it there. One might explore, in the light of today's knowledge, the alternative futures the metropolis might experience during a half century of change, say something about the probabilities and the desirabilities, but avoid any commitment to a particular option until the urgencies of some imminent action demanded the making of a definitive choice. One would not want to burn any bridges, so to speak, before crossing them.

What is the case here today? Have we some action option that justifies debate over how things may turn out a half-century hence? I think a contemporary choice is in fact implied in Professor Wheaton's paper; and I want to make this choice explicit and then to orient my own comments around it. In brief, we face this question: For what sort of future environment do we need to prepare our professional capacities? If the future is to mirror the technological quality of a Los Angeles or an Abercrombie-style London or a spread city like today's New York region, then we need only to develop more fully the methods of planning we already largely possess. But if a dramatically different type of urban structure is in the offing, then a correspondingly dramatic development in planning methodology will be demanded of us.

Thus a great deal does in fact hinge on how well we today anticipate the long-term future. This motivation justifies the next question: Is it possible to foresee fifty years with any degree of realism? In my own experience, I once satisfied myself as to the feasibility of looking thirty or forty years ahead by comparing 1955 land use and population estimates with the original forecasts of New York's Regional Plan, projections that had been based largely on 1920 census statistics. There had been remarkably close foresights, indeed. It is true, of course, that not a great many years of actual building were involved, given the intervening sixteen-year hiatus of the depression and the long war that stymied half the interval. Nevertheless, the evidence of a capacity to forecast patterns of land use, retail decentralization, and population change was impressive.

Looking for another example, preferably with an even longer lead time and testing period, I recalled once hearing about a book of predictions by H. G. Wells and happily found it in the library. The copyright said 1901. The title was *Anticipations** and the subtitle, "Anticipations of the Reactions of Mechanical and Scientific Progress upon Human Life and Thought." Here was an erudite and imaginative man of letters hazarding a hundred-year forecast. To make this author seem even more appropriate, 1966 turned out to be the hundredth anniversary of Wells's birth.

The second chapter, "The Probable Diffusion of Great Cities," proved ideal for our inquiry. The question posed is: How successful can a Wells or a Wheaton be in anticipating the very long future? Of course, the year 2000 is not yet here, though two-thirds of the interval spanned by Wells' predictions have gone by. It seems useful to check Wells both against what has occurred already and also against Wheaton's current expectations for the post-2000 world.

You have just learned Wheaton's verson elaborated in his paper. Let me quote 1901 Wells on some of the very same topics. For example, here is Wells on the geographic scale of the future urban region:

> It is much more probable that these coming cities will not be, in the old sense, cities at all; they will present a new and entirely different phase of human distribution. . . . (page 47.)

> [The] available area for the social equivalent of the [inner city riders] of today will have a radius of over one hundred miles, and be almost equal to the area of Ireland. The radius that will sweep the area available for such as now live in the outer suburbs will include a still vaster area. . . . [The] vast stretch of country from Washington to Albany will all of it be "available" to the active citizen of New York and Philadelphia before [the year 2000]. . . . (page 53.)

* New York: Harper, 1902.

As to population, Wells's prediction is virtually the same as Wheaton's, made as I have pointed out two-thirds of a century later:

> London, St. Petersburg, and Berlin . . . will go well over twenty millions, . . . New York, Philadelphia, and Chicago . . . forty million. . . . (page 54.)

Perhaps one would denigrate a mere projection of size and impose the sterner test: Could Wells anticipate the character of the future environment? Here is Wells' description of the most intensive urban districts of the year 2000:

> . . . and so, the centre . . . will be essentially a bazaar, a great gallery of shops and places of concourse and rendezvous, a pedestrian place, its pathways reinforced by lifts and moving platforms and shielded from the weather, and altogether a very spacious, brilliant, and entertaining agglomeration. . . . (page 62.)

> The American reader at least will promptly see, the much more practicable thing is that upper footpath, with those moving platforms beside it, running out over the street after the manner of the viaduct of an elevated railroad. . . . (page 33.)

Concerning the future nurturing of local and regional differences as precious heritages rather than regrettable vestiges, said Wells:

> The omens seem to point pretty unmistakably to a wide and quite unprecedented diversity in the various suburban townships and suburban districts. . . . It is evident that from the outset racial and national characteristics will tell in this diffusion. We are getting near the end of the great Democratic, Wholesale, or Homogeneous phase in the world's history. . . . (page 62.)

Wells jumped the gun on Professor Wheaton's Berkeley colleague, Melvin Webber, in his description of a new era of urban center type work done in the home:

> The business man may sit at home in his library and bargain, discuss, promise, hint, threaten, tell such lies as he dare not write, and, in fact, do everything that once demanded a personal encounter. . . . (page 66.)

And finally, lest you think I may warp Wells' ideas by paraphrasing them anachronistically in our current urban jargon, a final quote:

> Enough has been said to demonstrate that old "town" and "city" will be, in truth, terms as obsolete as "mail coach." For these new areas that will grow out of them we want a term. . . . We may for our present purposes call these coming town provinces "urban regions." Practically . . . the whole of Great Britain south of the Highlands seems destined to become such an urban region, laced all together not only by railway and telegraph, but by novel roads such as we forecast in the former chapter, and by a dense network of telephones, parcel delivery tubes, and the like. . . . (page 68.)

> Through the varied country the new wide roads will run, here cutting through a crest and there running like some colossal aqueduct across a valley, swarming always with a multitudinous traffic of bright, swift (and not necessarily ugly) mechanisms. . . . (page 69.)

I'm sure you will perceive these passages, as I do, to be amazing insights about the latent potentialities present in the year 1901 when Wells wrote. In this spirit, let us look now at Professor Wheaton's future vision for what it seems to imply about his view of the present —a view he extrapolates over the two-generation epoch we are about to enter.

Wheaton's metropolis will be exceedingly vast, varied, changing, intricate, intertwined. It will require exceptional ingenuity in the handling of extensive public services and the management of public controls. Its vitality and variety will rest on great economic and political freedom—on the creative use of the market and profit mechanisms and the continued exercise of local democratic institutions.

This happy state of being will result from a fortunate era of continued advance in technical virtuosity, private affluence, and corporate and government organizational invention. In Wheaton's concluding words:

> We are embarked upon a period of very rapid evolution in professional thought to devise new methods of foreseeing the forms which the future will generate and to accommodate our present actions and our proposals to that scale of change.

What concerns me here is the way this Wheaton model of the future would tend to focus the attention of the profession. Its stress is on those actions and proposals which will generate the new forms that relate to the particular kind of affluent and great society predicted.

I propose to sketch a somewhat different model of the future, a model based on a different reading of the present situation in America and the dynamics of our time.

Suppose, for example, we look at some current behavior not as necessarily indicative of long-term trends but rather as temporary and transitional actions marking a shift from one institutional or social behavioral pattern to another that is replacing it. This sort of phenomenon, frequent when times are dynamic, makes it very hard to tell whether a particular element that recently has been changing is about to stabilize upon reaching a new and different platform or is going to continue further in its trajectory—in the manner, say, of a circus clown who has missed the trapeze landing and gone careening off. For example, department stores once were all downtown. Then, especially after World War II, so many a year opened branches in the suburbs. Finally, in some metropolitan regions, virtually every suburban sector had branches of all the major stores and the rate of building new stores dropped precipitously. While the new pattern was being established, though, people tended to project future store construction well beyond the 100 per cent saturation point, simply assuming that more and more of the same would continue to happen.

Looking at certain pervasive behaviors of our own day, I wonder if we have misread them in the same fashion. It may turn out, for instance, that our national propensity for Sunday driving was just a temporary need after people achieved a new level of leisure time and before they learned what to do with it. In the year 2000, there may be hundreds of miles of underused recreational highways on Sundays. It may turn out that the vaunted shift from rail to rubber was really a pendulum-like swing that reversed around 1970, when the road-rooted romance ended and people became more chary about the use of their time and money. It may turn out that home ownership was a goal both alluring and enduring only for a particular generation who, born in the city, overshifted in the giddiness of great release after the Great Depression and the great World War and the great society. Maybe their suburb-born children will rediscover the man-made beauty of the city and the natural convenience of propinquity.

It may turn out that the rising birth rates of the post-World-War-II decades will be reversed in America by the backlash of our own pleas to the rest of the world. (Threatened with total population inundation, we urge them, take to the pills.) And it may turn out that the drive for affluence that dominated a generation of middle-class parents a generation out of being poor will prove less motivating for a generation of youngsters born to the middle class, who will substitute for our thirst for things their urgent search for the meaning of things in a crowded and trouble-ridden world, an earth drawn close by modern communications and virtually instant travel.

Several other possibilities are embodied in this alternative model. It views poverty as a stubborn condition claiming large groups and communicated from generation to generation—a modern version of original sin, not easily to be wiped out in a decade or two of instant affluence programs. It considers mental health very different from physical health. Physical health in most animals is a normal state unless specific disease or accident strikes. But mental health requires nurturing by mentally sound parents and teachers in healthy family and social settings that too frequently are missing to begin with. The model makes some assumptions too about the world abroad. Much of the expectation of early and continued affluence in America, it seems to me, is based on faulty perceptions about America's options in regard to the rest of the world. We seem to be in for heavy costs, whether we pay for destruction or for construction or for reconstruction, and whether the scene of our spending is Asia or Africa or America.

My working assumption is a long period of very hard work ahead for the next generations of Americans—and a continuing need to use resources sparingly in American homes, schools, transportation services, and work places—unless our children and later their children learn from us how to ignore the increasing billions of fellow human beings suffering extreme poverty on the other continents of the globe we share. In short, I do not believe we can separate American urban policy from American foreign policy and the intractable problems of the whole world.

Finally, most crucial of all is the issue: What assumption do we build into the model about purpose—not in this case the purpose of a fifty-year projection of metropolitan form but rather the fundamental purpose of the metropolis itself? After all, this purpose is the determinant of the basic function of the metropolis and ultimately of the appropriate metropolitan form in the physical sense.

Lewis Mumford, discussing "The Goals of Planning" at the 1948 American Society of Planning Officials conference, said of another great philosopher of cities:

> Ebenezer Howard was not, as you must know, a planner. He was not one technically capable of carrying out his proposals and his vision. But Howard had the audacity to ask himself a question which, of necessity, the day-to-day planner and replanner of urban congestion and urban blight did not dare ask himself: What should a city be—what must a city be—in order to further the utmost development of human personality?

The question, it seems to me, implies directly a twofold purpose of the metropolis: for each living individual that comes along, the furtherance of the utmost development of his personality (as Howard put it); for mankind as a whole, the never-ending nurturing of man as a social being and of mankind as a feeling, learning, aspiring, and loving species.

With such a definition of the purpose of the metropolis, and placing the American metropolis in its world setting, we return to the functions of this Metropolis Model Two.

What does it imply for the key concepts of education, of work, of leisure? Learning becomes no mere preparation for earning; work no mere servant of leisure; leisure no mere respite from work nor jobless time space to fill. And the metropolis becomes no mere place destined, in Professor Wheaton's marvelous phrase, for "sustaining the population, enabling it to consume."

Rather we well may see a transformation and redefining of the very meanings of such fundamental ideas as work, leisure, education, community, democracy, I, we, and they. The time indeed may come, as Professor Wheaton suggests fleetingly but significantly, when work and learning and deep enjoyment are as inseparable for masses of people as they have been through the ages for those we call artists. Work and play and education then would permeate every living district of the city. And the impact of such a development on the functions, the forms, the dynamic structure of the metropolis would be most profound.

Above all, the planning of such a metropolitan alternative would evoke a different demand, a different orientation, and a different response from the planning profession. My reservation about the main paper, then, is not so much with the glimpse it offers of the year 2017 as with the implications of that vision for planners in this year 1966.

SCOTT GREER
*Center for Metropolitan Studies,
Northwestern University*

Both Wheaton's and Fagin's remarks assume that government must play a role in the achievement of a better human environment; private enterprise cannot do the job alone. It is, therefore, important to consider what kind of government now handles our urban problems. Our governmental structure is an American solution to two dilemmas: the choice between the local political community and the nation, and the choice between private and public action. We are not yet sure what the role of government should be in the American economy. Because we are a mass democracy, our government is based on consensus; consensus of people who are not very many generations removed from illiterate peasants and farmers. We must develop a consensus among a people whose life styles vary tremendously. In listening to Wheaton's discussion of future kinds of neighborhood, it struck me that that is exactly the kinds of neighborhood we have now—I should think at least 400 types.

How do we develop consensus with all this variation? We have done it by segregation of unlike groups and by the "balanced ticket."

In the long run we have depended on education, on Americanizing the immigrant. We have done a great deal through the mass media. The tendency of such consensus is to multiply veto groups on the one hand and to move toward uniformity on the other. At present, government in most of our metropolitan areas is frozen in outmoded patterns. The center city is the only government of much scope in a metropolitan area, but it has inherited most of the difficult social problems of our society. It cannot really handle its job of creating area-wide consensus; it can only interact with other governmental units in the area. The metropolis is one housing market, one transport grid, one labor market. The center city, although the largest government structure, represents only a minority of the total population. The city of Portland is something like 43 per cent of the Portland metropolitan area.

We have, then, no competent political container for the metropolis. This is why we are now focusing so heavily on attempts to bring to life the dying downtown and gray areas when actually we should be paying more attention to the place where the action is—the outskirts, where there are few or no controls over land use, and where we are making very wasteful commitments that will have to be lived with for probably fifty years.

The minorities in the central city are not content to live with a do-nothing, caretaker government. These are the people whom public education has not fully drawn into our common culture; on the contrary, we must note the creation of subcultures. These are, I think, an extremely serious danger for a society which is so intricately interdependent and so vulnerable to sabotage. The civil rights movement has pioneered in the use of such weapons of sabotage as clogging transportation systems and making public space unusable. If these methods can be used for one purpose, they can be used for any number of purposes. Consensus is in danger.

The solutions, to the extent solutions have been suggested, have come from the national political institutions, not from the local units of democracy, whose governments are frozen and unable to move. They have no dynamics of consensus. Civil rights laws, originating in cities, have had to be enforced from Washington because of the failure of the local political community. We see other examples of extension of action from Washington because local metropolitan areas will not or cannot act: e.g., transportation and pollution.

The local democracy is limited by the political culture, which is frozen in the electoral game and in its constitutions and charters. Under these circumstances, it appears to me that a great deal of the initiative for new departures in urban policy will have to come from Washington. In many respects, the nation is perhaps the best unit to solve many of the problems we now think of as metropolitan. If, for example, we are really concerned with location theory, we might as well have a jurisdiction that takes in the whole playing field. Freedom of movement of the factors of production is of critical importance to metropolitan areas, and they have little or no control over it. At the national level we can control this through transportation decisions, through economic decisions, through the award of contracts. We could also tackle the problem of minimum standards, as we are now doing in the attack on poverty by defining minimum economic rights for citizenship.

I have the feeling that we are facing a very dramatic intergenerational change (as Fagin implied). By the end of this century the majority of adults will have had some sort of college education; also as average income increases, so will willingness to pay taxes. Organizational ability will increase and with it the ability to comprehend very large systems. Increasing use of the airplane is sure to bring wider intellectual horizons. In short, in another generation we may achieve a new consensus based on common values shared by the entire nation.

GIBSON WINTER
Divinity School, University of Chicago

It is becoming increasingly evident that the planner's world is a growingly complex one; he cannot escape dealing with the whole scope of human interests and potentialities. Obviously he has to select among them, as these potentialities are ordered in physical, social, and cultural patterns.

We are obviously approaching a new kind of political organization and decision-making process in which planners can play a key role. I think we are moving into a different kind of social process, for which we have to create the mechanisms. This process is going to be filled with deep conflict, as Scott Greer showed. I don't see how we can avoid the problem of representation in the planning process. In our tradition, men feel they have a right to have a voice in anything that affects their interests. They now realize that environment is not something caused simply by fate or automatic forces or private economic forces, but is part of the public sector.

Only planners can decide the levels for this total human world for which they can and will be held accountable—ecological, techno-logical, social, cultural. Perhaps planners will develop increasing speculation in the dimensions which they will explore. Wheaton's paper shows social patterns that are changing because of shifting ecological, technological, and economic forces. I don't agree with the model, but I don't negate it. These forces do condition, limit, and shape man's world in differing degrees in different historical epochs. Wheaton projects a very restricted perspective on this metropolis. This model can be very misleading if it is imposed on man's social and cultural world like a cutter on a mass of dough. Man's cultural values constitute a comprehensive set of functions which give different meanings to density and heterogeneity from those which Wheaton projects. They are considerations which ought to be interwoven with his technological possibilities in order to achieve the optimum environment.

In the framework of the two-year program of the AIP, I am sug-gesting that each of us work from some perspective on the nature of man. These perspectives are decisive for our selection of specific variables, or what Wheaton calls functions. The profound diversity of human potentialities, limits, and aspirations can provide a point of reference for integration of our various perspectives. We may order these values somewhat differently, but if we do take man as the measure, we shall work to include one another's perspectives rather than to exclude them. Planning will become what this confer-ence seems to be projecting—dialogue not only between the various disciplines but between various segments of the society.

Taking man as the measure furnishes no simple solution to the problem of values. However, most of us share an emerging historical view of man. We see him not only as constituted by his past and his environment, but also as responsible for the future, which he can shape. The richness of this historical view can maintain openness and inclusiveness in this planning process. The idea of man as both creator and creature of culture has posed radical threats to theological views of man because it opens man's future and recasts his understanding of ultimate fulfillment. It also projects a richer and more complex horizon for the planner, since it relativizes scientific projections like Mr. Wheaton's. It also affirms the scientific projections as crucial for coping with man's world. This frustrating complexity of our understanding of man, whatever its difficulties, opens the way to a promising dialogue among our disciplines and within our society. It can be a significant seedbed for a more responsible society.

VIII

Stephen Carr

Joint Center for Urban Studies of MIT and Harvard

The City of the Mind

When I think of the state of city design today I am reminded of that stage in the development of a child—which we all know so well—when he begins to ask "why?" For we city planners and designers are now beginning to seriously question the simple concepts of our conventional wisdom. We are struggling to emerge from a state of naive acceptance of "common knowledge" to the next stage of development in which we can begin to understand and thus to master our environment. If this seems a strange parallel, let me pursue it a bit.

In the process of intellectual development the child must create a stable and meaningful environment from the "blooming, buzzing confusion" of disconnected events that constitute the infant's world. He can only gradually free himself from his early bondage to the continuously changing vivid qualities of his surroundings: the particular shapes or textures or sounds of things. He does this by building up a model of the world by which he conserves his past experience, simplifies and connects it, and relates it to new experience. This model represents past experience in several ways: as learned sequences of action, in the form of visual imagery, and most powerfully in terms of language. It is largely by means of language that we progress from the distractable, novelty-bound state of early childhood to the relatively coherent and competent state of adulthood.[1]

197

For this gain in economy and control, however, we pay the price of a loss in our sense of the unique reality of direct experience and become victims of conventionality. We learn to use the traditional images and concepts of our society, its conventional wisdom, to organize our experience. In this process of "acculturation," society substitutes cultural bondage for the earlier bondage to continuously varying sense impressions. In time, we usually become "well adjusted" to existing conditions by means of these cultural norms. However, at some time rather early in this process the young child, perhaps sensing that there may be a way to escape this bondage too, begins to ask "why?"

We city planners and designers have been confronting the real blooming, buzzing confusion of our megalopolitan urban environment with the concepts of our conventional wisdom. We have a modest but growing vocabulary of techniques by means of which we represent and organize our world, whether in the form of land use maps or of verbal jargon. We know a "mixed use" when we see one. We have a few simple concepts like accessibility and dominance for relating the parts of a city. We know a few techniques for manipulating the urban environment and we once had a rather clear set of limitations on what it was our task to manipulate.[2] Yet we have finally reached the "why" stage, or so it would seem from the controversies of these last few years.

When a young child begins to ask why, we recognize that it is a critical moment in his life. He has now begun to question the simple commonplaces and seeming regularities of the limited world which had heretofore organized his short-sighted, day-by-day activities. He has become, one might say, a budding scientist and is therefore in need of very careful cultivation. At this stage he can be instructed in the acceptance of authority and conventional wisdom or he can be encouraged to form his own hypotheses about the way things are and to set out to gather the evidence necessary to test them.

We are embarking on a quest for the "good" day in an "optimum" environment. We ask why we should be concerned with the form of the environment and how city form might contribute to the quality of life. To be sure, we lack much relevant knowledge, but worse than that we lack a way of getting beyond our current conceptualizations of city form and its functions. Indeed, the most perplexing problem we face in attempting to improve the relationship of people with their urban environment is the persistence of conventional images and models of conceiving the city in the face of changing urban realities and human purposes.

We may surmise that the same dilemma faces ordinary city dwellers. For in a very real sense the city is what people think it is. The city that we know personally—the city of the mind—largely determines the world in which we have our life's experience and through which we strive to gain many of our daily satisfactions. The child's early model of his small world grows eventually to influence the form of all his interactions with the environment.

It is really the form in which people interact with the environment that should concern us as planners. But the interaction of people with their environment is a two-way process, shaped both by the form of the environment and by the psychological characteristics of people. As city planners and designers we have studied city form but have given very little study to the human half of the equation. It is time to try to understand something of this "city of the mind." For it is from such understanding, however limited at first, that we can most effectively develop new hypotheses about what would constitute a good city form. By shifting our perspective we may hope to get beyond our traditional approaches to design and, on the basis of our new hypotheses, to be able to propose more meaningful criteria and standards for city form and to invent new forms. Beyond that we will need to establish more constructive relationships with the people for whom we wish to design. For only their responses to our innovations can provide the test of potential effectiveness that we need. In the process we can hope to broaden their perspective as well, so that a better shape for the future metropolis might begin to emerge, both in the minds of people and as a concrete reality.

The Human Uses of Environments

You are well aware that planners are only human, but consider the news that all human beings are planners. What I mean by this is nothing mysterious, merely that most, perhaps all, of our interactions with the environment are intelligent ones. Notice I do not say rational or even conscious but rather "intelligent": guided by intelligence, by some mental plan or strategy, whether innate, learned to the point of habit, carefully worked out in advance, or invented on the spot. Each of these plans is intended to satisfy certain identifiable needs or to accomplish particular objectives.[3]

Since we are concerned with urban behavior, we need to know how the form of the city may facilitate or inhibit effective "planfulness." Take an example: Mrs. Jones' husband has just been transferred by his company, General Monopoly Incorporated, to Fringeville, where the family can expect to remain for 4.8 years. Mrs. Jones has a pressing need: she must adapt to Fringeville and if possible she must make it her own place. She will need to discover whether Fringeville is pleasant, to find her way to the shopping center and learn how to get to the grammar school, and to see what is required in the way of status symbols to bring the Jones' split-level ranch house up to the local standard. Beyond such utilitarian problems, Mrs. Jones will be trying to discover whether the form of Fringeville offers qualities to which she can come to attach deeper, more personal values and meanings. To accomplish all these purposes, Mrs.

Jones will need to develop and carry out appropriate plans for exploring the new environment and acquiring the information she needs.

For each of these purposes and plans the particular form of Fringeville may make Mrs. Jones' life easier and more satisfying or more difficult. The information she needs may not be organized and made visible or the qualities she seeks may be lacking. The pleasant areas of town may be hidden behind the crass facades of shabby main streets. The street patterns may be too complicated, making it difficult to find important destinations and hard to remember how to get there again once they are found. Or the available environmental means for expressing oneself may be so limited as to obscure meaningful differences among people. Even more likely, Fringeville may fail to provide any places to which Mrs. Jones can assign deeper meaning and significance. To be sure, even in the worst case Mrs. Jones will learn enough about Fringeville to serve her allotted 4.8 years there, but not without disappointments, frustration, and psychological strain. And as we all know, Mrs. Jones and Fringeville are not isolated cases in our urban society.

In cities, all of our daily activities and many of our satisfactions in life are dependent in some way on the form of our interaction with a man-made world. This built environment, among other things, reflects public purpose in its form, no matter how limited or misguided that purpose. I have suggested that we need to understand the nature of urban man's interaction with his environment in order to control it to better effect. Some relevant knowledge already exists. It comes mainly from experimental psychology but in part from our own primitive investigations. As we have seen, to pull scattered information together it is essential to have a model, a conceptual framework. Such a model must deal with those psychological characteristics of people which are relevant to their interaction with the urban environment. Linked to this is the question of which properties of the environment are most important in supporting or constraining the various forms of interaction.

I have found that the most fruitful way to organize my own thinking about these matters is in terms of phases of the man-environment interaction process. Any interaction with the environment can be subdivided into the following phases: (1) A *directive phase* in which some one of our many needs and purposes becomes sufficiently predominant to direct us to prepare to change our course of action. (2) An *intelligence phase* in which we search for new relevant information from the environment and organize it to be retained, usually in the form of memory representations. (3) A *planning phase* in which appropriate information is retrieved from such representations, or from other sources, and transformed to be used in the generation, evaluation, and selection of sets of possible actions. (4) An *action phase* in which the plan or set of plans judged most appropriate to our purposes is executed in a particular environmental context. (5) A *review phase* in which the effectiveness of the particular course of action is assessed in order to correct further action and to assign value and meaning to the experience

Notice that this formulation can apply to any level of planful interaction with the environment from personal planning through city planning to national planning. A course of action at any level need not explicitly involve all of these phases, but they are always implied. Routine habitual actions may require little articulation of need or purpose, gathering of new information, planning or review. Certainly the process is not always a conscious one. Sometimes it is only barely under control, as when we are caught in a stream of traffic, or are coerced to carry out plans relating to others' purposes but not our own.

Notice also that the phases of planful interaction are intentionally indifferent to the question of which dimensions of the environment happen to interest us.[4] The form of man's interaction with his built environment is determined by the social, spatial, and temporal structure of each environmental situation into which he enters (consider, for example, the first night of a long prison term), and also by the psychological characteristics of the individual. There seem to be general rules or strategies by which people deal with the environment which come into play in each phase of the interaction process. There are also characteristic group and individual differences both in psychological structure and in the purposes, knowledge, and plans which determine specific interactions. Here we can describe only what seem to be some of the most fundamental common psychological characteristics of people which might serve as a beginning in understanding the demands upon the form of the environment. Later, we will turn to the difficult question of how we might learn to take proper account of differences among people.

The Directive Phase: Needs and Purposes of Interaction

The determination of people's environmental needs and desires as a basis for the objectives of public policy is not a simple matter. The various lists of supposedly basic human needs are of very little help.[5] We can state minimum subsistence requirements for food or shelter, although our ability to prescribe tapers off rapidly as we leave the extremes. We can state some tentative standards for satisfactory air and water or light and noise levels, although man's physiological and psychological adaptability make even this difficult.[6] At best we can assert that it is not necessary to force people to adapt to obviously bad conditions and try to establish pleasanter levels of adaptation.[7] But even such a limited attempt at environmental standards is further complicated by the fact that pleasant levels of adaptation are determined in large part by the purposes of interaction. We can adapt to much higher noise levels if we are not trying to talk to someone.

Beyond such simple needs, we soon encounter the problems of individual and group differences, real but often unrecognized. Moreover, there is the knottier problem of how to legitimately raise people's levels of aspiration, how to help them realize what they might want if they were more fully aware of themselves and their needs.

Urban behavior is motivated by a tremendous variety of similar but basically unique needs, desires, and purposes. The potential expression of this diversity is, as we have seen, radically constrained by the limitations of a common language and set of cultural norms. It is further constrained by the limitations of the existing urban form. Imagine the richness of personal adaptation of the environment that would result if each family had the opportunity and the skill to select the site for their own dwelling and to design it—with whatever degree of professional assistance they desired—for themselves. The statistical trends of urban life, which we follow so assiduously and often take as an indication of "what people want," are at least as much a result of what is available for their choice as of what they might want.

The planner or designer, with his personal vision of a better world so different from present reality, often concludes that people's desires are apparently misguided and that their level of aspiration is too low. But we must also remember that people need what they want, even though as "impartial" observers we may feel that what they want is not always best for them. It has been a persistent technocratic ideal to imagine that the professional's special role is to determine people's needs, apart from their desires, to satisfy those "real needs" and then to wait for them to change their ways and express their gratitude. It is of course possible to change people's desires, at least superficially, by means of advertising and more profoundly through education.[8] Undoubtedly, the gradual and largely uncontrolled changes in the environment, especially in our technology, do alter people's wants in time.[9] We are generally agreed that we should attempt to change people's perceptions of the possible, and thus their desires, through education and exposure to wider environmental choices. We are just beginning to learn how city form itself educates, how it may help to broaden the individual's conception of the possible and thus raise his level of aspiration.[10] But that is quite another matter from imposing unwanted environments on people out of some higher conception of their needs which they do not share.

With all that, there may still be some fundamental psychological needs which, if understood, can determine performance standards for city form. These are the complementary needs for comprehension and for novelty, and there is a fair amount of evidence supporting their universality.[11] They are complementary because they call on the one hand for sufficient order in the environment to facilitate comprehension and on the other for sufficient complexity and change to stimulate curiosity and exploration.[12] In order to understand these requirements, however, we must first consider further how people operate in the environment.

The Intelligence Phase: Perceiving and Remembering the Environment

The environment is a bigger book than we can read. It contains far more potential information at any moment than we have the cognitive capacity to deal with. Because of our limitations, we are by nature selective.[13] Norbert Wiener remarked that the environment might best be conceived as a myriad of To Whom It May Concern messages, thus putting emphasis on the necessity for selection.[14] The counterpart of that statement might be that each of us is able to decide remarkably well which messages concern him and to ignore the rest. If this were not the case, we would fall into a state of confusion and paralysis from information overload—as sometimes happens, I am told, to unwary city planners. What is the secret of our selective powers?

We must understand, first of all, that perceiving and knowing are related processes. We begin by taking in an enormous amount of information through our eyes, ears, and other sense organs, most of which at any moment is irrelevant to our concerns. In order to put this information to effective use, to make something meaningful out of it, we must both condense it and relate it to the rest of our experience, past, present, and future. We have a number of more or less automatic mechanisms which sort and discard much information in accordance with an apparently fundamental human plan to seek and find simple features and objects whenever possible.[15] And what is simple in our experience is a question both of form and of familiarity. Thus we find again that by a kind of conventionality, by being most receptive to the recurrent regularities of our experience, we are able to select from the flood of incoming sense data that which most simplifies our lives. And of course we lose detail in the process.[16]

However, there are some details we cannot afford to lose. We strive to be ready to see those features of the environment which relate to our current needs and purposes, whatever their unfamiliarity. Even in a strange city we must be able to locate a restaurant efficiently when we are hungry. We must also be ready at all times to perceive at least some kinds of novelty, for what is unfamiliar may be dangerous. And we must be maximally receptive to other potential danger signals such as rapid motion or flashing lights. Moreover, sense data sometimes come in too rapidly, conflict or are incomplete, so that we have difficulty in formulating a satisfactory hypothesis about what is really "out there."[17] For all these reasons our elegant plan for organizing our perceptual experience by simple forms and nameable objects is often thwarted, especially in a fast-moving complicated environment such as the city. We may find ourselves confused, temporarily disoriented, straining to narrow even further those signals from the environment to which we will respond. Fortunately for us we can, within broad limits, make such an adaptation but we often do it at the cost of missing half our potential experience. We discover our loss when we return from a hectic trip abroad and suddenly see in our color slides hints of the richness we missed.

By analyzing how such perceptual selection operates in various types of environment and under varying conditions of planfulness and need, we can begin to understand one important human function of environmental form. Whatever the information we seek, our ability to achieve it is affected by the form of the environment, but people with different levels of familiarity with the same environment and carrying out different specific plans will attend to different features of that environment. An awareness of such diversity may make the designer's task more difficult but it may also make his designs more relevant to human use. In any case, in each specific environment only a few predominant types of plan are being executed, so the problem may be less serious than it at first appears. It should be possible to determine what those plans are and to direct design attention to the relevant features. Some designers attempt to do this in a rough intuitive way, but a radical improvement in our ability to create relevant forms can be achieved through research. We need only observe and question the users of various environments.[18]

The form of the environment influences not only our ability to achieve new information but also how we organize our experience in memory. Remembering continues the process of simplification. The task of memory is to represent an experience in a form which can be retained in the brain unused for an indefinite period and then located at an appropriate later time. As in any filing system, the need to retrieve information requires that we store it in as efficient a way as possible. This filing task occupies much of experience and we have typical strategies for accomplishing it economically under varying conditions. Thus,

while we may retain literal images of some significant events
or places, we normally use a few key perceptual features to
classify each unique experience under some simple, usually
verbal, category.[19] By that token the experience is not only simplified and condensed but is also automatically related to other
similar past experience. Thus, while we may also have a visual
image of it, we are likely to represent a street in memory as
"a high-class shopping street" with certain named stores, since
that is the most effective way of relating it to our other knowledge of the city and thereby make our memory of it more
accessible for future use. Within a common culture the attributes used in achieving such categories as "high-class shopping
street" are likely to be quite similar and predictable. The city
designer needs to discover what these critical features of the
city are.

There are some essential features of the urban environment
which cannot easily be translated into words, however. Perhaps
the most important is the visible form of its spatial pattern.
About ten years ago, Kevin Lynch began to investigate how the
form of the city affected people's ability to represent it to themselves in some coherent way.[20] Since *The Image of the City*
there have been a handful of other studies which have attempted to extend his work or to repeat it in other contexts.[21]
By now, the evidence seems to be that some of the variables
mentioned by Lynch besides clarity, simplicity, and dominance
of visible form are more significant in determining the memora-
bility of a city element than they at first seemed to be. On the
basis of current evidence, the relative social values which districts, streets, or buildings symbolize and the simple exposure
of these elements to the public eye would appear to be at least
as important as their visible form. Indeed, when we understand
how memory works to organize experience on the basis of its
significance to us—in part a question of perceived value and in
part of it familiarity or recurrence in our lives—it would be

surprising if social value and exposure were not crucial variables.

The relative visual and social dominance of various elements, while important, gives little indication of how people structure their representations of the city. Evidence on the structuring of spatial images of cities is still scarce. What there is indicates that here too we try to simplify and organize. As there are three basic human modes of representing the environment through actions, images, and words, there would seem to be three basic types of structuring subjective city models, the use of which varies in part with the form of the city and in part with our familiarity with it. Thus we may structure our memories of the city in terms of familiar sequences of visual images, in the form of extended spatial images of important areas, or schematically, as a simple over-all diagram, easily describable in words.[22] The particular spatial form of a city can facilitate or inhibit the development of such structuring.

The function of an extensive, well organized, economical, and *accurate* representation of the city is to facilitate planful action. As urban activities become dispersed we have an increasing need to get around in our environment without strain. We need to find many places of interest and thus to be able to execute more types of plans more easily. We already know some techniques for making city form more legible and we are gradually learning how to facilitate more effective structuring. But it is critical now to learn more about the intelligence phase, especially about how information on nonvisible activities or social values is integrated with visual-spatial representations—how our concepts about the city relate to our pictures of it.[23]

The Planning Phase: Using Our Model

Acquiring and retaining knowledge about the environment is not the same as putting it to effective use. To make a plan is to transform information in such a way as to generate a course of action different from that in which the information was originally gained. We may know what the river is like, but we cannot step twice into the same river in the same way. We must integrate information gained from past experience with information gained from other sources, including feedback from on-going activity. And we must integrate new plans with plans already in the process of being executed, with overriding life plans and with the plans of other people.[24] What most concerns us in all this psychological complexity is the influence of the form of the environment on the effectiveness of planning.

We have seen that the extensiveness and accuracy of our model of a city is affected by its form. The extensiveness and accuracy of this model determine our ability to predict the outcome of alternative courses of action in making our plans. Further, city form, through the model, affects accurate remembering, which is essential to effective planning. For example, the perceptual characteristics of environments may be ambiguous or mixed in incongruous ways so that they cannot be easily related to our verbal concepts and to social values. Thus what appears to be a "slum" may turn out to be a haven for struggling writers and painters, or a "residential street" may really be lined with institutions and professional offices. Such ambiguity or incongruity, while sometimes desirable for other reasons, inhibits accurate remembering. For remembering is a process of reconstruction in which we typically begin by recalling what we believe to be the most characteristic features and concepts and proceed to fill in the picture in whatever way is most consistent with these general features.[25]

On the other hand, environmental form can facilitate planning by making it less necessary to specify a plan in detail. The metropolitan world presently in the making is one in which it is becoming increasingly necessary to plan out our daily activities carefully. As functions separate and disperse, for example from town centers to spatially separate highway-oriented locations, we need more elaborate plans, more time and more patience to carry out our weekly round of activities. That the housewife has become a chauffeur is well known, but she is also becoming a dispatcher. As cities approach a formal state in which nothing is on the way to anything else, we also become unable to execute "spontaneous" plans, whether it be to stop off for a refreshing interlude in a bar or in a park or to make a needed but unplanned purchase. Areas of mixed use and character, if not so mixed as to be confusing or difficult to remember, clearly make planning easier by requiring less of it in advance.

Further influences of environmental form on our ability to formulate effective plans could readily be determined. All that is required is to set people from different environments problems to solve using their knowledge of those environments. The Lynch interview techniques, while developed for somewhat different purposes, are a model for this kind of research. Special purpose maps or trip descriptions showing how various types of activities would be carried out would give much information about the human uses of cities and also about the failures of city form. And such information would not be of merely theoretical interest. It would be directly useful in design.

The Action Phase: Supports and Constraints in the Environment

It is when we carry out our plans in real environmental situations that the consequences of form are most directly experienced. The form of the environment provides support for certain actions and constrains others. The significance of environmental form for human action, however, is as much a function of how people perceive supports and constraints as it is of the physical form itself.[26] No matter how skillful we become at measuring various end effects of environmental form, if we wish to understand the process of interaction of which such effects are the products, we must turn again to the city of the mind.

The environment is a potential field of human action but it does not become effective until we perceive what actions are possible and carry them out.[27] Thus if we plan to build a branch library in a neighborhood without one, what matters is that there are people in that neighborhood who would feel a need to use a library, who would perceive this particular library as one usable by them, and who would in fact have the time and ability to do so. Jane Jacobs has pointed out that planned environments, such as playgrounds in slum areas, sometimes fail to become effective ones.[28] The local residents may feel that it is an imposition, not needed in comparison with other more pressing needs, may not perceive it as a safe place to go, and may have insufficient time or be unable to supervise children who might use it. In any case, a different unplanned use may be perceived and the playground may become a battlefield for gang warfare.

The whole environmental field may be thought of as being subdivided into regions or settings for action, each of which determines, to varying degrees, the behavior which occurs within it.[29] We might say that although people have plans, the environment has "programs" built in which tend to coerce particular actions within a generally planful personal course of action. As we enter each setting, for example a traffic interchange or a shopping street, we must adapt our actions to the existing pattern of activity in the setting. Such action settings have both functional-physical dimensions and social-symbolic dimensions and they have a typical temporal scheduling of cycles of activity.[30] Environmental designers are used to thinking of their world as a nesting hierarchy of such interconnected settings beginning with a single room and running through neighborhoods and communities up to the scale of the metropolis.

We city planners have recently been scolded, with some justification, for conceiving of cities in an exclusively place-conscious fashion in the age of electronic communications.[31] There is no doubt that the boundaries between settings are increasingly permeable to interchanges of both communications and people. However, a basic characteristic of such settings is that they have a form—an ordered internal arrangement in time and space tending to determine human actions within them—which persists independently of particular actors. Our propensity to conceive of the environment in terms of such settings or regions is deeply rooted and justified; that they are becoming more interdependent does not make their real human functions less important.

By saying that, I do not mean to imply that all the functions of urban activity settings are well understood. Their economic and political functions are better understood than their social functions; their aggregate social functions are better understood than their specific psychological and behavioral functions. The effects of particular attributes of these settings, such as size or density, even though they have received some study, remain ambiguous.[32] For although the size of a community tends to be associated with desirable goods such as political power or choice, these depend on such factors as the degree of homogeneity or diversity within the community as well as on the particular structure of relationships that exists. Moreover, the achievement of power and diversity does not in itself indicate the degree of individual participation in these goods.[33] The same may be said for the human effects of density—for density cannot be separated from other variables operating in the dense region, as we find even with the rats which some writers are so fond of comparing to people in slums.[34] And so it goes with any single variable which we try to isolate from the multidimensional environment.

If we are concerned, as city designers, with predicting the more important effects of environmental form, it is likely that we will get much further, at least initially, by conceiving of the environment in terms of these multidimensional action settings and the relationships among them than we will by attempting to isolate single variables. For as we move from setting to setting, carrying out a plan of activity, so many variables change that it would be all but impossible to keep analytical track of them. By dealing with these settings we will be operating on units which have a relatively clear relationship to psychological and behavioral realities. They are the real units to which individuals must adapt their actions.

The Review Phase: The Meaning and Value of Environments

What can be said about how interaction with the environment produces meaning and value? I have suggested that the meaning and value of environments arise from a review function in which we assess the consequences of a course of action. But you will recall that I also began by asserting that the concepts by which we organize experience are imposed upon us by our culture and language. The explanation of meaning and value, then, must be in the nature of the relationship between conventional wisdom and personal experience.[35]

In simplest terms, meaning arises when we fill out the skeleton of culturally acquired concepts with the flesh and blood of significance derived from direct experience. Meaning is the increment to knowledge resulting from action—the subtle change in the shading of our environmental image produced by each unique experience of the environment. Each different house that we experience, provided we are attending to the experience, adds in some way to the meaning of "house." The amount it adds depends on the degree of its novelty and the state of our openness to new experience. That meaning arises from review simply means that in each meaningful experience there is an *effort* required to match new experience to existing categories.[36]

Similarly with value. In the normally developing individual, culturally derived values are continually tested against personal experience. By reviewing these tests we begin to create a personal system of values associated with various regions of the environmental field. These personalized values are closely linked with environmental meanings.[37]

Because we begin with a more or less common set of concepts and share many experiences with other people, especially with those of our class and local environment, many personal meanings and values are shared. We can therefore distinguish various realms of environmental meaning and value ranging from settings which may be personally meaningful and valuable for the great majority of citizens, for instance the Boston Common, to those which have meaning and value only to single individuals.[38]

Environmental meanings and values can also be differentiated by type and by mode of communication. In simplest terms there are functional, social, and esthetic meanings and values. Functional meanings are often expressed rather directly by visible forms or have a learned correlation with forms, which almost amounts to the same thing. Sizes and shapes of buildings and spaces and locational patterns may be immediately revealing to anyone familiar with the culture. And often, function is expressed explicitly by means of signs. Social meanings and values are seldom immediately apparent from the form and frequently lack even a conventional relationship to form. While obelisks typically mark a historic figure or event and domes are usually associated with public buildings, many parts of the environment with no particular distinguishing features may have historic or other social meaning and value. Social significance, usually as widely known to the residents of a place as functional significance, may be difficult to determine from the outside, except long familiarity, or more objectively, by surveying the local residents and noting frequency of agreement.[39]

Esthetic significance is an environmental quality about which there would likely be less agreement. Psychology has little to offer beyond psychoanalytic speculations and endless experiments on people's preferences for this or that type of visual pattern.[40] There is even considerable disagreement as to what constitutes an esthetic experience. My own preference is for a definition by Albert Guérard which states that: "Art is the quest of pleasure through the conscious expression of emotion."[41] I like it because it applies equally to the creation or appreciation of art, because it asserts that art is an active, never a passive, state, because it does not quibble about pleasure as the end of art, or about the necessity of consciousness, communication with a public, and emotion. If you disagree with this definition, no matter; I do not urge it upon you.

By agreeing with Guérard that the essence of art is "the quest for pleasure in conscious expression of emotion," I do not wish to exclude its other functions. Art, like science, can connect realms of experience previously separate in our minds and it has a special means for doing so: the metaphor.[42] Thus, the form of a house can represent the myriad forms of human sheltering: womb, cave, tent, tower, castle, palace.[43] How much more could the form of the city represent the richness of the world if we could master its metaphoric possibilities! While it has been suggested that art, which is after all a cognitive activity, will be found to conform to rules like those guiding other cognitive processes, we cannot write these rules of metaphor as yet.

Whatever our abilities as designers, city form becomes art willy-nilly. Pop Art shows us how to create our own "art" merely by observing the present environment. If such an inversion of value brings pleasure to some, it is not to be despised. By increasing the opportunities for sensuous involvement with the environment we can increase the chances for art, whether created by an "artist"-planner or by a "nonartist"-observer or both. Thus a city form which facilitates our more utilitarian activities can increase the possibilities for pleasurable city watching. For we need not always be bound by utilitarian concerns. We can learn, or relearn, to see the environment in its sensory richness, to see the abstract patterns of light and color, texture and movement where normally appear the useful objects of our daily lives. Such perception, while not the highest form of art, brings a kind of immediate childlike delight in the sights and sounds of the world. It is the sensuous foundation on which art, with its layers of cultural meaning, is built. Environments which are sufficiently orderly or sufficiently well known free us for this kind of perceiving, provided that the sensuous form is rich enough to reward our attention to it.

Perceiving and representing the environment, acting in it, and reviewing the consequences are the processes by which we create our personal city of the mind—our own "life space," as it has been called. The form of the environment can help to make that space narrow and confined or broad and open, constantly growing. By organizing the environment properly we can make ordinary city-using tasks simpler to accomplish. We can increase the scope of possible actions for any individual as well as his sense of competence in carrying them out. And we can increase his experience of meaning and esthetic pleasure.

One general question to be asked of environmental form, then, is whether it provides the required settings to support the socially desirable planful behavior of its residents and to bring increased meaning and pleasure to their lives. In other words, can the residents adapt the environment, by their pattern of interaction within the settings provided, to create a satisfying "life space"? Marc Fried's now famous study of the interaction of a working-class community with its local environment in Boston's now infamous West End is a case in point.[44] Fried found what he called a "sense of spatial identity," related to feelings of social group identity, in the attitudes of local people toward their environment and the places within it. He contrasted this feeling of identity or attachment to the settings of a particular territory with the typically selective and individualized middle-class use of space. From his finding that some 46 per cent of these people suffered some form of prolonged and "rather severe grief" upon being dislocated from their extended home, one might argue that the West Enders were too narrowly adapted at the cost of adaptability;[45] yet why not simply conclude that they suffered a real loss? For here may be a rather clear example of a relationship between the life image and satisfaction of a group of people and the form of their environment.

Taken in the context of knowledge that I have been describing, this study and others like it would seem to suggest, and here I will speculate, that under optimum conditions man's interaction with his environment is a kind of spiraling process of development. Having certain needs and purposes in mind, we interact in some way with a specific environment. This interaction, when successful, has adaptive value, either by increasing our adaptation to the environment or vice versa. By such adaptive interaction we gain in competence, we improve our image of the environment and our skill in manipulating it to our purposes. Increased competence, providing that we have a sense that the general environment is open and responsive, leads to the formulation and execution of plans of action directed toward satisfying new, more challenging needs, and so on. This, it seems to me, is the most useful of the many meanings of "mental health."[46] At any point in this process, however, we may come up against a dead end, either because the strains of adapting to a particular environment are so severe as to have crippled us or because we sense that the general environment beyond our haven is hostile or both. Thus the industry and positive striving reported to exist in many of the shantytowns of Latin America can be contrasted with the despair and frustration of a Watts.[47]

This perspective may help to interpret other findings on the psychological and social effects of environmental form. For instance, the much discussed relationship between friendship and proximity in homogeneous impermanent communities may be seen as an early stage of this adaptive process.[48] As confidence and competence increase in a new environment, friendships probably become more selective and less determined by spatial form. A higher state of development is always marked by an increasingly selective and creative use of the total environment. As we consider more developed states we necessarily change our focus from environmental determinants of behavior to qualities affecting the personal meaning and value of environments.

Some Criteria for Environmental Form

Given the current limited state of our knowledge about the relationship between the city of the mind and the city "out there," what criteria for environmental form can reasonably be deduced? In very general terms, we might conclude that a good environment should at least support socially desirable planful behavior and facilitate man's effort after meaning. However, such statements are not much help to the hard pressed city planner or designer. Much more research is needed of course, but even without it a number of still general but somewhat more operational criteria are suggested by what is known. Before stating these, I must stress that such criteria must be more in the nature of hypotheses than design tools at the moment. They are deductively derived and projected from present knowledge, testable but untested, capable of being made operational but not yet made so, and certainly incomplete. Further, since they are not applied to a specific case, they are unweighted and no attempt has been made to eliminate possible conflicts between them. They are, in short, very much like the other criteria we use in city planning. While some speculation is unavoidable, I will list only those criteria which seem to me to be rather well supported by current knowledge:

1. *Increase the exposure of people to a variety of environmental settings and potential interactions.* This will of course provide choice and allow for individual differences, but it should also have important effects on increasing people's sense of the possible and level of aspiration. For this reason it may be especially important for children. It can be accomplished by increasing the real variety of action settings, linked together in space and accessible within some limited time, or by increasing the mobility of people. When applied to the settings of daily activities or the routes of typical trips, increasing accessible variety means a reduction in the need for detailed planning of daily activities and increasing personal efficiency. What constitutes accessible variety depends in part on particular publics: a great variety of high-priced, upper-class stores nearby will offer few benefits to a population of poor Negroes. Finally, exposure to new or different environmental types can be accomplished by various special aids such as field trips or presentations by television or other media, with the implications for the quality of life made concrete.

2. *Stimulate and facilitate exploration of the environment.* While exposure may be helpful in this it does not by itself guarantee that seen environments will be explored. What is apparently required is the right level (not yet established) of novelty and complexity to stimulate curiosity plus sufficient openness and connectedness to allow easy access to new settings and experiences. Exploration can satisfy what may be a basic human need for new experience. By increasing individual interaction with novel and complex environments it leads to growth both by broadening the individual's categories and concepts about the world and by increasing his sense of competence and capacity to formulate and execute new plans. Increases in the rate and scope of interaction can also be accomplished by

means of special enrichment programs and techniques, but these are clearly more artificial and may be less effective than if the environment itself facilitates exploration.

3. *Increase the perceptual accessibility of city form.* We can make environmental elements and settings easier to recognize, identify, and remember by making sure that those few form attributes which are critical in recognition are most visible, as well as by simplifying and clarifying visual shape. Simplification of shape is easiest to accomplish at the moment because more is known about it. We may have a good intuitive sense of which attributes are critical in identification, mainly by attending to tradition and stereotypes, but not much is objectively known as yet. And of course the identity of some settings, such as slums, should probably not be clarified as such. Further, by decreasing ambiguity and incongruity in city form we tend to increase conventionality and reduce novelty and complexity. Thus this criterion might best be stated as a constraint on the facilitation of exploration or vice versa. Either way, there is a delicate balance to be drawn in design.

4. *Structure city form to facilitate the various modes of structuring mental representations.* This would require attention to sequential, areal, and schematic structures. By facilitating various modes of structuring we can make city form comprehensible to more types of people. Clearly some parts of the city such as commercial centers should facilitate all three types of structuring. In general, however, sequential structuring is most appropriate for habitual trips and the extended spatial structuring of an area where there is a concentration of heavily frequented action settings. Simplified schematic structuring may be most appropriate over large sectors of the city to facilitate fitting together sequences and limited spatial images.

A further help in structuring and in comprehension would be to increase the number and variety of available information aids and their correlation with city form. This may seem trivial but could be very important in facilitating more effective planning. In some European cities telephone books contain maps which indicate both street names and how the numbers run, a great aid in locating places. Information boards could be placed at strategic points, preprogrammed to light up the quickest or the most scenic route to any destination. Much could also be done to aid more important, longer-range planning. For example, detailed and generally accessible information on the real estate market in various parts of the city would greatly aid in house hunting.

5. *Enhance the unique qualities of environmental settings.* By emphasizing the special character of places we can encourage the formation of individual or small-group attachments and meanings. It is also a way of increasing variety and novelty. It may act as a further constraint on the conventional aspects of perceptual accessibility or it may in many cases be more highly valued than ease of recognition.

6. *Increase the relative exposure of city elements and settings of highest common significance, both functional and social.* This will increase the amount of real experience of these settings and thus increase the realization of their personal meaning and value for more individuals. It will also tend to reinforce their common significance, adding to group solidarity and perhaps impeding desirable changes or shifts in value. The need for continuity in change is doubtless real but indeterminate for the moment.

7. *Increase the plasticity and manipulability of city form to the actions of small groups and individuals.* This may be one of the most effective means for increasing the personal meaning and value of the environment as well as for increasing people's sense of competence and effectiveness. It should also increase variety and the uniqueness of places. The relatively greater degree of plasticity offered by the single-family house with its private manipulable yard has undoubtedly increased the indi-

vidual meaning and value of the environment, although there are system constraints on the expression of uniqueness.

8. *Facilitate a rhythm of behavioral and perceptual constraint and release in the organization of environmental settings.* This would increase the opportunities for contrast, comparison, and the formation of new mental connections between objects and events. It would also increase the freedom of action of the individual as he moves through the environment, executing his plans. It could be accomplished by the provision of alternative routes to the same destination, contrasting in type and character, or by juxtaposing quiet places to busy ones. It requires attention to the scheduling of events within settings to enhance temporal rhythms as well as spatial ones.

9. *Adapt the form of environmental settings to facilitate the predominant plans being executed within them.* This is obviously a catch-all, but an important one. To make it operational requires that we discover what plans are actually being carried out within various typical settings and develop client-centered techniques for establishing their relative importance. I would include here such physiological requirements as microclimate, light and noise levels since they are in general relative to the types of plans being carried out. Without being able to propose specific criteria in the abstract, I could suggest, for example, that in "general purpose" environments such as town centers, settings should be structured on several levels to facilitate the execution of several types of plans (utilitarian to pleasure-seeking) without conflict.

Although these criteria do not include all the performance characteristics that city form must satisfy, I believe that they may be some of the most useful and important for design. They can be tested both by attempting to apply them to design and by further research. We should proceed on both fronts at once.

If such criteria were developed into a consistent, weighted, operational set and imaginatively used in design, what would the resulting city form be like? At MIT, under the general direction of Kevin Lynch, we have been working to develop the implications of similar criteria for city form.[49] Although we have made some progress, inventing the future metropolis (as Britton Harris recently put it) is a demanding task. To develop my own ideas, based on these criteria, is worthy of another separate effort. But, although such utopian design research is much needed, significant advances could be made now in the practice of city design.

Tailoring the Form of the Future Metropolis to Its Users

The most fundamental problem for the practice of city design today is not the expansion and refinement of a set of performance criteria, or even the invention of new forms, as important as these may be. It is rather the identification, development, and meaningful collaboration with a client, or set of clients. Most city design is done today in a way not far different from the way it was done in the Renaissance. There is a patron, usually a director of planning or redevelopment, with some power to change the form of sections of the city. There is also the currently favored "urban designer," often not a planner and often brought in specially for the job. The amount of contact between this designer and the users of the environment is usually nil.[50] Since the shape of the environment will have a real effect on people's lives, as we have seen, this should not be a tolerable situation. Nor can we delude ourselves that the citizen groups, planning boards, and elected officials who will influence and make final decisions are truly representative of these users.

To say that the city designer should be a servant of the people is a proposition that we can all accept in the abstract. It means in practice that he will often need to become their advocate. But to be an effective advocate he will need to know as much about them as possible, as well as being an expert at his trade of relating their needs and purposes to proposals for city form. All of the existing political mechanisms plus others that have hardly been tried or are not yet developed will need to be employed for identifying the real clients of design and for establishing meaningful communication with them. The designer cannot be expected to be an expert in the development of these various kinds of knowledge, whether by anthropological field methods, attitude surveys, observation of behavior, or whatever. He can and should be involved with deciding what knowledge is to be sought and with interpreting the results.

His basic role, however, which only he can perform, is the development, evaluation, elaboration, and presentation of form alternatives which clearly relate to the needs, purposes, and values which have been identified. He must be centrally involved in establishing a process whereby new alternative forms for the city are presented to the relevant publics by various methods, their reactions assessed, revisions made, followed by new presentations, and so on. Only in this way can city form become truly a joint product of designer and the people who will use it. If in the process, the designer loses some of his cherished artistic license, it will be a small price to pay for better cities.

The city which emerges from this process will not be a unified total work of art. Rather it will be many cities in one—perhaps not all things to all men, but at least reflecting the true diversity of social groups, functions, and unique environmental settings of our urban world. To be sure, there are many economic and social barriers on the way to such an achievement. But we are now in the midst of a revolution to increase the participation of people in shaping the social, economic, and urban forms which in turn determine the quality of their lives. We city planners and designers by the traditions of our profession and the solemnity of our avowals that "the city is the people" must be with such a revolution.

And of course there is no end to it—no achievable "good" day in an "optimum" city which will suddenly put a happy ending to our dissatisfactions. For the specific needs, purposes, and desires which guide our striving are in constant flux as the conditions of our society change. That the future is uncertain and utopia unreachable, however, is no reason not to work for better days in better cities.

Comments on

Carr

PAUL VINCENT GUMP
Department of Psychology, University of Kansas

We are indebted to Dr. Carr for a sensitive and even-handed treatment of a complex set of issues. Within his comprehensive discussion it is possible to center upon two approaches to the person-environment problem. The first approach is connoted by the word "mind" in the title "City of the Mind": the city is what we experience, what we think it is. This point of view is explicit in the outline, which is organized around following an individual through stages of direction, intelligence, planning, action, and review. This orientation to our problem is *anthropocentric*; it seeks to understand wider and more complex phenomena by beginning with the person. The anthropocentric outlook focuses upon the individual, locates the significant organizing and dynamic forces within him, and speaks of how he selects from a variegated but passive environment.

The orientation we contrast to the anthropocentric one is explained later in the paper; here Dr. Carr describes the environmental field as being divided into regions or settings for action, each region determining to varying degrees the behavior which occurs within it. This approach we label *ecological*. It does not begin with particular behavior of individuals or with their particular needs and strategies; it attempts to comprehend the nature of the environment by starting with description of segments of that environment.

While it would be foolish to try to defend one or the other of these approaches as being superior intrinsically, it may be important to consider which, given the knowledge we possess, should have priority in research efforts. My own position would be that the ecological approach deserves primary attention if the desire is to understand how man and environment come together. The anthropocentric approach cannot, by itself, tell us what environments are really like. If one studies the environment by watching particular individuals one gets less than a comprehensive picture; as has been pointed out, individuals are selective and will not react to all parts of their environmental context. Even a very detailed and accurate description of an individual going through all phases from direction to review would yield a highly selected portrait of the environment.

It may seem strange for a psychologist to recommend research efforts that place the individual in less than first focus. Concepts and methods in our field are geared to study of persons and their individual behavior; even more compelling is the fact that individuals often *do* treat the environment as a passive array from which they select both perceptions and activity supports. Questioning the validity of this image may seem contentious.

But there are truths which obscure as well as illuminate. The truth that some persons are sometimes capable of a high degree of selection from, and self-determination within, their environments may be one of these obscuring truths. It is a truth which misleads on two counts: the coerciveness of the environment is often underestimated in favor of appeal to explanations of behavior relating to personality variables or to "case history" events. Even more crucial for science, the personality-determination truth diverts attention away from the study of environments qua environments. The truth promises, falsely we believe, that when we know more about the human person and about how he reacts to separate stimuli we will be able to predict his behavior and experiences in various environmental contexts.

Dr. Carr deals first with an anthropocentric approach and then with an ecological one. So far as research effort is concerned, we would urge a reverse order. The discussion we have heard refers to action or activity settings; certain of Dr. Carr's statements regarding these ecological units deserve underlining. He points out that if we do become able to handle such units as activity settings, "we will be operating on units which have a relatively clear relationship to psychological and behavioral realities." The behavior-influencing power of these regions is clear in the statement that "the environment has programs built in which tend to coerce behavior." Another term for activity setting is behavior setting, a concept developed by Barker and Wright[1] and Barker and Schoggen.[2] Along with Dr. Carr these authors also point out that the real locus of persons' behavior is in a behavior setting of some kind. Furthermore it has been shown how such ecological units are not merely places *for* behavior but are units created *by* behavior. Settings such as freeways, playgrounds, or schools are created by inhabitants' en masse behavior coordinated with the physical milieu. The quality of an array of settings can be quite coercive; for example the size of high school settings markedly influences the behavior and experience of students.[3]

Eventually we hope to establish a meaningful relationship between such disparate phenomena as high rise apartment houses and individuals' feelings of security, between zoning regulations and an individual's efforts for his family. How does one get from the more distal and nonpsychological environmental variables to the personal phenomena? The behavior setting would seem to be a bridge upon which the environmental and the personal come together. If this is true, the development of theory and method regarding these kinds of environmental segment is more than an interesting possibility among a number of alternatives—instead such development becomes a scientific priority.

Once such development is accomplished we are better prepared for problems at both ends of the bridge. We can study how particular individuals manage their plans in environments which we can describe adequately, and we can become interested in how larger and more distal environmental factors impinge on settings. Dr. Carr expressed this latter approach when speaking of environmental form: "One general question to be asked of environmental form, then, is whether it provides the required settings to support the socially desirable planful behavior of its residents and to bring increased meaning and pleasure to their lives."

G A R Y   H .   W I N K E L
Department of Architecture, University of Washington

Professor Carr has done a creditable job on a difficult task—the development of a conceptual model describing man's response to the urban environment. He has, I believe, correctly recognized the necessity of formulating such a model before extensive empirical research on urban problems can be undertaken. The development of models or conceptual schemes, however, is difficult. The model requires some degree of internal consistency. It must also be capable of yielding relatively unambiguous predictions. The model which Professor Carr has developed should be considered in light of these requirements.

In reading Professor Carr's paper I believe it is possible to detect a mixture of two relatively disparate approaches to an understanding of man as a user of urban environments. The first of these models is man-centered. Professor Carr speaks of man, the "planner," having interactions with his environment. Man "searches" for relevant information from the environment, "organizes" it, "retrieves" information from his "memory representations" to form a "plan," "acts" in accordance with that "plan," and finally "reviews" the effectiveness of his "plan" within some environmental context. As part of this sequence of activities, Professor Carr suggests that the "form" of the environment influences the particular kinds of "image" or "plan" man has and subsequently their behavioral expression. It is at this point that the focus of his discussion begins to change. The development of "plans" or "images" is dependent upon environmental characteristics rather than upon man as "planner."

This shift in emphasis raises some thorny questions: At what point does man cease to control his environment and does it begin to control him? Does the environment simply facilitate or hinder man's behavior or can it actively and significantly change it? Answers to these questions have relevance both theoretically and practically. Consider for a moment man as a "planner." If man actively organizes and evaluates his environment and if this occurs mentally, the "form" of the environment may be quite irrelevant because man can alter it to fit his own needs. The investment of time necessary to develop a set of physical forms based upon behavioral considerations may be wasted if man can easily alter them by verbal recoding to fit his own needs at the moment. This, of course, assumes that the planner is not explicitly trying to create an "unplanned" environment in which man is the master.

This problem may be clarified further by drawing an illustration from Professor Carr's paper. He suggests that man's need for novelty or variety should find a place in urban design. A number of the studies he cites would support his contention that man relies quite heavily upon altering sensory input from the environment. But the human being is indeed fickle. What is novelty one day may be drudgery the next. And indeed, the same studies cited by Professor Carr indicate that the effects of novelty on behavior are transitory. How can the city form be created so that it provides a continuing level of novelty if this is deemed to be important? A much more difficult problem would be encountered if a decision were made to optimize the character of novelty. In this case the "weakness" of the physical form might invalidate its incorporation in the city. On the basis of Professor Carr's paper it would be difficult to know whether greater effort should be devoted to the study of physical forms conducive to novelty or to the characteristics of man as a perceiver and encoder of novelty.

A suggestion that both should be studied could be poor research strategy, particularly if one approach were more likely to succeed than the other. In comparisons of the two approaches my own feeling is that a fuller investigation of the physical form itself has a greater likelihood of revealing significant relationships with human behavior. I feel that this direction is more fundamental because I do not think that enough attention has been given to the ways in which "images" of the environment have been developed in the first place. They must come from some kind of contact with the physical environment either directly or indirectly (i.e., mediated by formal and informal education). It seems hard to conceive of a set of images or plans which operate independently of an environmental context, no matter how "weak" or "strong" it may be. It seems logical therefore to spend a greater amount of time and effort investigating the physical environment itself—those characteristics which do alter behavior.

If one *were* to consider the characteristics of man as "planner," I think that the direction of research activities would involve a consideration of how man verbally codes his environmental experiences. If that process could be understood and if it mainly involved the manipulation of verbal symbols then the city planner might profitably spend more time educating people to change their verbal codes of the environment rather than manipulating the form characteristic of the environment itself.

In conclusion, I feel it necessary to stress the fact that my comments concerning Professor Carr's paper are directed toward a clarification of the implications of his position. At this stage of development it would be premature to assert the primacy of one approach over another. If my comments serve to stimulate some thought about the direction of future research then I shall have been amply rewarded. Professor Carr has already rewarded us by starting a dialogue which hopefully will lead to fruitful discoveries in a most difficult but most exciting area of investigation.

Stanley J. Hallett
Church Federation of Greater Chicago

Planning, Politics, and Ethics

We have gathered to reflect upon the condition of our cities, the state of our knowledge, and of the art of city planning, the choices that are open to us in the shaping of our environment, the structures and forms within which these choices must be made, and now some of the problems involved in making right choices.

Wandering the streets of Chicago the other night, I came across a new nightclub called The Happening. I was intrigued to discover that units of the show, which might be characterized as an improvisational theatre of the absurd, were called "Plannings." My first response was to feel that my professional dignity was offended.

But a couple of evenings later, I was out on the Near West Side standing among some of the public housing projects near a new university, listening to excited accounts by teenagers of their exploits of the night. They were just back from lobbing Molotov cocktails and generally adding excitement to the lives of police, firemen, reporters, and sundry civic dignitaries. Standing under a street light watching the red glow of a fire in the distance, one tall young man with a handkerchief around his head was interpreting the events. The flag held the key. "The blue field and white stars are the deceivers, and no one knows how many there are. The white bars are the years of white rule.

The red bars are the years of blood, and they are beginning."

And suddenly, the Plannings of The Happening didn't seem so absurd. The environment we have created in part of Chicago's West Side is at least as bizarre as the environment of the night club. The key difference is that out on the West Side no one is going to turn on the light and tell you that the show is over and you can go home now.

The Near West Side is, in a sense, a victory for planners. After many years of concern about how to relate the planning process to the political process, how to get plans implemented, we see a remarkable turning by the "decision-makers" to the planners for advice. Planning has been ensconced in the central control mechanisms of our large organizations. Plans that once gathered dust in the basement of City Hall are now being translated into an actual environment. What once were "Plannings" that never got past the dress rehearsal are now "Happenings."

There is an urgency about ideas that influence events; and one senses a new urgency in the discussions of planners. The academic game of exploring possible choices has been linked with the political game of acting on choices, and this sets in motion anxiety about making the right choices. It is the purpose of this paper to engage some of the problems in making right choices that will be explored in continuing consultations next year.

In approaching this task, I think it is useful to reflect upon the way our general consciousness is being torn between two images: the image of a mushroom cloud on the one hand, and that of a lunar probe on the other. The first stands as a symbol of unlimited destructive capability, and the second of infinite positive capability.

We are aware of the population explosion, urban growth, rates of change in information, communication, and education. These are commonplaces of our discussion; but one senses in our nation a loss of direction, and in many places a rising nihilism. Vietnam, race tensions in the cities, ideals of eliminating poverty seemingly caught in a morass of intractable stuff, changing sex styles and mores that produce at best an uncertain intimacy, elements of sickness in the youth culture, awareness of a polluted environment, and inefficient urban housekeeping that takes away with one hand what it gives with the other, requiring in commuting time what it yields in working hours—these are continuing themes.

An expansion of military systems in international affairs is matched by the domestic sale of guns, which reached astounding proportions in Chicago this summer, as it did in Los Angeles last summer. Military response overseas is matched by demands to support your local police here at home. We can see in the cities the pressures to express these attitudes, this spirit of man, in urban form, building new styles of the fortress city in apartment house complexes and suburban enclosures. This mood or spirit feeds an apocalyptic mode of thought that one finds in book titles: *Crisis in Our Cities, Sick Cities, Crisis in Black and White*, and so forth.

But it is also true that our consciousness is stretched these days in the other direction, toward unlimited possibilities: the elimination of poverty, the development of open cities, radical new technological systems which reduce the need for labor and open possibilities for significant work. The creative possibilities for shaping the environment in ways that contribute to human development seem infinite.

But even more awesome are the possibilities for shaping man, himself, through control processes which are now open to conscious decision and therefore in the ethical realm. This includes not only explosions in education but control of biological systems as well.

In this line stand the possibilities of regeneration of limbs, genetic control or manipulation, and mind-control or consciousness-expanding drugs with possibilities of increased intelligence capability. In one effort to project and date major developments of the next fifty years, British scientists estimated a breakthrough in mind-reading by 1996.

Bouncing around in this range of terror and hope, our minds and our culture respond with the pursuit of new moralities. The Playboy style takes the position that you can do what you must to get your share, the system will probably hold together as long as you are around, and any way there are always girls. The James Bond style exploits technology for toys, terror, sex, and humor. The religious institutions have been working to clear up the hangover from the nineteenth century (if not the thirteenth) amid the debris of the first half of the twentieth century with some beginning efforts to deal with the situation we now face.

We are caught in a curious irony. For although both the unlimited destructive capability and the rapidly expanding potentialities are products of human action, outputs if you will of the human community, there seems to be for each of us and perhaps for all of us a loss of control. It seems increasingly difficult to share in shaping the events which in other important ways are products of our own actions.

In reflecting upon these issues, we shall examine some root notions that may help to set some of the terms for discussing planning, politics, and ethics. I will argue that between planning and politics, politics is primary; and that between politics and ethics, ethics is primary. Within this framework, it will be argued that the emerging disciplines of planning have a critical and essential role in the development of ethics and politics, and therefore urban life.

To start with some commonplace definitions, as my colleague George Pickering put it, "Planning deals with choices; politics deals with choices; but on the other hand, ethics deals with choices." But planning, politics, and ethics deal with choices from somewhat different stances. Planning deals with the clarification of options or possible choices or sets of choices of individuals or groups. It seeks to clarify the field of action, projects or seeks to anticipate those elements in the field that are given or unchangeable (at least by the actors participating in the planned action) and hence, with which the actor or actors must come to terms. It analyzes those elements in the situation which are controllable, the alternative consequences or ends in view, and presents to the actors the options, among which, presumably, a choice will be made and action undertaken.

Politics deals with who gets to make what choices under what circumstances and with what ends in view. Put another way, politics deals with the distribution among groups of persons of the power to act. To the degree that this action is more than impulse and involves the anticipation of consequences, it involves planning. But since planning involves the presentation of options and persons may and frequently do select different options, politics involves the resolution of conflicting plans. A choice is made as to which plans will or will not be acted upon.

As soon as we engage the stuff of politics, we find ourselves asserting that each of us has the right to make some choices. We are unwilling to settle for the distribution of power to act purely on the basis of political accident. We start making claims about the rights of individuals or the rights of the community, and we have engaged the beginning question of ethics.

Ethics deals with right choice or right action or the pursuit of the good. Most positions in ethics assume with planners that there are alternative courses of action and some ground or basis for selecting among them. The clarification of this ground or basis of selection is the task of ethics.

Planning leads at some point to action. Action involves us in interaction with each other, or in politics. The effort to discern right action or action that leads to good ends is the task of ethics.

So far, so good. What could be simpler?

But let us go back over the discussion once more, and not so lightly. For one suspects that within the terms of the discussion, there may be some avenues for exploration.

Planning deals with the clarification of options or possible choices or sets of choices of individuals or groups.

Immediately a number of questions come to mind. Does this mean that all or only some of the options will be clarified or explored? Who decides which options will be explored (a political question), and will the right options be explored (an ethical question)? Whose task is it to clarify the options, what skills are needed, and how will these persons be trained, certified, and employed (the professional or vocational questions)?

Since the clarification of the right options may be related to who decided which options will be clarified, who will do the task, how they are trained, what methods they use, etc., it appears that we are thrown into the political and ethical questions before we can even get the discussion off the ground. That is, we must come to terms with whether or not there are right or wrong options, good or bad choices, and what is the basis for making such distinctions before we can even take the first step in the planning task—the selection of options to explore.

One way out is to suggest that all the options (or all the possible options) are being explored. This is one of the attractions of a matrix. It sets up the categories, the polarities and parameters, and explores the possible interrelationships of a range of variables. Theoretically, all the possible choices within the matrix can be explored. But the key word here is not matrix but *within.*

The Northeast Illinois Plan Commission in developing a set of options to be presented for public discussion used a set of categories that included residential concentration or dispersion, subarea functional integration or specialization, and the number of interchanges within or between subareas, and between subareas and the metropolitan center. These three sets of categories were elaborated into eighteen alternative plans, from which five were selected for presentation to the public.

But in an important sense, these were not an elaboration of eighteen options or even five. The choice of this particular set of categories can be regarded as one option. Another option might have been the exploration of plans to develop an open or racially integrated metropolis. A quite different set of options might have been developed if the explorations had started with the design of institutional structures or forms of community life through which persons might create a widely variegated pattern of land use development.

The point is that the range of options is large, indeed, and the choices within a matrix may not be as important as the selection of the matrix itself.

By and large, city planning through its history has tended to assume that the land-use and technological variables were the "givens" and the forms of community life or the institutions were the "takens." The planning of the new town of Columbia, Maryland, is a rare and interesting alternative. The planning started with the question put to behavioral scientists and institutional specialists (there wasn't an architect in the early planning work group): "What is it you are really trying to achieve in a human community?" This was followed by the question, "What institutional forms do you need to achieve it?" Only after serious exploration of these questions did the land-use and architectural questions get their day in court.

Columbia represents not only a reversal of work process but also of priorities which are increasingly important in our society. Technology has become the driving engine, as Scott Greer said, in an economy in which the decisions are secret and privatized to a very considerable degree. This technology lacks adequate control systems. It is not presently disciplined at crucial points by a meaningful design for community and for the institutions needed to give form to our common life.

As we noted, who decides which options to explore is a political question, and this becomes critical as the planning operations develop.

As the organizational systems for which planning is being

done become larger and more complex, the planning operation tends to become larger also. The work that a few isolated professionals were doing ten years ago is now being done by teams of twenty or thirty or more people. Budgets have increased correspondingly. Planning as it has become more elaborate and internally specialized becomes a function of large-scale organizations. The most elaborate planning operations are in the Pentagon, large corporations, major federal bureaucracies, core cities of our big metropolitan areas, and some specially developed units such as the Penn-Jersey transportation study and Resources for the Future.

It is reasonable to expect that when planning is related to the functioning of a large-scale organization, the selection of options would tend to include those which would extend the control, profitability, efficiency, and security of the organization. Furthermore, the high respect generally accorded to technical competence in our country means that the planning units tend to add legitimacy to the operation of the organization.

These political considerations should alert us when examining the ethical issues to: (1) the built-in biases of large-scale organizations which affect the options that are explored in planning; and (2) the use of the legitimizing power of technical planning to hide the biases or overwhelm opposition in public discussion not by the force of the argument, but by the status accorded to presumed scientific and technical competence. In clarification of options, then, politics is primary over planning and the uses to which planning is put.

An even more complex set of relationships can be seen between the definition of the field of action, the method of inquiry, and the ends or goals of action in both planning and politics. The field of action can be viewed as: (1) a series of disparate or interacting elements which can easily be quantified; (2) a locus of problems or possibilities; (3) a dynamic whole with a variety of polarities and structural aspects in tension; or (4) an historical field with important continuities and elements of uniqueness or unrepeatability in each situation. These views of the field of action tend to vary with the modes of inquiry which are seen as appropriate to the definition of the field. These may include: (1) a rationalistic-logistic mode; (2) a reflexive or problem-solving method; (3) a dialectical mode; or (4) an historical or semantic mode. A variety of combinations or variations of these modes or methods can be seen in the planning literature.

The goals of action also tend to vary with these definitions of field and of appropriate methods of inquiry. Freedom of particular units or systems-adequacy tend to be the goals when a rationalistic-logistic method is used. Reduction of frequency of certain symptoms or realization of particular values tend to be the goals of a problem-solving method. New patterns of relationship or the emergence of new stages of a developmental process tend to be the goals of a dialectical method. Openness to new situations and new meanings or affirmations of certain continuities tend to be associated with an historical or semantic method.

These definitions and methods, and the way they are played out in planning, politics, and ethics deserve more careful attention than can be given here. Richard McKeon, notably in *Freedom and History,* has examined ways in which the method of inquiry and definition of the field tend to vary together in political theory and ethical analysis.

In the historical development of city planning in the United States, there have been many variations on the theme that goals of action are separate, distinct, and private interests of actors, whether persons or corporations. Some have assumed that a hidden hand would work out the good of all. Others argued that there was built-in conflict which over a period of time would assure the survival of the fittest. These views share a notion of planning limited to private actors, individual or corporate, and reject the possibility of a public realm in which a community shares understandings and arrives at collective decisions about a common life which has a quality no private actor alone could achieve.

The problem of methods of inquiry can be seen in efforts to deal with problems of land use. Some ecologists and planners have assumed that it would be possible to arrive at optimums by analyzing statistically the patterns which develop and projecting them. Analysis, it seemed, could stop short of grappling with problems of values experienced by persons. The environment could be treated as an end in itself. The internal development of transportation planning models forced a new confrontation with publicly selected goals. As Melvin Webber pointed out, a transportation system can be designed to meet future land-use needs if you know where the people are going to live and where traffic generators will be located; but these factors depend on the development and location of the transportation system. The circularity is obvious and presents a degree of freedom which can be resolved by public choice which considers the shaping of the environment to meet the needs of persons in the community. The public can relinquish the right to make this choice by capitulating to the pressures of limited-interest groups like highway construction contractors, or it can face the options realizing that there are genuine choices to be made. At this point, the question of the "right" choice becomes too obvious to avoid, and we are in the midst of a political and ethical issue—there is something concrete at stake, miles and miles of it. The internal dialectic even of land-use and transportation planning moves us beyond the mere questions of efficient means to confrontation with problems of ends in view, and the processes of political choice. Once land-use planning gets this far, there is no turning back, except for those who content themselves with mapping flood plains.

The relationship between methods of inquiry, institutional forms, and the ends of action comes into even sharper focus when housing and urban renewal are examined.

Consider for a moment the problem of identity and identification and its impact on the relationship of persons to physical
objects. In a neighborhood to whom does the school belong?
And the streets, the shops, the parks, and even the homes?
"To the people who live there, of course," you say. But how
does their sense of identity expand to include the physical surroundings?

One way is to see in one's surroundings the imprint of labor.
A house becomes your home when it gets your pictures on the
wall, the new paint in the bathroom, screens on the sunporch,
or the other thousand and one little modifications that you make
when you live in a house. Ownership contributes the right to
make modifications without asking anyone for approval, except
perhaps your wife, and adds to the feeling of belonging if you
are happily married.

But let us consider an apartment building, or more particularly public housing. The buildings are designed to be indestruc-
tible and unmalleable. They are managed by professional bureaucrats. Special guards are hired to protect the projects, although as Charles Swibel, head of the Chicago Housing Authority, said in a moment of unusual candor, "They are to protect the property, not the people." The management has the
right to check to see how many people are living in your apartment and how much income you have. In many such developments, there is the awareness that they were built eighteen
stories high in order to avoid the necessity of finding sites outside the walls of the ghetto. That is, they are a part of a com-
pound built in the center of the city for persons who are
regarded as unacceptable neighbors and fellow citizens.

It is not enough to criticize the design as "warehouse *Homo
sapiens*" or alternatively to praise the architect for having
worked out a design which could permit the construction of
high-rise buildings and still meet the federal limits. The point
is that there is no separating the design, location, and style of

construction of facilities from the social institutions which are operative in them. The public housing compounds and over-crowded ghettos in our cities are silent witnesses to the scream-ing racism seen in crowds in Gage Park, Bedford-Stuyvesant, and Hough. If these social institutions are rotten at the core, if they are based on racism and the fundamental denial of the personal worth of the residents, then the physical design must of necessity become symbols of that evil. In biblical language, they might be called "whited sepulchres," or in less biblical language, "brick outcast houses."

There is no building of an optimum environment that does not consider the symbolic value of land-use patterns and facili-ties; and if what they symbolize is rejection, brainwashing, or coercion, then there is no health in them. The safest, most effi-cient, healthiest, and cleanest housing in the country is in Leav-enworth, Kansas, and it even provides security, maximum security.

In housing and urban renewal issues, it is more events than internal developments in planning that are forcing a reconsid-eration of goals, and there is a serious question whether this does not also force a reconsideration of the method of inquiry and definition of the field. It is not surprising to see planning turning from architecture and engineering to social sciences. As this happens, what these sciences have to offer becomes in-creasingly important.

Since World War II in the United States social science has had an increasing concern for the social consequences of values, norms, and meaningful beliefs. This has been accompanied by a growing interest in the sociology of religion, the processes of decision-making, and the power structures of society. It is ob-vious that if human values, norms, and beliefs make a difference in shaping social structure, political processes, economic devel-opment, technology, and even land-use patterns, then those fac-tors which influence values and beliefs—including economic conditions, social roles, the family, religion, and ethics—are significant for dealing with problems of urban development. That this perspective emerged only recently helps to explain why a history of modern city planning which relates the growth of city planning to developments in social theory, value systems, religious institutions, meaningful beliefs, and the power structures and conflicts within American cities has yet to be written.

The new uses of social science and the problems of methodology of planning, politics, and ethics are seen in the efforts to construct games of models of urban development that Meiers, Drake, and others are attempting. In these games, the rationalistic-logistic method is useful in handling quantifiable data, well-known patterns of relationship which can be translated into computer language that permits the handling of large amounts of data in complex sets of relationships.

But there are other aspects to the decision-making process which cannot be reduced to computer language. They call for judgment in areas where the relationships are not fixed and the variables not quantifiable. A problem-solving or reflexive method of thought is required. Persons playing the game of metropolitan development are called upon to make choices, and some of the consequences of these choices are not known until other players of the game make subsequent choices.

The game itself may be said to be designed by persons using a dialectical method in which the various dynamic elements are brought together in ways that illustrate how the various aspects finally contribute to and are in turn shaped by the whole pattern of urban development.

When the players and designers of the game turn to a real city, they face problems of an on-going historical process which includes uniqueness, unrepeatability, and extensions of meaning, requiring appropriate methods of inquiry.

These four methods of analysis which have historic roots in philosophy do not simply collapse into one another. They may not even be reconcilable at the theoretical level. But they are, as McKeon suggests, reconcilable at the practical level. They do combine to make up a game, that is, if people will let them. Some of the critical ethical issues begin to be clarified in the construction of such games. Games of metropolitan development can be played by fewer than a dozen actors. This reflects the concentration of control systems and the limited points at which significant policy discretion can be exercised. If this is so, what of the life space within which the other millions of actors move? What, for instance, is the relationship between large and small units in the society?

Current social science tends to ignore this problem or to make several assumptions which are questionable at best. The Parsonian social system model, for example, tends to assume that everybody has a voice in the parliament, that there is at least some equality of power to participate, and that the basic pattern of relationship is persuasion. This may be applicable to Harvard faculty meetings, but it is not very useful in dealing with some of the critical problems we face in our cities. There are a few men like Dr. Merrill Jackson at the Center for Conflict Resolution who are working on problems of social relationships characterized by hierarchical patterns, powerlessness, and brainwashing or coercion. Yet these are the patterns which characterize the system of race relations in our cities, and have immense importance for forms, methods, and goals of planning. They involve political forms in which the ethical issues are crucial.

Hannah Arendt in her suggestive diagnosis argues that both the public and the private realm have collapsed into a maze of necessity and manipulation on the one hand and false intimacy on the other. The creation, expansion, and enrichment of the public realm calls for institutional reconstruction and the development of qualities of integrity, courage, and openness in our ethical life. Some important thinkers are working along this line, including John Seeley, who has been looking at the nature of leadership and authority, and the problems of internal and external control.

These concerns come into focus in a question posed by a Negro youth on 47th Street who was discussing some community problems. He finally said, "Is this somebody else's pool game? Or do I also hold a cue?"

As the central control systems of large-scale bureaucracies become stronger, with even the voting process in the central cities dominated by administrative patronage, the rationalistic-logistic style of planning is extended in ways that treat this youth as a pool ball. Even our language taken from established social science strips away personhood. "Culturally disadvantaged" and "economically deprived" are labels that reduce expectation of responsiveness and justify coercive extensions of the bureaucratic control systems. Even the "helping" professions extend hierarchical relationships while making the pill easier to swallow.

In these relationships, the ethical issues central to politics and planning become clearer. Ethical issues which are at the heart of the very existence of a city have come home recently to a group of eighty young corporation lawyers in Chicago who are working in eight different churches in the slums with legal advice programs. They started out providing case services, but as they got involved with people, they discovered that there are substantial numbers who feel that the processes of the law are not for them. "The courts just chop you up if you get caught in them," is a frequent judgment based on more than a little experience.

The lack of procedural justice for the black or the poor, the inability to get redress of grievances, tears apart the very fabric of the minimum levels of affirmation in the society. These lawyers have discovered that the laws do favor the landlord over the tenant, the creditor over the debtor. These young lawyers are concerned about the question of what happens when a substantial body of people in the heart of a city feel that it is no longer their city in any meaningful sense; that the laws belong to somebody else; that the system that includes the politicians, the cops, the bankers, and the courts, and, yes, the planners, is somebody else's system.

These illustrations point to the absence of the minimum level of consensus or affirmation of certain basic ethical norms which may be essential to the very survival of the city. Racism illustrates a system of mutual rejections and denials. If we are going to talk meaningfully about the kind of communities we are intending or planning, then we must grapple with the ethical issues involved in finding a minimum set of universals necessary to sustain a complex urban community, that may still permit pluralism and diversity to flourish. These are ethical issues which are primary in any discussion of politics and planning.

To reiterate the argument, in the relation between planning, politics, and ethics, ethics is primary over politics, and politics is primary over planning. Modes of inquiry, definitions of the field of action, and goals pursued tend to vary with all three.

It needs to be seen, however, that the exercise and disciplines of planning have an important contribution to make to the development of any adequate ethic. At some point, there is need for the clarification of genuine options. Regardless of the theoretical perspective used, there are points at which actors must encounter each other, share interpretations of the situation and appropriate lines of action, and work out the problem of what is to be done. Apart from this, there can only be a self-destructive nihilism. When parts of our society are denied the opportunity to engage in the action, denied the resources to understand, plan for, and shape the action, then we can expect the kinds of protest that veto not only what might be but even what is.

We need planning that enriches a variety of centers of action, not just the upper floors of corporate skyscrapers or City Hall.

We need planning that enables us to state intentions, clarify a range of options, and open up public spheres of interpretation and interaction. Forms of planning can help to push the decision-making processes of society to deal with genuine choices, to take account of the intractable stuff of things, and the open responsiveness of persons.

We stand at a critical point in the history of our country when we need to dream a new American dream that is at once more inclusive and more pluralistic. We stand between the mushroom cloud and the lunar probe, between a wide range of terror and hope, between fascination with our new possibilities and a desire to escape from them. We are called to a fresh, searching reflection and analysis. This is a job to which the major institutions and professions need to commit themselves.

We need to reaffirm what we want to conserve and to consider carefully what we want to create. Hopefully, we may develop a planetary society embracing great cities containing many communities of meaning that have passed beyond the point where, like an intoxicated man, they stagger from crisis to crisis struggling to recover their balance. Instead, our cities may have developed that internal control and balance that enables them to move with grace and form into scarcely dreamed-of realms of art and science and politics, of personal development and meaningful community life.

Comment on
Hallett

CALVIN S. HAMILTON
Director, Los Angeles City Planning Commission

Chicago—Los Angeles; Molotov cocktails, violence, housing discrimination, charges of police brutality, minority ghettos; these are the ingredients of these long, hot summers. We planners in Los Angeles last summer were faced with a sort of instant urban renewal. As Dr. Hallett said, "There is an urgency about ideas that influence events. And one senses a new urgency in the discussion of planners. For the academic game of exploring possible choices has been linked with the political game of acting on choices, and this sets in motion anxiety, and concern about making the right choices."

Speaking from the perspective of the ninth largest urban region in the world, I can assure you that there is an urgency about the issues to which he addresses his paper. If anyone here still thinks city planning can be limited to physical planning, he has clearly missed the entire meaning of Hallett's paper, and in fact, of this entire proceeding. What do I mean by the urgency of human values, norms, and beliefs as they shape planning in Los Angeles?

You've all heard of Watts! After being Director of Planning for Pittsburgh, Watts looked to me like a nice suburban residential community. The streets are paved, it has better parks than all of Pittsburgh, larger schools on ample sites, wide major thoroughfares. But it seethes. Obviously, the reality of conflict, dissatisfaction, and tension in Watts won't go away because of a multicolored land-use plan, or even a workable program. It is clear that the future of Watts and all of southeast Los Angeles is tied to economic and social problems, psychological identity, open housing, and all the other problems facing minority and disenfranchised ghettos in our major cities.

How are we to achieve a regional planning program that is opposed or seriously questioned by local politicians, the Birchers and their fellow believers, and uninformed or apathetic citizens; a program covering 20,000 square miles, ten million people, and roughly 200 political entities? The physical planning will be the easiest step; the tough assignment, as Hallett said, is "the nature of the political institutions within which planning is carried on."

The San Fernando Valley has one million people, almost five times the land area of Pittsburgh, and most of those one million people couldn't care less about Watts. I know, I've asked many of them. They feel alienated from the central city (even though they are a part of Los Angeles); they feel largely alienated from government and planning, which they feel is not responsive to their individual desires, and frustrated by a lack of communication between planners and citizens as to their needs, ideas, and values.

Angelenos who live in the mountains want to be left alone; they want the mountains saved from the bulldozers and high rise. Everyone who drives wants and needs his own car, but many can't afford even one, let alone two or three autos.

When we are looking at goals we are looking at the value system. How do you create a vehicle so that the citizens of this vast area can: first, express their fundamental human needs and desires; second, obtain a sense of participation in the determination of ultimate goals—what kind of urban civilization do they want in southern California?; third, sense an opportunity to follow through in the process of developing policies and plans to achieve these goals.

In Los Angeles we have organized this program in the following way:

1. We have divided the total conceptual goals program into four areas: human and social determinants; economic determinants; physical determinants; technological determinants.

2. We have considered the input of citizens in determining these goals on several levels. *First,* we have organized technical and professional groups of specialized orientation, such as an interreligious council; Jews, Catholics, Protestants, and others; physical environmentalists (architects, landscape architects, etc.); aerospace industry; social scientists, etc. Each of these we are asking to staff their groups full-time, independent of our department staff. *Second,* we work with economically or socially representative groups, such as labor unions, chambers of commerce, and Leagues of Women Voters. *Third,* we use geographically oriented groups, representing an occupational, economic, and social spectrum, such as neighborhood congregations. These will be discussing the results of the preliminary findings by the professional groups, first in their local group, then with the neighborhood churches, service clubs, local chambers of commerce, and neighborhood property owners' associations. The most difficult task is to get cross-fertilization between neighborhood groups such as the Negro ghetto and white affluent middle-class neighborhood groups.

You ask a citizen to "participate in the planning process," and he doesn't know what you are talking about. You ask him to help determine, with a variety of fellow citizens, what kind of urban civilization he wants in the future, and he responds favorably and generally with enthusiasm. For example, this is the first time that the three major religious groups have focused on a common task (except for the racial issue). So many have said: "This is the first time we have ever been asked by government to help shape our own destiny."

The Los Angeles Goals Project is designed to let the citizens decide what objectives should be explored. Out of this exploration will come their determination of alternatives. The most important part of this process is to emphasize the inherent needs, the capabilities, the desires of the individual in his many-faceted relationship to the city, and to shape, hopefully, a future that allows for the development of each individual.

Another part of this project is to identify the principal issues that face Los Angeles, the present policies of the city and the region concerning these issues (on some issues there is no policy), and to come to grips with the implications of the preferred goals for public policy.

In our opinion, city planning must allow the citizens a major voice in selecting the objectives for future study. We must, as planners, break away from simply planning land use, and must totally embrace, as fundamental guides for our work, the goals, values, and beliefs of the citizens. These are fundamental before we can meaningfully study alternatives. We must break away from the planners' imagination of what we think the citizens want.

I strongly feel that planners have a responsibility to help carry to the citizens and their designated and elected representatives the moral and ethical issues of our urban civilization. We must pose the problems as we see them, stimulate, delineate, clarify. We must build the mechanism for a pluralistic approach to the development of citizen involvement in planning preparation.

Only after consulting as many people as possible can the planner be assured that the plan adopted will be that of the people, will reflect their choices, and will be sound ethically, politically, and technically.

This type of plan, with everyone involved in the process, will stand a much better chance of being effectuated than a plan that is simply presented for citizen approval after being prepared by the planning agency alone.

X

Moshe Safdie

Architect for Habitat '67
Montreal exposition, 1967

Habitat '67

Of the forces which are bringing about change in our urban patterns, some are obvious and much discussed: population growth, changing economic base, and general expansion of the economy. Some are more subtle and have to do with the desires and aspirations of the population.

We want to live in a small intimate community; yet we want to have all the amenities of the great metropolis. We want a dwelling with privacy, identity; yet we want the setting of a rich social life. We want to be near open country; yet we let the city spread endlessly. We want all the things suburbia has to offer; but we also want the amenities of the downtown area. What we really want is Utopia, but we are not clear about what Utopia is. The planner's and the architect's task today is to resolve these contradictions.

There is, of course, no economic reason why, particularly on this continent, we should not achieve Utopia. There is no reason why every family should not live in a spacious dwelling, why every dwelling should not have a view and sunlight. There is no reason why a pedestrian should ever have to cross the path of a car, nor why a car should ever have to stop for a red light.

Five decades ago, the wealthy North American descending

to the slums within his city disassociated himself—he did not feel responsible. Twenty years later, descending to the slums, he did not feel responsible but he did feel compassionate. Today, he has learned to share a moral responsibility—he cannot disassociate.

The political realities of our time add another force which we must satisfy in conceiving our Utopian environment. In the past, it was possible to consider the environment in terms of national economy and resources. Today, it is essential to consider these in terms of global economy and resources. Just as it is no longer possible today within a country to justify an extremely uneven distribution of wealth which results in slums on the one hand and mansions on the other, so it is becoming impossible to justify extreme wealth and prosperity in one country and poverty in another. As we have evened out the distribution of wealth within national boundaries in the past, we are now entering a phase in which this is taking place globally. Consequently, the need for economy in using land, labor, and natural resources becomes even more critical. The image of Utopia must have universal application. To the planner and the architect today, economy is a moral obligation.

But do we have the image?

Our democracy operates through selection. Our environment is a result of selection and inertia. To exercise selection, there must be an image so simple and clear that a pressure is created upon our system to achieve it. After the Second World War, we had such an image in North America. It was the image of the single-family house, detached on its own lot in the green suburb. So simple, clear, and strong was the image that our entire system of legislation and of financing was transformed to make it possible to obtain our dream. But the image was limited. It did not take into account many facets which are essential aspects of the environment's totality and survival. It did not take account of the concentration of business and industry. It did not take account of our social needs and the variety demanded in daily life. It did not relate to our land resources or to our transportation systems. But the image was clear and it was pushed through. Today, through experience, we have become aware that we must evolve a more concentrated environment; that we must transform technically to achieve economies in the construction of the environment, such as we have achieved in other industries through mass production and automation. But we are unable to exercise selection because we have no clear image of what we want.

We must explore in two directions: the potentials of urban systems on a regional scale—the pattern of settlement that determines the environment. This involves transportation systems; the relationship between communities; between the open country and urbanized country; between industrial and agricultural facilities. From these considerations must grow the new form of our regional cities.

And then, we must explore the scale of construction itself. No longer can we think of the city as a two-dimensional pattern consisting of detached buildings. The city is evolving into a continuous three-dimensional system in which all the land uses that make up the environment are integrated. A mass-produced system must be designed to satisfy an infinity of "structures," that is: stability, sunlight, air movement, circulation, grouping of elements, service, sense of location, and others.

In the process of achieving this, we are undergoing two revolutions. One is in the field of transportation, and the other is in the field of construction. The revolution in the field of transportation will expand the mobility of man. It will expand the limits of the size of cities from the one-hour travel limit of 20 or 30 miles to 300 or 400 miles. This will make it possible for the regional city, made up of many smaller interdependent communities, to group 10 or 20 million people sharing all facilities. It will make it possible to integrate the agricultural and industrial segments of the environment, as well as the open recreational space, with the built-up urban space. These new means of surface transportation will be the primary determinants of the regional urban pattern.

The development of three-dimensional building systems would permit the reorganization of the land uses within the environment from a two-dimensional pattern to a three-dimensional pattern in space. This would permit a more concentrated environment without losing the amenities which we consider essential.

It is with this conviction that Habitat '67 has evolved, and it was in recognition of this that three Canadian governments, federal, provincial, and municipal, who are building Habitat, have supported it. They have considered it as a research project where the aspects of a mass-produced building system will be explored. As a building system, Habitat '67 attempts to find and offer solutions to the problems of the environment today:

1. Habitat attempts to provide appropriately for families within a high-density development and to preserve the amenities of the single-family house in a multistory urban structure.

2. Habitat attempts to integrate within a community all the urban functions: residential, commercial, industrial, institutional, and recreational. These functions are rearranged from the conventional city pattern into a three-dimensional structure with each function attempting to complement the others.

3. Habitat attempts to introduce a building system which utilizes mechanization and mass production methods already used by other industries toward the achievement of a more economical construction of higher quality, capable of production in volume to answer global housing needs.

4. Habitat is located so that it will affect the growth of the city of Montreal. It is a beachhead, a catalyst on the riverfront which would accelerate the redevelopment of the waterfront of Montreal and bring about the reopening of the city toward the St. Lawrence River, now separated by industry and the habor.

Typical housing and commercial development shown in cross section

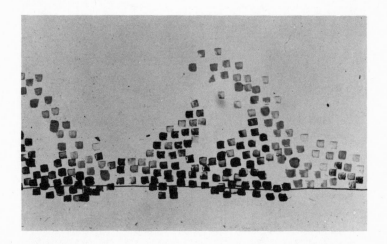

A "ventilated" manmade hillside of housing units, shown schematically. Shopping and public facilities in the center at ground level

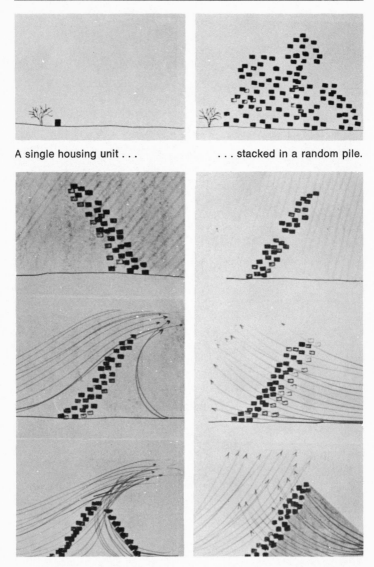

A single housing unit . . .   . . . stacked in a random pile.

The architect's sketches, showing wind, rain and sun in relation to
the basic Habitat sloping hillside of housing units

Habitat '67 at the Montreal World's Fair. Over 200 prefabricated units at a density of 110 units per acre plus public facilities. Moshe Safdie & David, Barott, Boulva, Associated Architects, 3 Place Ville-Marie, Montreal, Quebec

The most imaginative recent attempt at prefabrication. Concrete stalls stacked into an eleven-story "hillside" for EXPO '67

XI

W. L. Rogers

Aerojet-General Corporation

Aerospace Systems Technology and the Creation of Environment

It is amazing and somewhat frightening to consider the rate at which our environment is increasing in complexity. By adding two states to our union, the number of political interfaces on the state level has increased almost 2,500-fold. By adding one new cabinet post to the existing ten, the number of departmental interfaces has increased by eleven-fold, not by 10 per cent. In all areas one can see that each component added to the political or physical environment increases its complexity factorially and not linearly, and correlation and control of this proliferation of components require greater and greater analytical skills as well as much more rapid evaluation techniques.

As scientific knowledge and industrial and agricultural practices increase in sophistication, greater and greater specialization of the skills of individuals, as well as the activities and products of regions, states, and nations will be induced. One can foresee a time when North America and Australia could be the breadbasket of the world, while nations such as Japan, Great Britain, and Germany would be primarily suppliers of industrial goods with relatively small capability of supplying agricultural products to the world, or even to themselves. Hopefully, proper combinations of specialized individuals or regions may be integrated to provide an ever-increasing per capita output of goods and services, leading to higher standards of living and improvements of the welfare of mankind.

If we define environment to be all things outside of an individual's skin, then we would include all of the political, social, and economic aspects of man's relationship to himself, as well as the physical, geological, and ecological characteristics of the planet. Changes or progress in man's knowledge and practices may affect any or all of the components of the environment and, as specialization increases, the number of interfaces between specialties will be increased. Of equal importance, changes in technology and in national and international social institutions will undoubtedly alter the balance of environmental components, so that entirely new problems will develop, for which there are no historical solutions.

We can readily see that increases in urban population density, related to changes in agricultural technology, as well as increases in specialization of individual skills, have presented knotty problems in such areas as urban transportation, law enforcement, garbage collection, and public administration. Examples of the disadvantages that accompany advances in industrial, agricultural, and service industries are numerous. However, without enumerating them, we can recognize that, if it is allowed to grow uncultivated or uncontrolled, the structure of the environment of tomorrow has only an infinitesimally small probability of approaching an optimum for the welfare of mankind. We must therefore devise means of assuring that expansion of technological capabilities and material output are not achieved at the expense of social welfare; and, as long as man is restricted to living on this planet, or even in the solar system, we must husband our resources and not pursue present advantages at too great future costs. We are rapidly beginning to recognize that future generations will have to pay a stiff price in actual expenditures as well as in imputed losses of productivity and recreational value for the pollution of our lakes and streams resulting from attempts to maximize the profits of some industries by using these natural resources as dumping grounds.

To survive in today's nationally and internationally competitive markets, industrial firms must make maximum use of modern managerial tools. Each firm must solve its special technical, manufacturing, and marketing problems in a timely and economic fashion or be relegated to the fate of the dinosaur and disappear from the scene. Our successful, large, diversified companies daily demonstrate their special problem-solving capabilities. The same capabilities can and must be brought to bear to solve the present and future problems of our environment.

The aerospace industry has solved vast and extremely complicated problems using what is termed "systems technology." Although this technique has received great attention in recent years, it is neither new nor peculiar to the aerospace industry.

In 1930, RCA used the systems approach to plan the development of a television broadcast system. The Bell Telephone Laboratories began to use the term "systems engineering," in today's meaning, in the early forties. It is also likely that some form of systems engineering was used to construct the pyramids and the Roman aqueducts.

As used in the aerospace industry, this old but new technology follows the general pattern of: (1) establishment of mission requirements; (2) derivation of general system requirements; (3) separation of the system into identifiable components and subsystems; (4) system analysis to identify optimum combinations of subsystems; (5) establishment of design and operational criteria; (6) testing to determine that system objectives have been met; and finally, (7) manufacturing, assembling, and operating the system.

In many cases, several alternate systems may be synthesized to see which will meet the mission requirements. Final selection of the most desirable system is then made, based on economy, timeliness, or other constraints.

Separation of the system into definable components is one of the more critical aspects of systems engineering. The purpose of this procedure is to display the component parts in such a fashion that the influence of the characteristics and performance of the components on the overall performance of the system may be quantitatively identified. It is then possible to construct a model of the system, and by varying the characteristics of the subsystems, arrive at an optimally feasible over-all system. The same model may also be used to indicate desired areas of advanced research and development for which no mission has yet been defined.

Systems analysis of environmental problems will undoubtedly uncover many areas of research, independent of specific missions, but leading toward the eventual improvement of our understanding and control of the environment.

Special attention must be paid to the interfaces between subsystems. If varying one subsystem produces a square peg as its interface with the adjoining subsystem, there must be a square hole in the mating component to receive that peg, or both components must be varied until a proper match is achieved.

As one might expect, maximizing the performance of any single subsystem or all of the subsystems does not necessarily provide optimum characteristics for the system as a whole. Only by judicious trade-offs of subsystem characteristics do we reach the desired optimum.

From this brief and simplified description of systems engineering we can see that systems technology is really only a methodical analysis of the vehicle by which we hope to reach some objective. It permits quantification of the effects of variations within the system and hopefully permits objective selection of the best feasible solution of a complex problem. When we speak of utilizing systems technology to create the future environment we can use the word "create" only in the sense that the end product is derived by the skillful and systematic use of logic and computational tools, rather than by evolution.

Whether one is considering development of a new product line or a new weapons system, there is a lag between the conception of the goal and its accomplishment. The lead time required for marketing a new commercial air transport may be five years or more. Similarly, space exploration goals have lead times of five to ten years. Where disparate and diverse disciplines are required, where research programs must be accomplished to achieve technical feasibility, lead times may be measured in decades rather than years. Solution of environmental problems, or achievement of environmental goals, will call upon almost every established discipline taught in the colleges and universities of the country. Almost without exception, research programs must be instituted in every discipline, to provide qualitative and quantitative knowledge for understanding the environmental components and eventually establishing and accomplishing environmental goals. We can expect, therefore, that lead times in achieving environmental goals will be long and that much effort and money must be expended before these goals may be reached.

Our very lack of knowledge of our environmental problems is a serious deterrent in the solution of these problems. If we do not know that use of some insecticides is deleterious to health we have little motivation to eliminate their use. Even worse, we may not recognize the cumulative effect of air or stream pollution until streams are practically barren of fish or respiratory diseases increase to an alarming extent. Water shortages are most noticed when water is rationed. Air pollution is only "shop talk" for city planners until you fly over your city and see the noxious blanket that obscures the buildings.

One cannot condemn the average citizen for his lack of interest in the vigorous pursuit of environmental control. Human beings cannot be expected to rise up in arms over the sulfur dioxide content of the atmosphere unless they are informed of its effect and the degree to which their activities increase this pollutant. The key to overcoming apparent public apathy toward undesirable trends in our environment is first, the identification of these trends and then judicious public dissemination of information on their character and effects.

This requires an enlightened view on the part of the body politic and industry. Our elected and appointed officials *must* cease to pass on inherited practices and procedures which prevent paying more than lip service to improving our environment. They must enlist the aid of, rather than fight, lobbies of special groups attempting to maximize the benefits of their subsectors of our society. Firms and industries must be informed of the potential costs in taxes and lost revenues associated with a deteriorating environment, whether their activity is a root cause of the deterioration, or whether they are only remotely contributors. There must be a rapprochement between political administrators and industrial managers so that the vast technical capability of the United States industry may be called upon to point the way toward a better environment and the skills of our political leaders may be used to accomplish desirable and feasible environmental goals.

Governor Pat Brown of California took a giant first step in achieving this rapprochement. In early 1965 he enlisted the services of North American Aviation Company, Lockheed Missiles & Space Company, Space General Corporation, and Aerojet-General Corporation, all systems-oriented aerospace firms, to study four critical and urgent problems of the California environment. These studies included: the design of a statewide waste management system; a system to provide for the detection, rehabilitation, and institutionalization of the juvenile delinquent and criminal population; an information system using advanced techniques to provide timely advanced planning for public needs; and a complete, integrated transportation system. Their goals were to anticipate requirements and developments over the next thirty to fifty years. These studies were an experimental effort to use systems technology to solve socioeconomic problems.

In Aerojet's Waste Management Study, we could readily identify sources of agricultural, industrial, and domestic waste. It was clear that by redesign of existing plants, control of design of future plants, or development of special waste disposal systems, much of the effluent and residues of California's industries and agriculture could be eliminated or rendered less noxious. But at what permissible cost? Over what time period? By what means of administration and control? Most important of all, to what degree?

These questions could not be answered by rejuggling the variables or developing new mathematics or new models, because no standard optimum could be clearly stated. We certainly could and did develop plans for improving components of the environment. Hopefully, this subsystem optimization will be in the direction of improving the total system.

I think we have made progress toward most effectively utilizing systems technology to solve socioeconomic problems. These are not sacred words, but those of you who may contemplate systems technology as a tool for creating our future environment might consider these suggestions:

First, the establishment of goals for our changing environment will be politically dictated—and here I use the word political in the Greek sense of: "the exercise of the rights and privileges by which the individuals of the state seek to determine or control its public policy." Under these circumstances, the elected or appointed representatives of the people must follow the example of California's Governor Brown, and solicit the assistance of organizations experienced in the management of large, complex, multidisciplinary programs. One of the keys to effective systems management and systems analysis is the availability within an organization of highly competent specialists in all of the disciplines pertinent to the system's requirements, together with systems-oriented generalists capable of integrating the output of these specialists and guiding the program toward its objectives, with a minimum of digression and wasted effort.

Second, and departing from aerospace systems engineering, mission requirements must be determined before establishing the mission. This probably requires a little explaining. Aerospace mission requirements are generally based on the need or desire to accomplish a specific goal such as "place a three-man vehicle in a 200-mile circular orbit to perform these specific experiments." The mission is either currently technically feasible or will be feasible after specific research and development programs have been successfully accomplished. Economic and time constraints are added in later trade-off studies.

In establishing environmental goals, it is necessary first to determine what is socially and politically feasible—and this includes the effects of the program's costs on the existing socioeconomic structure. Only then can a mission be clearly stated, and systems requirements established and analyzed. Except for severely hazardous environmental changes, the element of time will probably be considered to be less important than costs.

Third, the validity and effectiveness of a systems-engineered environment will be directly proportional to the degree to which we can quantify social parameters such as health, convenience, esthetics, and happiness. This is not a signal to throw up your hands in dismay. It means that we must continue or even accelerate our research programs in public health, psychology, economics, and the like so that we may clearly state in terms of dollars or longevity or per capita expenditures on mental institutions the effect of changes in our environment.

Secretary Udall has said, "We can have abundance and an unspoiled environment if we are willing to pay the price." I might add, the price we pay for a spoiled environment may be infinitely larger than the expense of bringing to bear all of our skills and technology to determine what we can achieve in improving our environment and then taking the steps to make it that way.

XII

George T. Bogard

General Electric Company

The Role of Large-Scale Enterprise in the Creation of Better Environment

Creating a better living environment through the present process of development and construction has failed to keep pace with a highly industrialized society in a climate of rapidly changing technology and a steadily expanding economy. Building is the second largest industry after food, and the only major industry failing to participate in the greatest economic boom the world has ever known. This industry has been on a long-term plateau for more than a decade, building 1.5 million housing units annually, plus or minus 100,000. The two things that continue to rise are the cost of developed land and the cost of construction. Increased values, at least in the eyes of never-more-prosperous potential customers, just have not materialized. Thus housing's share of consumer spendable income continues to lose out to more attractive goods and services.

Our concern as both citizens and members of a major business operation, interdependent with the community, extends to such things as: (a) a rapidly growing crime rate (500 per cent faster than population gains); (b) the inability of our educational system to keep pace with explosive demands; (c) inefficient and unsatisfactory municipal services; (d) the breakdown in public

transportation and circulation within cities; (e) wasteful and in-
effective land use; (f) the failure of the building process to progress into the twentieth century along with other major industries (it is still largely a handicraft industry, with little cost
control, little innovation, and a signal lack of progress); (g) the
failure of cultural recreational opportunities to keep pace with
increased leisure time and growing affluence; (h) inadequate
health, sanitation, and medical facilities to serve a rapidly expanding and longer-lived population; (i) rapidly skyrocketing
costs of all amenities, services, and construction; (j) steadily accelerating per capita tax costs for community services.

We do not believe that the federal government should assume all responsibility for meeting these challenges; or that the
problems are too monumental for private enterprise to tackle;
or that either can find the solutions alone. But there is strong
evidence that the many relatively small entrepreneurs engaged
in building and developing cannot bring about an evolution in
building process and the creation of vastly better environmental values.

A year-long study by a carefully selected team, comprising
six men trained in different disciplines, with diverse business
and professional backgrounds, resulted in certain findings and
conclusions which have led General Electric to consider a new
role in the building and development field. After careful observation and investigation of the lack of progress in meeting
the problems of building and development, it became clear that
progress was essentially blocked by the interaction of prolifer-
ating, restrictive, inflexible planning and zoning regulations;
archaic, conflicting codes and inspection practices; union work
rules and limitations; the highly fragmented character of the
construction industry (thousands of small firms, with limited financial capacity and unequal bargaining power); unwillingness
of mortgage lenders to support builders who might want to in-
novate and experiment.

In other words, the cards are effectively stacked to discourage innovation, experimentation, and development of new systems and techniques. Regardless of what a builder-developer might want to do, he could not risk a 5 or 10-million-dollar mistake because, in all likelihood, it would put him out of business. As a matter of fact, practically no long-range, city-scale development plan can be seriously undertaken because of a lack of financial staying power in the face of unforeseen adverse market conditions.

Recognizing the problems and finding widespread agreement among experienced leaders of the building industry was comparatively easy. What to do about the roadblocks to progress was something else! In considering alternative solutions, the conclusion was soon reached that a large, diversified, financially strong enterprise, with broad interests running throughout the entire fabric of a community, might contribute importantly to the development of new prototype communities which would offer more human values, greater living satisfaction, at less investment cost and lower per capita operating costs than existing cities afford. Here appeared to be an excellent opportunity to serve society, assist government in meeting its goals, and move the building industry toward transition and growth, while demonstrating that a large, diversified company has an important role to play in the quality of urban life.

From all past experience we are conscious of the value of a systems approach to solving complex problems. To put it another way: "If the end results are established and carefully defined, a kind of reverse critical path can then be followed which identifies all necessary inputs and required sequences of application to produce desired results." Therefore, if we can decide on what constitutes a better community, or know exactly what values we want to end up with, it should be less difficult to create the kind of city people would really like to have, and at costs far below those we are now forced to pay.

We believe great economies can be achieved in building planned communities. Such communities offer opportunities for new products and systems based on new technology and new understanding in areas such as information storage, retrieval, processing, display; transportation and communications; individual and community safety; health and education; new materials and construction techniques; better land planning and use. The success of new cities will, of course, depend on offering superior environmental and human values in competition with other housing alternatives—a classic competitive situation.

A diversified enterprise such as General Electric is equipped by financial, technical, manufacturing, and marketing capabilities to meet this king-size challenge. Contributions that could be made include: (a) the necessary financial staying power to undertake a 15 to 20-year development program of a city of more than 100,000 population; (b) wide diversity of technologies and engineering capabilities which can be brought to bear on design and construction problems; (c) experience and facilities for broad-scale research and planning and long practice with systems analysis; (d) a product and manufacturing scope which covers almost the complete spectrum of community services, embracing power production and distribution; water management; waste, trash, and sewage disposal; transportation systems and traffic control; communications—educational, entertainment, and security; information accumulation, processing, and control; educational systems—print and electronics; medical electronics systems; indoor climate control; environmental lighting; building materials; household service functions; financing—conditional sales, mortgages, and leasing; and electric product service and maintenance; (e) experienced management trained to cope with large and complex projects; (f) acknowledged responsibility, integrity, and public confidence.

With all these things going for us, it appears promising to direct those resources toward creating prototype communities on a larger scale and, hopefully, of a quality not as yet achieved; to provide tens of thousands of homes (probably no less than 30,000) characterized by a diversity of incomes, occupations, cultures, age groups, and interests; to provide for the full cycle of life with a wide range of educational, recreational, entertainment, and cultural opportunities; to create basic employment for the majority of the residents who would be within easy commuting distance to a wide variety of employment; to provide better answers to the problems of air and water pollution, waste and sewage disposal, transportation and circulation within the community; to add a high order of beauty and esthetic appeal to structures, public and private lands; to improve the efficiency of municipal services in order to deliver a lower per capita operating cost. For example: an information utility performing essential functions for municipal operations and sharing time with commerce, industry, schools, and hospitals in the community.

The kind of planned, multifunctional community on a city scale that is envisioned means more than physical planning, mechanics, and esthetics—it must incorporate economic and social planning to make it a viable self-defined, self-sufficient city. Thus far, most of the so-called planned communities are a collection of physically planned neighborhoods or villages. Most lack economic planning with provisions for primary employment and hardly any are very sophisticated in their approach to human or social planning. This is an era in which builder-developers and industry have the least knowledge and experience. We must look to the experienced planners, sociologists, anthropologists, and psychologists for guidance. I am sure that no one has all the answers, but by a process of trial and (I hope) not too many errors, we should be able to achieve large-scale improvements.

In carrying out our aim of creating a better urban life, there are important by-products to be achieved along the way. What is badly needed is an accelerated evolution in the building process comparable to that which has been under way in all other major industries. Without added product features which appeal to customers, without cost reduction programs which result in lower prices and higher values (the refrigerator is an example), the building industry is pricing itself out of business at a rate which has stymied any growth in volume for more than ten years. Working with the Bureau of Standards, trade unions, contractors, architects, and consulting engineers, we believe that General Electric can develop a modular concept of components in electromechanical systems which can reduce in-place costs of all essential services provided in new construction. If a transition can be made from material specifications to performance specifications, it will greatly accelerate the introduction of new materials and construction techniques into the building process.

Although we have confidence that all can be accomplished, there is a large element of risk; a likelihood of making mistakes costly to correct; the uncertain element of time; difficulty in securing understanding and approval; accepting the possibility of substantial losses. We still believe the stakes are so great for the future health, progress, and prosperity of our country, and the continued development of our society, that it is appropriate for a large-scale enterprise to utilize all its resources to develop a better environment for living.

XIII

John T. Howard

Department of City and Regional Planning
Massachusetts Institute of Technology

Some Thoughts on the Future

I think we have learned quite a good deal about man and about environment, about past and present man, about present and future environment. We've learned something about the interaction between man and environment. We, who began, at least, as physical planners, and always did think that our tampering with the physical environment had a bearing on the needs and wants of man, have been comforted to find out that this is, indeed, apparently so, and that what we have been involved with is of some significance and importance. By Dr. Dubos and by others, we have been assured that man is infinitely varied, infinitely various, that this degree of variation is influenced by his immediate environment, that in terms of his potentials for adapting, he's about the same as he has been for the last fifty thousand years, and that for the next fifty thousand he will presumably remain about the same as he is now, in genetic composition and in his capacity to interact with his environment. We have learned that although man is astonishingly adaptable, many of these adaptations occur at a price, and that he has the privilege of responsible choice for his destiny.

We have learned a good many things in these three days, but probably the most outstanding thing is that the various disciplines that are met here to consult on this topic share a rather

GREED

extensive body of ignorance. We have derived no prescriptions, no final answers, nor do we expect to in 1967, either. We do not expect the members of the many other disciplines and fields with whom we are seeking to consult to be able to tell us just exactly what we ought to be accomplishing, nor just how. But there are a few things that are, it seems to me, derivable from what we have been listening to. Some, perhaps, are new to us; most, I believe, confirm the way we have been previously thinking.

If we are to look to the next fifty years as a time of moving forward, of bringing about improvement, it seems to me that there are a number of what might be called national policies, consensuses, which need to be brought into being in this country. I do not mean federal government policies or consensuses. I mean points of view, attitudes, which need to be generally shared by all our people if we are going to succeed in moving in the directions that we think are important. Pre-eminent among these is the necessity of dealing with poverty, inequality of opportunity, and social injustice. Obviously, such policies are not the private property of the planning profession, or of any profession. They are worth pursuing for their own sake, but even the physical planner who refuses to become a social and an economic planner, who recognizes that his competence is only in dealing with the relatively small-scale physical environment, must recognize that we shall not be able to deal with the purely physical urban and metropolitan environment until this social and economic problem has been reduced.

I have another suggestion. In view of the lag in American society and in the planning profession, in developing either the goals or the methodology for devising an optimum environment, I suggest that this country needs to slow down. I propose, as a step essential to the future well-being of this country, a policy of population limitation. Our present rate of growth is jeopardizing even limited accommodation between men and their en-

Appendixes

A: Matrix Tables

B: Program of Portland Conference

I. Matrix of Controllable Variables

	Climate	Air	Water	Solid Wastes	Noise	Intake	Safety	Privacy	Number	Density	Duration	Frequency
Climate												
Air												
Water												
Solid wastes												
Noise												
Intake												
Safety												
Privacy												
Number												
Density												
Duration												
Frequency												

Meaningful combinations of any number of the variables can be sought by using the technique known as principle component analysis. With this technique it is possible to identify clusters of variables that tend to vary simultaneously. The matrix can then be subjected to factor analysis. Furthermore, the large number of variables to be manipulated can frequently be reduced by the application of conical correlation analysis.

II. Technological Functions Matrix

	Climate	Air	Water	Solid Wastes	Noise	Intake	Safety	Privacy	Number	Density	Dura-tion	Fre-quency
Home												
School												
Shopping												
Commuting												
Work												
Recreation (spirit)												
Leisure and re-creation												
Experiences of nature												
Healing												

Using combinations that have been derived from analysis of the controllable variables, it is possible to relate functions to variables.

III. Trade-Off Matrix (Relation of Function to Function)

	Home	School	Shopping	Commuting	Work	Re-creation (Spirit)	Leisure and Recreation	Experiences of Nature	Healing
Home									
School									
Shopping									
Commuting									
Work									
Re-creation (spirit)									
Leisure and recreation									
Experiences of nature									
Healing									

Only by such sophisticated mathematical and statistical techniques as interactive matrix manipulation, simulation, and random sampling can we progress from the Technological Functions Matrix to the Functions Trade-Off Matrix.

I wish to acknowledge the refinement to the matrix concepts made by Myron B. Fiering, Ph.D., Assistant Professor of Engineering and Applied Mathematics on the Gordon McKay endowment, Harvard University.

Program of Portland Conference

MONDAY
Morning Keynote Session

Introduction of Mayor Terry Schrunk, by LLOYD KEEFE, AIP, Director, City Planning Commission, Portland
Welcome by Mayor TERRY SCHRUNK
Report on AIP's Two-Year Consultation, by HARLAND BARTHOLOMEW, AIP, Chairman, AIP's 50th Year Consultation
Introduction of Dr. René Dubos, by GORDON WHITEHALL, AIP, Consultant in Planning and Government, Los Angeles
Keynote Address, Man Adapting: His Limitations and Potentialities, by DR. RENÉ DUBOS, microbiologist, Rockefeller University
Response by C. DAVID LOEKS, AIP, Director, Twin Cities Metropolitan Planning Commission, St. Paul
Introduction of John W. Dyckman, by EDGAR M. HORWOOD, AIP, Director, Urban Data Center, University of Washington
City Planning and the Treasury of Science, by JOHN W. DYCKMAN, Chairman, Center for Planning and Development Research, University of California, Berkeley
Responses by DANIEL CARSON, Department of Psychology, University of Michigan; BENNETT BERGER, Department of Sociology, University of California, Davis

Luncheon Highlight Session

State of the Institute, by C. DAVID LOEKS
Aerospace Systems Technology and the Creation of Environment, by WILLIAM L. ROGERS, Von Karman Center, Aerojet-General Corporation
Role of Large-Scale Enterprise in the Creation of Better Environment, by GEORGE T. BOGARD, Community Systems Development Division, General Electric Company

Afternoon Critique of University of California Paper

WILLIAM C. LORING, U. S. Public Health Service

Afternoon Discussion Groups (see below)

Evening Presentation of Rare Films

"Man, Iron and Fire"; "America on the Edge of Abundance"; "Human Response to the Visual Environment"; "City of the Bees"

TUESDAY
Morning Presentation

Introductory Remarks, by MYER R. WOLFE, AIP, Chairman, College of Architecture and Urban Planning, University of Washington

The City as a Mechanism for Sustaining Human Contact, by CHRISTOPHER ALEXANDER, Department of Architecture, University of California, Berkeley

Critique by H. PETER OBERLANDER, Head, Program of Community and Regional Planning, University of British Columbia; PHILLIP THIEL, College of Architecture and Urban Planning, University of Washington; ROBERT F. WEHRLI, Department of Architecture, University of Utah

Introductory Remarks, by GEORGE A. DUDLEY, Dean, School of Architecture and Planning, University of California, Los Angeles

The City of the Mind, by STEPHEN CARR, Department of City and Regional Planning, Massachusetts Institute of Technology

Critique by PAUL VINCENT GUMP, Department of Psychology, University of Kansas; GARY H. WINKEL, Department of Architecture, University of Washington

Afternoon Discussion Groups (see below)

Evening Highlight and Awards Dinner

Remarks by IRVING HAND, AIP President Elect, Executive Director, Pennsylvania State Planning Board

The Environment We See (slide presentation), by HERBERT H. SWINBURNE, architect, Philadelphia

Awards Presentations
  Honor Awards: Camden, New Jersey; Capitol Region of Connecticut
  Distinguished Service Award: Howard K. Menhinick, AIP
The City of Man: A Social Systems Reckoning, by BERTRAM M.
  GROSS, Director, National Planning Studies, Maxwell Graduate
  School of Citizenship and Public Affairs, Syracuse University
Habitat '67, by MOSHE SAFDIE, architect, Montreal

WEDNESDAY
Morning Presentation

Goals for Our Metropolitan Regions, LYLE FITCH, President, Institute of Public Administration
Introduction of William L. C. Wheaton, First Catherine Bauer
  Wurster American Life Lecturer, by ROBERT L. WILLIAMS, AIP
  Executive Director, American Institute of Planners
Form and Structure of the Metropolitan Area, by WILLIAM L. C.
  WHEATON, Director, Institute of Urban and Regional Development, University of California, Berkeley
Critique by HENRY FAGIN, Department of Urban and Regional
  Planning, University of Wisconsin; SCOTT GREER, Director, Center for Metropolitan Studies, Northwestern University; GIBSON
  WINTER, Divinity School, University of Chicago
The Link between Parts I and II of the Consultation and Introduction of Stanley J. Hallett, by WILLIAM R. EWALD, Jr., AIP, Development Consultant
Planning, Politics, and Ethics, by STANLEY J. HALLETT, Church
  Federation of Greater Chicago
Comments by CALVIN S. HAMILTON, AIP, Director, Los Angeles
  City Planning Commission

Afternoon Critique Session

Some Thoughts on the Future, by JOHN T. HOWARD, AIP, Head, Department of City and Regional Planning, Massachusetts Institute
  of Technology

Reports from Discussion Groups (see below)
The Journalists' View, by DONALD J. STERLING, Jr., *Oregon Journal*;
GEORGE FAVRE, *Christian Science Monitor*; MITCHELL GORDON,
Wall Street Journal
A Final Word and Announcement, C. DAVID LOEKS

DISCUSSION GROUPS

1. *The Seven Ages of Man*

    Chairman, CHARLTON R. PRICE, Technology Management Programs, Stanford Research Institute; *Co-Chairman*, CALVIN S. HAMILTON; A. L. FROST, Metropolitan Youth Commission, Portland; PAUL VINCENT GUMP; EDWIN E. PETERSEN, Metropolitan Youth Commission, Portland; JOHN H. WAGNER, Jr., National Council of Churches, Los Angeles; GARY H. WINKEL; MRS. CLIFFORD E. ZOLLINGER, National Council on Aging, Portland

2. *The Daily Functions of Man*

    Chairman, RICHARD IVES, U. S. Department of Housing and Urban Development; *Co-Chairman*, LYLE FITCH, Institute of Public Administration; DONALD BERGSTROM, Traffic Engineer, Portland; HENRY C. HIGHTOWER, Assoc. AIP, Department of City and Regional Planning, University of North Carolina; DONALD D. KUMMERFELD, U.S. Bureau of the Budget; DOROTHEA LENSCH, Recreation Director, Portland; VINCENT J. MOORE, Assoc. AIP, Division of the Budget, State of New York; RT. REV. MSGR. THOMAS J. TOBIN, All Saints Church, Portland; REV. GEORGE TODD, United Presbyterian Church

3. *Man's Housing and His Neighborhood*

    Chairman, ALAN TANIGUCHI, School of Architecture, University of Texas; SOL ACKERMAN, Department of Housing and Urban Development; DR. IDO DE GROTT, epidemiologist, Taft Sanitary Engineering Center; GEORGE A. DUDLEY, School of Architecture and Planning, University of California, Los Angeles; WALTER GORDON, architect, Portland; JOHN B. KENWARD, AIP, Portland Development Commission; NATHANIEL J. PARISH, Raymond and May Associates; WILLIAM K. WITTAUSCH, Housing Research, Stanford Research Institute

4. *Man's Spirit, His Rights, Mental Health and Identity*

    Chairman, REV. J. V. LANGMEAD CASSERLEY, Seabury-Western Seminary; *Co-Chairman*, WILLIAM C. LORING; DONALD CLARK, Sheriff, Multnomah County, Oregon; NORMAN A. HILMAR, U.S. Public Health Service; ROSS MILLER, Parry Center for Children, Portland; GEORGE 'SCHERMER, George Schermer Associates; REV. PAUL SCHULZE, Portland Council of Churches; RABBI MATTHEW SIMON, Los Angeles Regional Goals Project; DR. GIBSON WINTER

5. *The Research and Education Man Needs to Build Optimum Environment*

    Chairman, BARCLAY G. JONES, Assoc. AIP, Department of City and Regional Planning, Cornell University; *Co-Chairman*, CORWIN R. MOCINE, AIP, University of California, San Francisco; GRADY CLAY, Editor, *Landscape Architecture*; RENÉ DUBOS; KENNETH R. GERVAIS, Portland State College; GLENN GREGG, Lewis and Clark College; CHARLES MCKINLEY, Consultant, Portland City Planning Commission; DR. JAMES METCALFE, University of Oregon Medical School

6. *Pollution of Man's Environment*

    Chairman, OSCAR SUTERMEISTER, AIP, U.S. Public Health Service; JOHN P. EBERHARD, National Bureau of Standards; RICHARD HATCHARD, Portland Health Bureau; PAUL M. REID, AIP, Metropolitan Area Regional Planning Commission, Detroit; KENNETH SPIES, Director, Oregon State Sanitary Authority

7. *The Forms for Man's Cities*

    Chairman, CHARLES A. BLESSING, AIP, City Planning Commission, Detroit; A. P. BERHART, University of Toronto; WALTER CREESE, School of Architecture and Allied Arts, University of

Oregon; SIMON EISNER, Planning Consultant, Eisner-Stewart & Associates; WILLIAM HALL, U.S. Bureau of Public Roads; FRANCIS J. IVANCIE, Assistant to Mayor of Portland; LLOYD T. KEEFE; RAI Y. OKAMOTO, Regional Plan Association; GEORGE T. ROCKRISE, Department of Housing and Urban Development; CHARLES TIEBOUT, University of Washington; THOMAS VAUGHAN, Oregon Historical Society

Notes

III. Dyckman: City Planning and the Treasury of Science

1. D. M. Wilner, R. P. Walkley, T. Pinkerton, and M. Tayback, *The Housing Environment and Family Life* (Baltimore: Johns Hopkins University Press, 1962).

2. L. M. Howard and Robert A. Scott, "A Proposed Framework for the Analysis of Stress in the Human Organism," *Behavioral Science*, Vol. 10, No. 2, Apr. 1965.

3. Note especially Kurt Lewin, *Principles of Topological Psychology* (New York: McGraw-Hill, 1936).

4. John B. Calhoun, *The Ecology and Sociology of the Norway Rat*, U. S. Public Health Service Publication No. 1008 (Washington: Superintendent of Documents, 1963).

5. B. F. Skinner, *Science and Human Behavior* (New York: Macmillan, 1953).

6. Meyer Weinberg, "Aspects of Southern Urbanization and Social Segregation," report for Equal Educational Opportunities Program, U. S. Office of Education, 1965, mimeographed.

7. René J. Dubos, "Emerging Patterns of Disease," in *Man Under Stress*, Conference No. VII of the series on California and the Challenge of Growth, University of California, 1963.

8. A. H. Maslow, *Motivation and Personality* (New York: Harper, 1954).

9. The President's Science Advisory Committee, Environmental Pollution Panel, *Restoring the Quality of Our Environment* (Washington: Superintendent of Documents, Nov. 1965).

10. D. H. Carson and B. L. Driver, "Environmental Stress," resource paper prepared for the 1966 AIP Conference.

11. Z. H. Surti and E. F. Gervais, "Peak Period Comfort and Service Evaluation of an Urban Freeway and an Alternative Surface

Street," National Proving Ground for Freeway Surveillance, Control and Electronic Aids, Detroit, Michigan, Jan. 1966.

12. Henning E. von Gierke, "On Noise and Vibration Exposure Criteria," *Archives of Environmental Health*, Vol. 11 (Sept. 1965), pp. 327-39.

13. A. Cohen and H. E. Ayer, "Some Observations at Airports and in the Surrounding Community," *Industrial Hygiene Journal*, Vol. 25, No. 5 (Sept. 10, 1964), pp. 134-50.

14. M. M. Zaret, "The Laser Hazard," *Archives of Environmental Health*, Vol. 10 (Apr. 1965), pp. 629-30.

*15. Janet Abu-Lughod, "The City Is Dead—Long Live the City: Some Thoughts on Urbanity," resource paper prepared for the 1966 Annual Meeting of the AIP, mimeographed, May 1966.

16. J. B. Calhoun, "Population Density and Social Pathology," *Scientific American*, Vol. 206 (1962), pp. 139-49.

*17. Richard Meier, "Policies for Urban Settlement Intended to Minimize Losses from Conflict and Violence," resource paper prepared for the 1966 Annual Meeting of the AIP, mimeographed, May 1966.

18. Abu-Lughod, cited.

19. L. Festinger, S. Schachter, and K. Back, *Social Pressures in Informal Groups* (New York: Harper, 1950).

*20. Nagel, quoted in Senn, "Goals and Planning: Research Notes toward a Reconstruction of Planning Theory," resource paper prepared for the 1966 Annual Meeting of the AIP, mimeographed, May 1966.

21. J. S. Mill, *A System of Logic*, 8th ed. (New York: Harper, 1874), p. 656.

22. Martin Meyerson, "Building the Middle-Range Bridge for Comprehensive Planning," *Journal of the American Institute of Planners*, Vol. XXII, No. 2 (Spring, 1956).

23. Maynard M. Hufschmidt, "Environmental Planning: With Special Relation to Natural Resources," resource paper prepared for the 1966 Annual Meeting of the AIP, mimeographed, July 1966.

24. Ibid.

25. Behavioral Sciences Subpanel, Life Sciences Panel, Presi-

*These papers will be published in a book in 1967.

dent's Science Advisory Committee, Strengthening the Behavioral Sciences (Washington: The White House, Apr. 20, 1962), p. 2.

Loring: Comment on Dyckman

1. John B. Calhoun, "Population Density and Social Pathology," *Scientific American*, Vol. 32, No. 206, pp. 139-46 (1962).
2. John J. Christian, "Phenomena Associated with Population Density," *Proceedings of the National Academy of Science*, Vol. 47, pp. 429-49 (1961).
3. A. E. Martin, *Environment, Housing and Health*, World Health Organization, mimeo., WHO/Env. San./66.144, Geneva.
4. W. C. Loring, "Housing Characteristics and Social Disorganization," *Journal of Social Problems*, Vol. 3, No. 3 (Jan. 1956), and "Residential Environment: Nexus of Personal Interactions and Healthful Development," *Journal of Health and Human Behavior*, Vol. 5, No. 4, pp. 166-69 (Winter, 1964).
5. E. M. Gruenberg, M. D., "Community Conditions and Psychoses of the Elderly," *American Journal of Psychiatry*, Vol. 110 (June 1954), pp. 888-903.
6. P. and M. Chombard de Lauwe, *Famille et habitation*, Centre National de la Recherche Scientifique, Paris, 1959.
7. L. Rosenmayr and H. Strotzka, *Wohen in Wien*, Der Ausbau, Mono. No. 8, Vienna, 1956.

Carson: Comment on Dyckman

1. P. T. Young, "Studies of Food Preferences, Appetite and Dietary Habit. VIII. Food-seeking Drives, Palatability and the Law of Effect," *J. Comp. Phys. Psych.*, 41: 269-300 (1948).
2. M. D. Van Arsdol, Jr., G. Sabagh, and F. Alexander, "Reality and the Perception of Environmental Hazards," *J. of Health and Human Behavior*, 5: 143-53 (1964).
3. C. W. Nixon, "Effects of Sonic Boom on People: St. Louis, Missouri, 1961-1962," *J. of Acoustical Society of America*, 38: 913 (Nov. 1965).
4. P. N. Borsky, *Community Reactions to Sonic Booms in the Ok-*

lahoma City Area, Biophysics Laboratory, Aerospace Medical Research Laboratories, Wright-Patterson Air Force Base, Feb. 1965.

5. A. Verwoerdt and R. H. Douvenmuehle, "Physical Illness and Depressive Symptomatology, Aspects and Awareness," *J. of Gerontology,* 19: 330-35 (1964).

IV. Alexander: The City as a Mechanism for Sustaining Human Contact

1. Emile Durkheim, *The Division of Labor in Society* (Paris, 1893), trans. by George Simpson (Free Press, 1933).

2. Melvin M. Webber, "Order in Diversity: Community without Propinquity," *Cities and Space,* ed. Lowdon Wingo, Resources for the Future (Baltimore, 1963); Webber, "The Urban Place and the Nonplace Urban Realm," in Webber et al., *Explorations into Urban Structure* (Philadelphia, 1964), pp. 79-153; Marshall McLuhan, *Understanding Media* (New York, 1964); Richard Meier, *A Communications Theory of Urban Growth* (Cambridge: MIT Press, 1960).

3. Of course, people do occasionally have intimate contact with one another, even when these two conditions are not fulfilled. This happens between old friends, who now live 3,000 miles apart and see each other every few years for a day or two. But even in these cases, there must have been some period in the past when the two conditions *were* satisfied.

4. C. H. Cooley, *Social Organization,* first published New York, 1909; reprinted Free Press, 1956, pp. 23-31.

5. Edward A. Shils, "The Study of Primary Groups," in Lerner and Lasswell, *The Policy Sciences* (Stanford University Press, 1951), pp. 44-69; W. I. Thomas, *Social Behavior and Personality,* ed. E. H. Volkart (New York, 1951); George Homans, *The Human Group* (New York, 1950).

6. Homans, pp. 456-57.

7. Ralph Linton, *The Study of Man* (New York, 1936), p. 230.

8. For instance, Clarence Stein, *Towards New Towns for America* (Chicago, 1951).

9. Webber, cited; Ikumi Hoshin, "Apartment Life in Japan,"

Marriage and Family Living, 26 (1964), pp. 312-17; Rudolf Heberle, "The Normative Element in Neighborhood Relations," *Pacific Sociological Review* 3, No. 1 (Spring, 1960), pp. 3-11.

10. Ruth Glass and F. G. Davidson, "Household Structure and Housing Needs," *Population Studies*, 4 (1951), pp. 395-420; S. P. Brown, *Population Studies*, 4 (1951), pp. 380-94. This is also the same as saying that one-fifth of all adults in urban areas are either single, separated, widowed, or divorced. See U. S. Census, Vol. I, *General U. S. Statistics* (1960), Table 176.

11. Durkheim, cited; Cooley, cited; Louis Wirth, "Urbanism as a Way of Life," *American Journal of Sociology*, 40 (1938), pp. 1-24; J. Beshers, *Urban Social Structure* (New York, 1964); Janet Abu-Lughod, *The City Is Dead, Long Live the City* (Berkeley: Center for Planning and Development Research, 1966).

12. H. Gans, *The Urban Villagers* (Free Press, 1962); Michael Young and Peter Willmott, *Family and Kinship in East London* (London, 1957); M. Fried and P. Gleicher, "Some Sources of Residential Satisfaction in an Urban Slum," *AIP Journal* (1961), pp. 305-15.

13. Abu-Lughod, cited.

14. The numbers three and four have no special significance. I have chosen the range three to four, simply because one or two are too few, and more than about five too many to sustain at the level of intimacy I have defined.

15. R. E. L. Faris and H. W. Dunham, *Mental Disorders in Urban Areas* (Chicago, 1939), pp. 82-109.

16. Ibid., pp. 54-57.

17. Alexander Leighton, *My Name is Legion*, The Stirling County Study, Vol. I (New York, 1959); Charles C. Hughes, Marc-Adelard Tremblay, Robert N. Rapoport, and Alexander Leighton, *People of Cove and Woodlot*, The Stirling County Study, Vol. II (New York, 1960); Dorothea Leighton, John S. Harding, David B. Macklin, Allister M. Macmillan, and Alexander Leighton, *The Character of Danger*, The Stirling County Study, Vol. III (New York, 1963).

18. Hughes et al., p. 267.

19. Ibid., p. 297.

20. Leighton et al. (1963), p. 338.

21. T. S. Langner and S. T. Michael, *Life Stress and Mental Health* (New York, 1963), p. 285.

22. A. M. Rose, "Mental Disorder and Socio-economic Status," *Mental Health and Mental Disorder* (New York, 1955), Summary Table 4, pp. 102-104.

23. Langner and Michael, p. 286.

24. Ibid., pp. 287-89.

25. Neil A. Dayton, *New Facts on Mental Disorders* (Springfield, Ill., 1940), p. 464; C. Landis and J. D. Page, *Modern Society and Mental Disease* (New York, 1938), p. 163; Benjamin Malzberg, *Social and Biological Aspects of Mental Disease* (Utica, 1940), p. 70; Benjamin Malzberg, "Statistical Analysis of Ages of First Admission to Hospitals for Mental Disease in New York State," *Psychiatric Quarterly*, 23 (1949), p. 344; H. F. Dorn, "The Incidence and Future Expectancy of Mental Disease," *U.S. Public Health Reports*, 53 (1938), pp. 1991-2004; E. M. Furbush, "Social Facts Relative to Patients with Mental Disease," *Mental Hygiene*, 5 (1921), p. 597.

26. Malzberg (1940), p. 116; C. Landis and J. D. Page, *Modern Society and Mental Disease* (New York, 1938), p. 69; L. M. Adler, "The Relationship of Marital Status to Incidence of and Recovery from Mental Illness," *Social Forces*, 32 (1953), p. 186; Neil A. Dayton, "Marriage and Mental Disease," *New England Journal of Medicine*, 215 (1936), p. 154; F. J. Gaudet and R. I. Watson, "Relation between Insanity and Marital Conditions," *Journal of Abnormal Psychology*, 30 (1935), p. 368.

27. Harry F. Harlow and Margaret K. Harlow, "The Effect of Rearing Conditions on Behavior," *Bull. Menninger Clinic*, 26 (1962), pp. 213-24.

28. Harry F. Harlow and Margaret K. Harlow, "Social Deprivation in Monkeys," *Scientific American*, 207, No. 5 (1962), pp. 136-46.

29. Anna Freud and Sophie Dann, "An Experiment in Group Upbringing," *Readings in Child Behavior and Development*, ed. Celia Stendler (New York, 1964), pp. 122-40.

30. Herman R. Lantz, "Number of Childhood Friends as Reported in the Life Histories of a Psychiatrically Diagnosed Group of 1000," *Marriage and Family Living* (May, 1956), pp. 107-108.

31. R. E. L. Faris, "Cultural Isolation and the Schizophrenic Personality," *American Journal of Sociology*, 40 (Sept. 1934), pp. 155-69; R. E. L. Faris, *Social Psychology* (New York, 1952), pp. 338-62; R. E. L. Faris, *Social Disorganization* (New York, 1948), chap. 8; Paul Halmos, *Solitude and Privacy* (New York, 1952), pp. 88-92; Carle C. Zimmerman and Lucius F. Cervantes, S.J., *Successful American Families* (New York, 1960); R. Helanko, "The Yard Group in the Socialization of Turku Girls," *Acta Sociologica*, Vol. 4, No. 1 (1959), pp. 38-55; D. Kimball, "Boy Scouting as a Factor in Personality Development," Ph.D. Thesis, Dept. of Education, University of California, Berkeley, 1949; Melvin L. Kohn and John A. Clausen, "Social Isolation and Schizophrenia," *American Journal of Sociology*, 20 (1955), pp. 265-73; Dietrich C. Reitzes, "The Effect of Social Environment on Former Felons," *Journal of Criminal Law Criminology*, 46 (1955), pp. 226-31; E. Gartly Jaco, "The Social Isolation Hypothesis and Schizophrenia," *American Journal of Sociology*, 19 (1954), pp. 567-77; Aldous Huxley, *Island* (New York: Bantam, 1963), pp. 89-90; Arthur T. Jersild and Mary D. Fite, "The Influence of Nursery School Experience on Children's Social Adjustments," *Child Development Monographs*, 25 (1939); Helena Malley, "Growth in Social Behavior and Mental Activity after Six Months in Nursery School," *Child Development*, 6 (1935), pp. 303-309; Louis P. Thorpe, *Child Psychology and Development* (New York, 1955); K. M. B. Bridges, *Social and Emotional Development of the Pre-school Child* (London, 1931); W. R. Thompson and R. Melzack, "Early Environment," *Scientific American*, 194(1) (1956), pp. 38-42.

32. This is, in effect, the same as the classic thesis of Cooley and George Herbert Mead, which says that the individual self appears only as a result of interaction with others, and that it is liable to disintegrate when these interactions are not available. Mead, *Mind, Self and Society* (Chicago, 1934); Cooley, cited.

33. Glass and Davidson, p. 400.

34. "The person who is diagnosed as suffering from schizophrenia perceives himself as bombarded by a multiplicity of personal and family problems he is not able to handle." L. H. Rogler and A. B.

Hollingshead, *Trapped: Families and Schizophrenia* (New York, 1965).

35. Robert Sommer and Humphrey Osmond, "The Schizophrenic No-Society," *Psychiatry*, 25 (1962), pp. 244-55.

36. Durkheim, pp. 283-303.

37. J. G. Miller, "Input Overload and Psychopathology," *American Journal of Psychiatry*, 116 (1960), pp. 695-704; Richard Meier, cited.

38. E. T. Hall, *The Hidden Dimension* (New York, 1966).

39. Ministry of Housing, *Families Living at High Density* (London, 1966), pp. 29-33; John Madge, "Privacy," Transactions of the Bartlett Society, University College, London, 3 (1965), p. 139.

40. Leopold Rosenmayr, *Wohnverhltnisse und Nachbarschaftsbeziehungen*, Der Aufbau, Monograph No. 8 (Vienna, 1956), pp. 39-91.

41. Hans Strotzka, *Spannungen und Losungsversuche in Stadtischer Umgebung, Wohnen in Wien*, Der Aufbau, Monograph No. 8 (Vienna, 1956), pp. 93-108.

42. Nelson Foote, Janet Abu-Lughod, Mary Mix Foley, and Louis Winnick, *Housing Choices and Housing Constraints* (New York, 1960), pp. 107 and 392.

43. Ibid., pp. 223-63, and Peter H. Rossi, *Why Families Move* (Free Press, 1955).

44. Ibid., pp. 187-93, and Irving Rosow, "Homeownership Motives," *American Sociological Review*, 13 (1948), pp. 751-56.

45. Center for Urban Studies, *Aspects of Change* (London, 1964), chap. 8, "Tall Flats in Pimlico." Santa Clara County Study, unpublished, 1966.

46. Charlotte Buhler, *Proceedings and Papers of the Ninth International Congress of Psychology*, 1929, pp. 99-102.

47. A few of the mothers who try to get their children into nursery school are, of course, trying to get greater freedom for themselves. However, at least one survey has shown that the majority of mothers do so, not because they want more freedom for themselves, but because they want their children to have more contact with other children. Cambridge Association for Advancement of State Education, *Report on Nursery Schools* (Cambridge, England, 1966).

VI. Gross: The City of Man: A Social Systems Reckoning

1. For the term "turbulent environment"—as distinct from a "placid" or "disturbed reactive environment"—I am indebted to Fred Emery and Eric Trist of the Tavistock Institute of Human Relations and their paper, "The Causal Texture of Organizational Environments," *Human Relations*, Feb., 1965.

2. Walt W. Rostow, *The Stages of Economic Growth* (Cambridge University Press, 1960).

3. Ben J. Wattenberg and Richard M. Scammon, *This U.S.A.* (New York: Doubleday, 1965), pp. 86-87.

4. This discussion is based on the discussion of "The Urban Revolution" in *Space-Time and Post-Industrial Society*, Occasional Paper, Comparative Administration Group, American Society for Public Administration, March, 1966.

5. Ibid.

6. Lauchlin Currie, *Accelerating Development* (New York: McGraw-Hill, 1966), p. 53. This book won the prize offered by the Society for International Development for the best book on development by a citizen of a "developing" country. Dr. Currie is Director of the Department of Economics in the National University of Colombia and of its new Institute for Investigations in Development.

7. These and other aspects of man-resource social systems are analyzed in much greater detail in my *The State of the Nation: Social Systems Accounting* (London: Tavistock Publications, 1966). This book is also incorporated in Raymond A. Bauer, ed., *Social Indicators* (Cambridge: MIT Press, 1966).

8. For a more detailed identification of the varieties of social systems, the section "The Complexity of a National Society," *The State of the Nation: Social Systems Accounting*, cited.

9. Eltor Mayo, *The Human Problems of an Industrial Civilization* (Boston: Harvard Business School, 1933), pp. 138-47.

10. The case for broader annual reports at the national level is presented in detail in my "The Social State of the Union," *Transaction*, Nov./Dec., 1965, and "Let's Have a *Real* State of the Union Message," *Challenge*, May/June, 1966.

11. Evelyn M. Kitagawa and Philip M. Hauser, "Social and Economic Differentials in Mortality, United States, 1960," unpublished report based on paper presented at Annual Meetings, Population Association of America, New York, April 29-30, 1966.

12. Sir Geoffrey Vickers, "The End of Free Fall," *The Listener*, Oct. 28 and Nov. 4, 1965.

13. Frank Manuel, "Great Societies: Past and Future," paper presented at the Arthur F. Bentley Seminar on the Great Society, under the auspices of the National Planning Studies Program, Maxwell Graduate School of Citizenship and Public Affairs, Syracuse University, March, 1965. To be published in Bertram M. Gross, ed., *The Great Society* (New York: Basic Books).

14. The most important Jerusalem rebulider is Teddy Kollek, the "new style" politician who is now Mayor of Jerusalem.

15. For a detailed analysis of these concepts, see my "Activating National Plans," Chapter 7 in Bertram M. Gross, ed., *Action under Planning* (New York: McGraw-Hill, 1966).

16. Ibid.

17. Bertram M. Gross, "National Planning: Findings and Fallacies," *Public Administration Review*, Dec., 1965, pp. 263-73.

18. Bertram M. Gross, *The Administration of Economic Development Planning: Principles and Fallacies*, Public Administration Branch, United Nations, Aug., 1966.

19. Adapted from the prophetic book "Milton" by William Blake.

VII. Wheaton: Form and Structure of the Metropolitan Area

1. Louis Wirth, "Urbanism as a Way of Life," *American Journal of Sociology*, 44, July, 1938.

2. Janet Abu-Lughod, "The City Is Dead—Long Live the City: Some Thoughts on Urbanism" (Berkeley: Center for Planning and Development Research, University of California, 1966).

3. Sebastian De Grazia, *Of Time, Work and Leisure* (New York: Twentieth Century Fund, 1962).

4. Leo Grebler et al., *Capital Formation in Residential Real Estate*, National Bureau of Economic Research (Princeton: Princeton University Press, 1956), Chapter V.

5. There is also another catalogue of terminology which deals with the detailed physical composition of subdistricts, zones, or buildings. This language is largely architectural and is in considerable degree, though not entirely, separate from the language in which the form of the metropolitan area is described.

6. Cf. the work of Bennett Berger, W. B. Dobriner, Walter Firey, Herbert Gans, Charles Seelye, Lloyd Warner, and William H. Whyte, Jr., for example.

7. Greenleigh Associates, *Diagnostic Survey of Tenant Households in West Side Renewal Area of New York City* (New York, 1965); *Home Interview Study of Low-Income Households in Detroit, Michigan* (New York, 1965); and Arthur D. Little, Inc., *Renewal Attitudes Study, City of San Francisco* (Cambridge, 1965).

8. Marc Fried, "Grieving for a Lost Home," in Leonard Duhl, ed., *The Urban Condition* (New York: Basic Books, 1963), and other chapters of the same. Cf. also Alvin L. Schorr, *Slums and Social Insecurity* (Washington: U.S. Department of Health, Education and Welfare, 1963).

9. Reginald R. Isaacs, "The Neighborhood Theory: An Analysis of Its Adequacy," *Journal of the American Institute of Planners*, Vol. XIV, No. 1, Spring, 1948.

10. Wallace-McHarg Associates, *Plan for the Valleys* (1963); Phillip H. Lewis, *Recreation and Open Space in Illinois* (University of Illinois, Sept. 1961), and Eckbo, Dean, Austin & Williams, *Urban-Metropolitan Open Space Study*, prepared for the California State Office of Planning, Sacramento, Nov., 1965.

11. Thomas Reiner, *The Place of the Ideal Community in Urban Planning* (Philadelphia: University of Pennsylvania Press, 1963).

VIII. Carr: The City of the Mind

1. See chapter 1 in J. S. Bruner, R. R. Olver, P. M. Greenfield, et al., *Studies in Cognitive Growth* (New York: John Wiley, 1966). In the chapter cited, Bruner describes this process and makes quite clear the great economy and power of language. The other modes of representation do not disappear of course. A tennis stroke must still be represented in terms of action. Many aspects of form can be

represented only in visual imagery, etc. See also L. S. Vygotsky, *Thought and Language* (Cambridge, Mass.: The MIT Press, 1962), Benjamin Lee Whorf, "The Relation of Habitual Thought and Behavior to Language," reprinted in *Language, Thought and Reality* (New York: The Technology Press and John Wiley, 1956), pp. 134-59, and Roger W. Brown, *Words and Things* (Glencoe, Ill.: The Free Press, 1958), especially "Naming and the Mental Image," pp. 83-92.

2. The limited but challenging role of the city planner as an interpreter of human objectives in terms of the physical form of the city was clearly set forth as an ideal by Kevin Lynch and Lloyd Rodwin in "A Theory of Urban Form," *Journal of the American Institute of Planners*, 24 (Nov., 1958), pp. 201-14. On page 203 they say: "City and regional planners operate primarily upon the physical environment, although mindful of its complex social, economic, or psychological effects. They are not experts in all the planning for the future that a society engages in, but only in planning for the future development of the physical and spatial city: streets, buildings, utilities, activity distributions, spaces and their interrelations. Although cries of dismay may greet such a reactionary and 'narrow' view, the currently fashionable broader definitions lead in our judgment only to integrated, comprehensive incompetence."

3. See G. A. Miller, E. Galanter, and K. H. Pribram, *Plans and the Structure of Behavior* (New York: Henry Holt, 1960), especially chapters 1 and 4.

4. It is true that city planners by tradition and the present definition of their role manipulate mainly spatial variables. Lately, however, we have begun to broaden our scope to include some temporal dimensions, to attempt to design processes of change rather than final forms. More recently still we have been urged to operate directly on the social structure through the design of social action programs. Whether or not we are presently competent to assume such broadened responsibilities, there is little doubt that they are being thrust upon us by the pressure of events. In the continuing reassessment of our role, however, controversies between "physical" and "social" planners will probably be resolved. This will happen as we come to realize that what city planners and designers are really

doing is helping to shape the *form of interaction* of people and environments. Such interaction, while socially conditioned, is also and always affected by the particular setting in space and time.

5. For an attempt to develop such a list relative to the city see R. Dewey, "Needs and Desires of the Urbanite," in Coleman Woodbury, *The Future of Cities and Urban Redevelopment* (Chicago: University of Chicago Press, 1963), pp. 309-68. The classic long list of "basic" psychological needs was compiled by Henry Murray and his associates at Harvard and appears in his *Explorations in Personality* (New York: Oxford University Press, 1938). Some of these seem to be relevant to city form, but there is much disagreement as to their universality.

6. See chapter 10 in René Dubos, *Man Adapting* (New Haven: Yale University Press, 1965).

7. A group at the University of Michigan has attempted to compile the relevant material with reference to establishing criteria for school environments. For a summary see D. H. Carson, "The Interactions of Man and His Environment" in *SER-2, School Environments Research: Environmental Evaluations* (Ann Arbor, Mich.: University of Michigan, 1965), pp. 13-52.

8. Studies of advertising have shown that while it is possible to change people's desires for one brand name over another, it is very difficult to change their relative desires for various real goods. See for example R. Reeves, *Reality in Advertising* (New York: Knopf, 1961).

9. For a brilliant if often questionable development of this thesis see Marshall McLuhan, *Understanding Media* (New York: McGraw-Hill, 1964).

10. See John Dyckman, "The Changing Uses of the City," *Daedalus* (Winter, 1961), pp. 111-31.

11. On the need for comprehension and mastery of the environment see R. W. White, "Motivation Reconsidered: The Concept of Competence," *Psychological Review*, 66 (1959), pp. 297-333, and the summary chapter in his "Ego and Reality in Psychoanalytic Theory," *Psychological Issues*, III (No. 3, 1963). On the need for complexity and novelty see chapters 2 and 8 in D. E. Berlyne, *Conflict Arousal and Curiosity* (New York: McGraw-Hill, 1960), H.

Fowler, *Curiosity and Exploratory Behavior* (New York: Macmillan, 1965) and D. Fiske and S. Madoi, *Functions of Varied Experience* (Dorsey Press, 1961), especially chapter 13, pp. 380-401.

12. The importance of this need for complexity and novelty in the environment is suggested by a study just carried out by Marcia McMahon, a graduate student at MIT. The research follows a lead from this currently very active area of research in psychology, that there should be a relationship between environmental complexity, exploratory behavior, and curiosity. The subjects of the study were lower-class Negro children, aged eight to eleven, living in three different areas of Boston which differ substantially in complexity. Since there was no simple, single dimension for measuring complexity, the number of differing action settings which the children used in each area was taken as the most meaningful indicator. Surprisingly enough, both the children's patterns of exploration in the city and their level of curiosity in responding to new situations were found to vary consistently with this measure of the complexity of their environmental experience. While the sample was small and the methods imperfect, the findings, if true, have striking implications for the potential usefulness of environments in facilitating exploration and intellectual development. Marcia Lee McMahon, "The Relationship between Environmental Setting and Curiosity in Children," unpublished Master's thesis (MIT: Department of City and Regional Planning, 1966).

13. See, for example, George A. Miller, "The Magical Number Seven Plus or Minus Two: Some Limits on Our Capacity for Processing Information," *Psychological Review*, 63 (1956), pp. 81-97.

14. Norbert Wiener, *The Human Use of Human Being* (Boston: Houghton Mifflin, 1964).

15. The best current review of the subject appears in R. L. Gregory, *Eye and Brain* (New York: McGraw-Hill, 1966).

16. For a general description of this process of economical transformation in perception see F. Attneave, "Some Informational Aspects of Visual Perception," *Psychological Review*, 61 (1954), pp. 183-93.

17. J. S. Bruner describes these problems in perceiving in his article, "On Perceptual Readiness," *Psychological Review*, 64 (1957), pp. 123-52.

18. I am presently carrying out some research of this kind which uses a special camera to record what people look at as they move through the environment. This behavioral data can be compared to their later memory of the trip to bring out the features of the environment which are critical in the process of perceiving and remembering. We can vary people's familiarity with a given environment and we can change the instructions, or plans under which they operate.

In the relatively "planless" state, when the individual is operating under a highly general plan such as "look around for something interesting," perception will be almost entirely determined by the form characteristics of the immediate environment. For example, in an environment new to him an individual, operating under such a plan for general exploration, will begin by noticing those features which are simplest, in the sense of standing out as easily recognizable forms and in the sense of fitting his general expectations. Once the individual is oriented and as he becomes more familiar with the environment his attention will be increasingly attracted by the novel and changing features such as people, traffic, or weather conditions. Given some knowledge of degree of familiarity, we seem to be able to predict the average performance of ordinary "planless" perceivers quite well by analyzing form characteristics. This means, of course, that we can also design that average performance, if we wish to.

19. G. A. Miller discusses this process of economical encoding of experience in his "The Magical Number Seven Plus or Minus Two." For a more comprehensive treatment of the whole topic of categorization, see chapters 1 and 2 in J. S. Bruner, J. J. Goodnow, and G. A. Austin, *A Study of Thinking* (New York: John Wiley, 1956).

20. Kevin Lynch, *The Image of the City* (Cambridge, Mass.: MIT Press, 1962).

21. Those published are by John Gulick, "Images of an Arab City," *Journal of the American Institute of Planners* (Aug., 1963), pp. 179-97, and Dirk de Jong, "Images of Urban Areas," *Journal of the American Institute of Planners* (Nov., 1962), pp. 266-76. Several others are in progress at MIT and the Joint Center for Urban Studies of MIT and Harvard.

22. Interview investigations which I have carried out in Rome indicate that perhaps most frequently people remember the city as

sequences of images along main routes through it. This is the image of the habitual automobilist, the young resident who has not yet built up his familiarity with whole areas of the city, or the newcomer unaided by a map. Although these sequential images may be linked together at key intersections, the over-all image which results is typically a rather distorted and often disorganized picture of the whole, with many significant gaps between routes. Beyond this, people may build up rather accurate spatial images of the extended areas of cities with which they are most familiar, their own neighborhood or the central areas of cities such as Lynch studied. These images are typically built up by the detailed interlocking of sequences—whether automobile or pedestrian. This tends to be a self-correcting process but may nevertheless produce significant distortions depending on the degree of ambiguity in the form. Finally we attempt, where the form allows it, to achieve very simple, diagrammatic representations, somewhere between a simplified map and a verbal description. Some patterns of course make such representation easy, as when we realize that Manhattan is an oblong gridiron "with its long, wide, named streets far apart and running north-south and its short, narrow, numbered streets close together and running east-west." When the pattern is complex or we are dealing with the whole city, such a simplified diagram may be achieved only by long familiarity, if ever.

23. Anselm Strauss has reviewed the many verbal concepts of the American city in his *Images of the American City* (New York: The Free Press of Glencoe, 1961).

24. See chapter 7 in G. A. Miller, E. Galanter and K. H. Pribram, cited.

25. An excellent readable review of the general characteristics of memory can be found in I.M.L. Hunter, *Memory: Facts and Fallacies*, rev. ed. (Baltimore: Penguin Books, 1964). The classic work, also highly readable, is F. C. Bartlett, *Remembering* (Cambridge: Cambridge University Press, 1932).

26. The original work here is by Kurt Lewin. A good short review can be found in chapter 6 of F. H. Allport, *Theories of Perception and the Concept of Structure* (New York: John Wiley, 1955). See also Isidor Chein, "The Environment as a Determinant of Behavior," *Journal of Social Psychology*, 39 (1954), pp. 115-27.

27. Herbert Gans discusses the notion of potential and effective

environments in an unpublished paper, "Some Notes on Physical Environment, Human Behavior, and Their Relationships," prepared for the Conference on Social and Physical Environment Variables as Determinants of Mental Health of the National Institute of Mental Health, September 14, 1958.

28. Jane Jacobs, *The Death and Life of Great American Cities* (New York: Random House, 1961).

29. See Edward Tolman, "The Model," chapter 2 in Part III of Talcott Parsons and Edward A. Shils, eds., *Toward a General Theory of Action* (Cambridge: Harvard University Press, 1951). Tolman develops Lewin's topological field theory and discusses the environmental field in terms of "behavioral regions." Perhaps the psychological development of this idea most closely related to the concerns of planning and design is by Roger G. Barker and his associates at Kansas. Barker and H. F. Wright use "behavior settings" as their unit of analysis in their intensive study of the interaction of children with the environment of a small midwest town, *Midwest and Its Children* (New York: Harper and Row, 1955). See also chapter 3 in Erving Goffman, *The Presentation of Self in Everyday Life* (Garden City, N. Y.: Doubleday, 1959) and chapter 9 in his *Behavior in Public Places* (New York: The Free Press of Glencoe, 1963). Edward T. Hall has developed an anthropological perspective on personal space, which he calls "proxemics," and which takes some account of settings. See chapter 9 in his *The Hidden Dimension* (Garden City, N. Y.: Doubleday, 1966). While his formulation may prove useful in analyzing a particular small setting, such as a room, it has little relevance as yet to city design.

30. For an extremely provocative treatment of the many functions of scheduling in society, see Charles Hackett, "Scheduling," in F. S. C. Northrop and H. H. Livingston, eds., *Cross-Cultural Understanding* (New York: Harper and Row, 1964).

31. Melvin M. Webber, "The Urban Place and the Nonplace Urban Realm," in *Exploration into Urban Structure* (Philadelphia: University of Pennsylvania Press, 1964), pp. 79-153.

32. For a study of the effects of school size on rate and type of interaction, see R. G. Barker and P. V. Gump, *Big School, Small School* (Stanford, Calif.: Stanford University Press, 1964).

33. Ibid. Barker and Gump found that although big schools of-

fered a decidedly greater variety of settings, individual participation in a number of settings was greater in the small schools.

34. The much discussed study by John B. Calhoun in which various forms of social pathology, and eventually a "behavioral sink," resulted from overcrowding Norway rats is summarized in L. J. Duhl, ed., *The Urban Condition: People and Policy in the Metropolis* (New York: Basic Books, 1963), pp. 33-44. One of the most extreme attempts to apply these findings to slum conditions is to be found in chapter 13 of Hall's *The Hidden Dimension,* cited. There are many obvious differences between Calhoun's experimental situation and even the worst slum conditions, even if we except the rat-man leap. While they have many constraints, slum buildings are not closed animal pens. Moreover, even slum dwellers have moral precepts and defense mechanisms, wear clothing, etc. And of course there are many more obvious economic and social conditions in slums which could be used to explain "social pathology." For all that, the relative density, or human intensity, of settings undoubtedly has important, if largely unknown, consequences on behavior within them.

35. For a review of the many meanings that environments may convey, see David Lowenthal, "Geography, Experience and Imagination: Toward a Geographical Epistemology," *Annals of the Association of American Geographers,* 51 (Sept. 1961), pp. 241-60. Anselm Strauss, cited, is suggestive on the various public meanings and values of cities. The basic text in experimental psychology is C. E. Osgood, G. J. Suci, and P. H. Tannebaum, *The Measurement of Meaning* (Urbana: University of Illinois Press, 1957).

36. F. C. Bartlett, cited, discusses our "effort after meaning" in this sense.

37. On the relationship between value and meaning, see Charles Morris, *Significance and Signification* (Cambridge, Mass.: MIT Press, 1964).

38. On the reality of these common social values attaching to places, see Walter Firey, "Sentiment and Symbolism as Ecological Variables," *American Sociological Review,* X (Apr. 1945), pp. 140-48, and his *Land Use in Central Boston* (Cambridge, Mass.: Harvard University Press, 1947).

39. See, for example, William Michelson, "Value Orientation and

Urban Form," an unpublished dissertation in the Department of Social Relations, Harvard, 1965. Although his findings are somewhat ambiguous, Michelson develops a very useful interview technique for relating people's preferences for various housing and neighborhood forms to their general set of values. His method could easily be applied to determining public values in relation to specific places.

40. Two of the more interesting examples are, on the psychoanalytic side, Anton Ehrenzweig, *The Psychoanalysis of Artistic Vision and Hearing* (New York: Julian Press, 1953) and, on the experimental side, W. L. Valentine, *The Experimental Psychology of Beauty* (London: Methuen, 1962). The art historian E. H. Gombrich has made an admirable attempt to marry art and psychology in his *Art and Illusion* (New York: Pantheon Books, 1962). See especially chapters 7 and 9.

41. Albert L. Guérard, *Bottle in the Sea* (Cambridge, Mass: Harvard University Press, 1954), part II.

42. See "Art as a Mode of Knowing," in J. S. Bruner, *On Knowing* (Cambridge, Mass.: Harvard University Press, 1962).

43. The writings of the French philosopher, Gaston Bachelard, are particularly evocative of these qualities. For a poetic analysis of the myriad human functions of the house as universe, see his *Poetics of Space* (New York: Onion Press, 1964), chapters 1 and 2.

44. Marc Fried, "Grieving for a Lost Home," in Leonard J. Duhl, cited.

45. How narrow adaptation can become is indicated in Lee Rainwater, "Fear and House as Haven in the Lower Class," *Journal of the American Institute of Planners*, 32 (Jan. 1966), pp. 23-30.

46. See chapter 3 in Marie Jahoda, *Current Concepts of Positive Mental Health* (New York: Basic Books, 1958).

47. On the basis of her experience in Venezuela, the anthropologist Lisa Peattie did just that in a recent lecture at Harvard on "Social Issues in Housing," one of the Catherine Bauer Wurster Memorial Lecture Series, sponsored jointly by MIT and Harvard.

48. The classic work is by Leon Festinger and his associates. See his "Architecture and Group Membership," *Journal of Social Issues: Social Policy and Social Research in Housing* (1951), pp. 152-63.

49. The most recent discussion of city design by Kevin Lynch is

"The City as Environment," *Scientific American*, 213 (Sept. 1965), pp. 209-19.

50. Reality is much more complicated than my caricature. In fact, nearly all contemporary city design in this country has been accomplished within the context of urban renewal. The social failures of urban renewal have encouraged administrators to attempt to "plan with people," that is, with neighborhood groups. Such groups are not inevitably unrepresentative of the whole affected community, but they tend to be only the articulate middle class. Most urban renewal design continues to be an internal affair among politicians, administrators, planners, architects, and developers from which user clients are rather effectively excluded. For a review of some of the design inadequacies of this process, see Roger Montgomery, "Improving the Design Process in Urban Renewal," *Journal of the American Institute of Planners*, XXXI (Feb. 1965), pp. 21-30.

Gump: Comment on Carr

1. R. G. Barker and H. F. Wright, *Midwest and Its Children* (New York: Harper & Row, 1955).

2. R. G. Barker and P. Schoggen, "A Quantitative Study of Environmental Change over a Decade within an American and an English Town," final report to the National Science Foundation, 1966.

3. R. G. Barker and P. Gump, *Big School, Small School* (Stanford: Stanford University Press, 1964).